In the Company of Diamonds

De Beers, Kleinzee, and the Control of a Town

In the Company of Diamonds

*De Beers, Kleinzee, and
the Control of a Town*

◆

PETER CARSTENS

Ohio University Press
Athens

Ohio University Press, Athens, Ohio 45701
2001 by Ohio University Press
Printed in the United States of America
All rights reserved

09 08 07 06 05 04 03 02 01   5 4 3 2 1

Professor Ninian Smart and Fithian Press, Santa Barbara, Calif., have generously given permission for quotation the whole of the poem "The Paterson Scale (A Method Anglo-American Uses to Grade People)" at the beginning of chapter 10.

Figure 4.1 is a reproduction of the photo published in the *1888–1988 Centenary Supplement* of De Beers Consolidated Mines Limited. Courtesy of the De Beers Archive in Kimberley. Middlebrook Studio, Kimberley, took the original photograph. Figures 4.2, 5.1, 5.2, 5.3, 5.4, 5.5, 7.1, 7.2, 7.4, 7.5, 7.6, 8.2, and 8.3 were taken by C. G. Trevett, resident engineer at Kleinzee from 1929 to 1932. Figures 10.1 and 10.8 are reproductions of previously published material. Courtesy of De Beers Namaqualand Mines. Figure 5.6 is the remnant of a photograph located in the archive of the Kleinzee Museum. Figures 10.4, 10.5, 10.6, 10.7, 10.9, and 10.10 were made from miscellaneous color slides (almost certainly of De Beers origin) obtained in Steinkopf. Figure 1.6 is a reproduction of a photograph taken in 1927 by an employee of Consolidated African Selection Trust and published with permission of Rio Tinto-Zinc Corporation and the archive of the London School of Economics and Political Science. Figures 1.1, 1.2, 1.3, 1.4, 1.5, 2.1, 4.3, 4.4, 7.3, 8.1, 8.4, 8.5, and Appendix 1 are from the William and Jack Carstens collection. Figures 7.7, 7.8, 8.6, 8.7, 10.2, 10.3, 10.11, 10.12, 10.13, and Epilogue 1 are from the author's collection.

Cover photos: (top) Waiting for Their Men, from the author's collection; (middle) De Beers Board and Officials, 1937, courtesy of the De Beers archive; (bottom) White Pick-and-Shovel Workers, 1930, by C. G. Trevett.

Library of Congress Cataloging-in-Publication Data

Carstens, Peter.
    In the company of diamonds : De Beers, Kleinzee, and the control of a town / Peter Carstens.
    p.   cm.
    ISBN 0-8214-1377-5 (cloth : alk. paper) — ISBN 0-8214-1378-3 (pbk. : alk. paper)
        1. De Beers Consolidated Mines—History. 2. Diamond industry and trade—South Africa—Kleinzee—History. 3. Diamond miners—South Africa—Kleinzee—History. 4. Blacks—Employment—South Africa—Kleinzee—History. 5. Industrial relations—South Africa—Kleinzee—History. 6. Capitalism—South Africa—Kleinzee—History. I. Title.

HD9677.S64 D423 2001
338.2'782'0968719—dc21

                                                                00-065765

Contents

Part 1
Early Years: From Prospector to Company

Part 2
Oppenheimer's New Empire

Maps and Figures

Tables

Preface and Acknowledgments

My association with the people of the Namaqualand region of South Africa as a social anthropologist goes back to the late 1950s and early 1960s, when I carried out research on the Steinkopf Coloured reserve. My work at that time focused on, among other things, the nature of people's socioeconomic relationships with the wider world. The residents of Steinkopf and its four sister communities (Concordia, Komaggas, Richtersveld, and Leliefontein) regarded themselves as stock farmers; when good rains had fallen, some families also practiced a little agriculture. In practice, though, much of the people's livelihood depended at that time on the remittances received from the many migrant workers who sold their labor to mining companies in the region. By the 1990s, very little had changed. In fact, with the decline in farming, the increased cost of living, and more mouths to feed, income contributed by migrant workers had become even more crucial for survival. In addition to that research in Steinkopf,[1] my earliest links with Namaqualand are more personal and go back even further. From 1930 to 1940, I was a full-time (if very junior) resident of the "old" alluvial diamond mining town of Kleinzee; a visiting resident from 1940 to 1947, during vacations from boarding school in Cape Town; and an occasional visitor afterwards until 1956.

I left South Africa in 1964 to take up a visiting lectureship at the University of North Carolina, Chapel Hill, in the United States, and the following year I accepted a regular faculty position at the University of Toronto. In 1970, I became a Canadian citizen, thereby forfeiting my South African citizenship and passport. I corresponded with a few people on the Steinkopf reserve over the years, but it was not until 1990 that I was able to obtain a visa to return to South Africa for a few weeks, when I managed to fit in brief excursions to both Steinkopf and the "new" mining town of Kleinzee. It was then that the idea of writing this book was conceived. Two years later, I carried out a full year's research in South Africa, from July 1992 to July 1993.

While my earlier work in Namaqualand focused on the socioeconomic life and culture of Steinkopf, one of the communities that supplied labor for the Kleinzee mine, this book deals with the company that has employed those migrant workers over the years. It is, therefore, more than a community study of a company town, and special attention has been paid to Kleinzee's ties with the wider world and with its history. Linking the present to the past was the most challenging part of the project. To extend the focus through time, and to sharpen it, I needed to adopt a sort of "zoom lens" approach; I wished to examine, in some detail, the early prospecting and digging days, as well as the various intermediate periods in the life of the town and the local industry. Without these historical detours, I would never have understood the intricate schemes adopted by the Anglo American and De Beers companies to gain control of the Namaqualand diamond industry and maintain dominion over it.

With regards to the processes of time, I have generally followed the convention of detailing the sequence of important events and historical periods that led to the formation of a company, the building of a town, and the evolution of the industry from its simple, crude, pick-and-shovel beginnings, with tent and shack dwellings, to the introduction of complex technology and the "suburbanization" of daily life. I have, however, endeavored to go beyond the mere chronicling of events over a seventy-year period to explain the relationship between historical processes and everyday intercourse.[2] And while my interpretations of the sociocultural processes of company-town life are informed by social anthropological (and sociological) perspectives and free use of the comparative method, my ideas have also been influenced by the work of those geographers and historians who have been pioneers in the study of company towns. With regard to my use of the comparative method in this study, readers should note that comparisons are made, not only between various kinds of company towns but also with other social formations characterized by their relative isolation and economic and institutional dependence on the outside world (e.g., military bases, native reserves, boarding schools, etc.). This method of analysis and enquiry brought to light not only what might be called the cultural landscape of closed communities but the effects of "closedness" on the quality of their lives as well.

I must now elaborate briefly on my kinship and other connections with Kleinzee when I was growing up, and the particular perspective those years gave me in writing this book. My father, Jack Carstens, worked for the company as the mine pit superintendent from 1928 to 1956, a position he acquired through his close association with the diamond industry as a prospector. He was the first discoverer of diamonds in Namaqualand—near Port Nolloth, in August 1925; and the following year he made a second discovery, at Kleinzee. My mother, a teacher, pioneered primary education at Kleinzee—first as an unpaid volunteer and then as an employee of the company from the mid 1940s to her retirement in 1956. The vantage point from which I experienced this mining community as I was growing up thus was unlike that of the son of a mineworker, but it did provide me with the credentials in later years to reflect on the nature of the hierarchical structures in company towns and to recall that everyone employed by the company, regardless of class or rank, was at the mercy of the authority exercised by consultants and directors. Even the senior staff (management) could be fired on the strength of a telegram from head office in Kimberley. One manager, for example, was dismissed without reason from the services of the company in 1930. Several years later, two other managers were recalled because they did not perform to the satisfaction of head office. The senior security officer was mysteriously fired in 1929, while on leave, without being permitted to return to pack his bags.

My father, I now recall, was always terrified that he would be sacked from his superintendent's job if the full story of his misfortune as a prospector were to be interpreted as his being critical of the De Beers company—or worse, of Oppenheimer himself. When I started my research for this book, I had little interest (apart from curiosity) in his hard-luck story, which seemed irrelevant to this study. But my informants told me otherwise; and when I started to poke my nose into the dusty files, I soon discovered that the saga was intricately related to company power, of which my father must have been acutely aware. In fact, so deep-rooted was his fear of reprisals that, when as a pensioner of De Beers he published his memoirs, he used a fictitious name (Albert Truro) for George Scott Ronaldson, the man who had deprived him of his share of the alluvial diamond fields that were taken over by Oppenheimer's companies in 1927.[3] Ronaldson became a director of Cape Coast Exploration Ltd. in 1928.

The direction and success of social research involving different time periods depends on a number of factors. These include the availability of reliable primary and secondary sources, a lively oral tradition, and, equally important, the opportunity to integrate intensive contemporary fieldwork with the historical dimension. My early socialization in Kleinzee stood me in good stead while I was evaluating mine records and identifying photographs. There were many

xiv ◆ *Preface and Acknowledgments*

faces and names that I recognized, each with their own legends and special anecdotes. On the whole, though, it was the wealth of detail contained in the mine records, especially those from 1926 to the mid 1960s, that contributed most to the reconstruction of history. These priceless documents, incidentally, had been rescued from a garbage dump, a few months before I arrived, by an enlightened employee, and given to the local museum for safekeeping.

While this archival gold mine at Kleinzee formed the basis of my historical reconstruction, I also had open access to the holdings in the De Beers Archive at Kimberley and restricted access to a few files in the Anglo American Archive in Johannesburg. The Deeds Office in Cape Town provided most of the answers that I needed to questions relating to land transfers. Other archival material comes from the United Kingdom, from the London School of Economics and the Rio Tinto-Zinc Corporation in London and Newbury; it was in their collections that I discovered full details of the part played by Consolidated African Selection Trust in the founding of Kleinzee.

Fieldwork is never easy, and my 1992–93 experience was no exception, nor was it helped when my wife and I were unable to obtain permanent housing in the "closed town" of Kleinzee. This was due largely, I suspect, to our not being employed by the company, and because we should not, in theory, have been there at all. We did not fit into any "normal" slot, and this made the allocation of a house impossible in terms of company rules. However, we overcame the problem of accommodation by renting a house in McDougall Bay, near Port Nolloth, and most days we commuted on the terrible road to Kleinzee, where we were housed during the day in the spacious quarters of the local camera club, which became our research base. Commuting was extremely tiring. We had to check out whenever we left town and check in again when we reentered. However, after a few months, several trusting families going on leave at different times invited us to live in their houses in return for looking after their pets.

Most of the research and preparation of this book were made possible by a generous grant from the Social Sciences Federation of Canada (1992 to 1996), which included time in which I was released from teaching during the 1992–93 academic year. The University of Toronto granted me a sabbatical the following year. I am most grateful to both institutions for their support. I must also thank the University of Cape Town for awarding me honorary affiliation and for taking care of visa issues and research permissions while I was in South Africa.

De Beers Namaqualand Mines (and its head office in Kimberley) kindly granted me permission to undertake the research, and I am extremely grateful to Brian Magrath, the Kleinzee general manager at that time, for sharing his astute insights into the culture of the mining world with me, and to Dr. Richard Molyneux, chief geologist (now president and chief executive officer of De Beers Canada Corporation) for his support and encouragement. Dr. Moonyean Buys, De Beers archivist in Kimberley, gave me special assistance in locating the Kleinzee holdings.

Rio Tinto-Zinc Corporation generously made all their Selection Trust material available to me, and I am grateful to Jane Loadman and Daphne Deacon at the London and Newbury offices for their special interest in my research. Dr. Angela Raspin, archivist, and her staff at the London School of Economics were most generous with their time in locating relevant material from their Selection Trust holdings.

I must also express special gratitude to the many Namaqualanders, past and present, especially from Kleinzee and Steinkopf, who contributed to this book in a variety of ways. The list is long and I must thank them collectively; however, the specialized contributions of four Namaqualanders require special acknowledgement because of their superior knowledge and understanding of the company-town phenomenon, having themselves lived both in Kleinzee and other mining communities for long periods: Jennifer Cloete, Lydia Cloete, Paddy Marx (née Wilson), and Glenda Von Zeil (née Hughes). A rough calculation reveals that, between the five of us, we spent a total of about two hundred years in Namaqualand, with half of those years in Kleinzee.

At Tumbler Ridge, British Columbia, where for a brief time I did research, I am greatly indebted to Michelle Coughlin and the staff at the town hall; I also want to thank April Moi and her staff at the B.C. Travel Centre and Business Info Centre, and Quintette Operating Corporation, who provided my wife and me with pleasant accommodation in a furnished flat.

I am very grateful to Robert Halupka, Nick Harney, Diane Mew, Jeremy Mouat, Colin Newbury, and Robin Oakley for reading earlier drafts of this book and for their comments. Bonnie Erickson kindly gave advice on the tables and graphs. The maps and graphics were prepared by Byron Moldofsky in the Department of Geography at the University of Toronto. I also wish to thank Susan Lichingman and Pam Gravestock at University College for clerical assistance. I benefited enormously from the critical evaluations of four anonymous readers while preparing the final manuscript. And I am especially grateful to Gillian Berchowitz, senior editor of Ohio University Press, for her special interest in my book at all stages of its preparation. Dennis Marshall, the copy editor, was both devastatingly accurate and pleasingly skillful in revision of the text, and I am greatly indebted to him for the many improvements he engineered.

Finally, I must thank my wife, Chantal Carstens, another social anthropologist, who shared the field experience with me and contributed enormously to this work, both in South Africa and at Tumbler Ridge.

Note on Currency and Exchange Rates

Comparative exchange rates over long periods of time are always trouble-some, and the following notes may prove useful.

Up to January 1961, £1 (South African) equaled £1 (British). In February 1961, South Africa introduced the rand, which was equal to 10s. (ten shillings, British) or $1.40 (U.S.). More recent year-average currency exchange rates between rand and the U.S. dollar (based on *IMF Year Book*) were $1.2840 in 1980, $0.4399 in 1988, and $0.2943 in 1993.

In the Company of Diamonds

De Beers, Kleinzee, and the Control of a Town

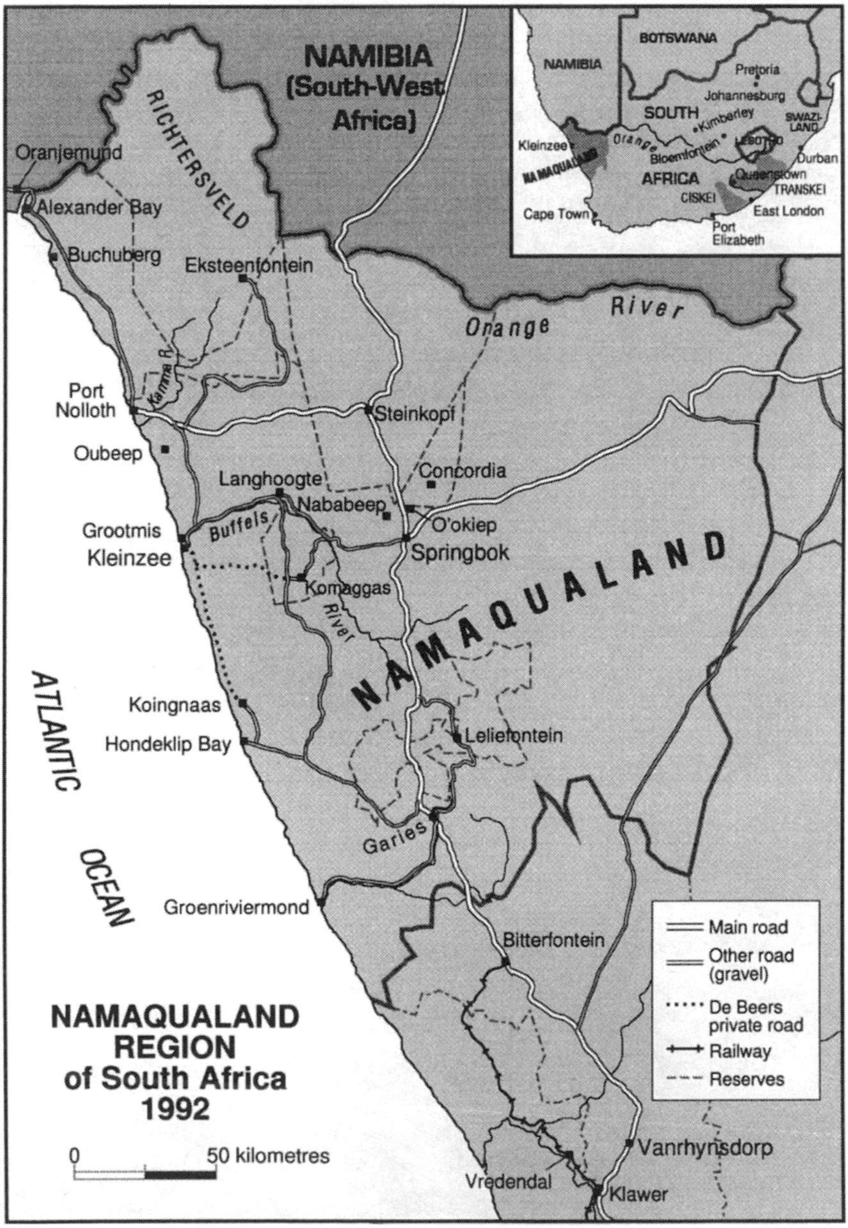
NAMIBIA (South-West Africa)
RICHTERSVELD
Oranjemund
Alexander Bay
Buchuberg
Eksteenfontein
Orange River
Karma R.
Port Nolloth
Steinkopf
Oubeep
Concordia
Langhoogte
Nababeep
O'okiep
Grootmis
Kleinzee
Buffels River
Springbok
Komaggas
NAMAQUALAND
ATLANTIC OCEAN
Koingnaas
Hondeklip Bay
Leliefontein
Garies
Groenriviermond
Bitterfontein
Vanrhynsdorp
Vredendal
Klawer
NAMAQUALAND REGION of South Africa 1992
0
50 kilometres
Main road
Other road (gravel)
De Beers private road
Railway
Reserves
BOTSWANA
NAMIBIA
Pretoria
Johannesburg
SOUTH AFRICA
Kimberley
SWAZILAND
Kleinzee
Orange
Bloemfontein
LESOTHO
Durban
NAMAQUALAND
Queenstown
TRANSKEI
CISKEI
Cape Town
East London
Port Elizabeth

Namaqualand Region of South Africa

Company Towns

An Introduction

ompany towns, as institutions of production and profit, have been part of the industrial age all over the world for a long time. And in mining and other extractive industries, the building of company towns in remote, underpopulated parts of the world is very common.[1] Despite their gigantic industrial value, the moral and aesthetic assessments of company towns have never been particularly commendable: Mark Twain's view of the old coke towns was that they suggested "hell with the lid off"; more recent and no less critical was Mumford's devastating pronouncement that the whole of the industrial age has been a period of environmental plunder, pollution, and despoliation—a period of *abbau*, the unbuilding of the world.[2] Company towns have come to symbolize the wrecking of the environment, especially those towns associated with extractive industries such as mining and lumber milling.[3]

But there is more to the character of company towns than their destructive effects on flora and fauna and the rest of the environment. Typical company towns (*typical* in the sense of possessing the majority of common attributes) are inhabited entirely by employees of the company. They are unincorporated, and the company owns all the real estate and infrastructure and controls and administers both the town and the industry for which the latter was created. Thus, everything associated with the settlement—the houses, shops, schools, hospitals, and recreational facilities—is subordinated to the business enterprise and the will of its owners. Employees and workers know this very well from the manner in which they are differentiated and ordered

3

by their companies according to occupation, ethnic affiliation, and other so-cial criteria, especially when the allocation of housing and access to recre-ational facilities are involved. Many company towns are never planned; they grow haphazardly as the extractive enterprises linked with them expand.

Housing, and its cost to the employer, is a significant indicator of each employee's status in the industry, determining and reinforcing the nature of the relationship between employer and employee. Moreover, while company housing may be a roaring success from the standpoint of labor management—and may even provide employees with somewhat better housing than they might otherwise have enjoyed—it has hidden handicaps in the long run for worker-tenants. The company's combined roles of township manager, land-lord, employer, and owner give rise to insecurity of tenure, favoritism in the allocation of houses, a correspondence between the payment of low rents (or no rent) and low wages and compulsory overtime, and bunkhouse and com-pound systems. Moreover, even if employees have the financial means to ac-quire real property locally, opportunities are not available. All forms of private enterprise are prohibited, which places yet another restriction on em-ployees while they are working for a particular company.

The major task for company-town management has always been the se-lection of appropriate (generally cheap) labor for the particular needs of the industry. Once the labor is recruited, decisions have then to be made as to the most effective ways of controlling it, and of keeping workers contented while in service. This helps explain why mining companies, in particular, attempt to recruit their workers from the same ethnic group. In Southern Africa, many companies also find it advantageous nowadays to transport their labor to and from their homes because it helps in the establishment of contractual rules (especially with new workers) and paternalistic links between management and the home villages of their workers.

Thus, the most efficient administrative design for every company is a sys-tem in which paternalism, as the hegemonic ingredient of company power, can be appropriately extended to all employees in a manner that takes care of their basic needs, according to what is morally acceptable to company direc-tors and materially acceptable to employees. For example, the bunkhouses of the logging and mining camps of the U.S. and Canadian frontiers would be unacceptable by contemporary standards on both counts, as would the low-ering of housing standards for foremen and white-collar workers in any mod-ern company town. This kind of paternalism is not new. Writing in 1556 about the important duties that good mine managers *(praefectus fodinae)* need to perform, Georg Agricola cautioned them in his scientific treatise on mining to be well-informed on many things, including arithmetic, law, surveying, and architecture. "[But the mine manager must also know medicine] that he may be able to look after his diggers and other workmen." Agricola also advised that mine owners look for a site (assuming there was a choice) where there are good roads and access to civilization, and he included stern guidelines for consulting engineers *(jurati)*, saying they should visit all mines for periods of fourteen days.[4]

Company towns are often regarded as "closed" communities, and many companies fence in their towns and place guards at the entrances to protect their properties from theft and vandalism and their workers from the influence of "undesirables" such as hucksters, peddlers, and agitators. Security on diamond mines is fraught with additional problems associated with diamond theft: elaborate and unique measures of surveillance are considered necessary. But "closedness" must also be seen in a structural and symbolic sense relating to the quality of workers' links with, and access to, the outside world.

There are diverse approaches to the study of company towns, but most writers, in defining what a company town is, agree on a cluster of criteria not too different from those presented above; they would not, however, necessarily agree on all of them.[5] Some writers ask for refinements that would exclude many modern company towns. James Allen, for example, argued in his pioneering comparative study of two hundred or so company towns in the American West that mining communities in which there is "private home ownership and self-government and the dominance of independent business firms" should be excluded.[6] Thus, in Allen's scheme, Bisbee, Arizona, did not qualify as a company town because almost all of the homes were privately owned—that is, not under the direct control of Phelps Dodge Corporation. To exclude Bisbee and similar communities, including many Appalachian coal towns and Tumbler Ridge in British Columbia,[7] from the "company town" list is theoretically retrograde; such exclusion gives the impression that mining companies need to strengthen their power by involving themselves in the provision of housing, recreation, and other social services for their workers and employees. Most mining companies enjoy so much power and hegemonic influence that excursions into matters such as town planning, housing, and social services are undertaken only when necessary (as in remote areas, for example) or to conform with state regulations. Thus, while I would agree with Martin Bulmer that every company mining town where the company is party to all the principal economic transactions carried on within it provides an example of a pure capitalistic mining community,[8] I do not think that less company involvement in worker welfare is necessarily an indication of weakness in a company's power base.

At the other end of Allen's scale was Morenci, Arizona, where the company owned all the homes, business buildings, and public utilities, as well as the store that dominated the business life of the town. But, somewhere in the middle of the continuum, was Ajo, also in Arizona. There, the company owned about half the land upon which residences and other buildings were located, plus all the buildings constructed on its land—criteria that qualified Ajo as a company town in Allen's scheme.[9]

In an intriguing analysis of Ajo (after the publication of Allen's comparative study), Larry Stucki demonstrated how the company, Phelps Dodge Corporation, "totally control[led] the lives of [Ajo's] employees" even during lay-offs and a prolonged eight-month strike, despite the fact that many economic transactions in town were carried on by parties other than Phelps Dodge. He shows that the company always got its way to further its own ends because the "systems leaders" developed schemes for gaining total knowledge of every aspect of the "environment's microstate." This strategy of gaining control over people's lives included the weeding out from the workforce all those men who had "undesirable" work habits and "bad" personal characteristics, retaining only those who met the company's standards.[10] The process is very reminiscent, as I show later, of the techniques used in South Africa by Cape Coast Exploration Ltd. in its labor recruitment during the late 1920s and early 1930s. There the company kept in touch with the "desirable" workers during closures with a promise of reemployment when operations resumed, thereby "eliminating the weaklings."

Kleinzee

Kleinzee is a near archetypal company town located on the coast of the lower reaches of the semidesert region of Namaqualand, South Africa. All the four thousand or so inhabitants of this alluvial diamond mining community are employed by, or have some connection with, the formidable De Beers company. The latter not only owns, controls, and operates the mining areas but owns and controls most of the contiguous coastal strip of stock farming land extending south from Port Nolloth for about two hundred miles. It also controls and restricts the movement of all its employees.

Unlike the inhabitants of the first camp built in the late 1920s, today's residents enjoy the benefits of an ample supply of fresh water, piped in from the Orange River, and electricity, drawn from the ESKOM grid system. There are trees, lawns, and well-kept gardens, tarred roads, a large supermarket, good housing for many, a well-equipped hospital, and schools and restaurants; a golf course and rugby and cricket fields are resplendent with lush green turf. To the unenlightened, the suburban quality of this utopian oasis may appear to differ little from many modern towns of similar size in the Western world.[11] But Kleinzee remains a single-industry company town, built, owned, and controlled by De Beers Consolidated Mines Ltd. to be the headquarters of all its alluvial diamond mining operations in the region.

To what extent can Kleinzee's social institutions be said to mirror those of South African society in general? Kleinzee has its black, Coloured, and white workers, a compound system, and conventions that with regard to racial segregation and discrimination are comparable to those in the rest of South Africa; similarly, the whole system of social differentiation and stratification is modeled on the conventions of the wider society. However, as the image of the "New South Africa" began to emerge in the late 1980s, company policy was, for various reasons, at the vanguard of several reforms in race relations. By 1990, plans were being made to desegregate the schools in Kleinzee, and residential segregation had begun to be less rigid. More men and women of color had begun to occupy positions hitherto denied them. By 1992, the company's jet was piloted by a black South African and the schools were fully integrated. Racial stereotyping became a serious offence in the eyes of management, while a new program, known as operational renewal, encouraged the whole workforce, irrespective of race or rank, to be on first-name terms with each other. In theory, there was to be equal pay for equal work, and a new program of job and wage allocation was introduced to stamp out racial discrimination on payday.

Most of the themes dealt with in this book are pertinent to other company towns in different parts of the world. I have kept in mind the importance of providing a broad, comparative focus alongside the more empirical detail of sociological analysis. I have also attempted, at another level of presentation, to tell the story of Kleinzee through the socioeconomic hierarchy created by "head office" to facilitate the administration of every aspect of mining, including matters such as housing and recreation.

The book begins with the prospecting days and the original discovery, in August 1925, of alluvial diamonds in the Namaqualand region, when prospectors together with their workers braved the elements with a naive spirit of optimism, only to lose every gain to "the diamond ring" soon after. I have addressed the often-complex relationship between prospectors and mining companies: the latter were waiting in the wings until the time was ripe to incorporate the work of others into the world of company directors and consulting engineers. I use the term *complex relationship* because the situation also involved a rather ugly tapestry of "negotiation" by middlemen (including a few women) who, lacking real capital and industrial chicanery and toughness, were easily outmaneuvered by the captains of industry at the expense of the prospectors and discoverers.

My research shows, not surprisingly, how naive and misinformed prospectors and their circle were of the power wielded by the business and corporate elites at all levels in the industrial world. Directors of big companies seeming always to be too busy with the affairs of industry and commerce (and with their shareholders) to waste time negotiating with small fry such as prospectors and diggers, low-level business transactions were always done for them by brokers closer in rank and status to the prospectors; the middlemen—equipped with special cunning and efficiency—were well able to outmaneuver the pick-and-shovel pioneers.

Most of the first part of the book (chapters 1 to 8) focuses on the origin and emergence of the first mining camp at Kleinzee and its subsequent development a few years later. After the early mining syndicates had obtained options to purchase Namaqualand farms on which to prospect and mine, various powerful companies acquired interests in these ventures. In 1927, Chester Beatty's Consolidated African Selection Trust Company, based in the United Kingdom, acquired a 50 percent interest in the properties of the George Scott Ronaldson syndicate. The following year, Ronaldson, a Kimberley businessman, sold his half share to a newly formed company known as the Cape Coast Exploration Ltd. Cape Coast had been established in February 1928 by Ernest Oppenheimer (Anglo American Corp.). Later, in 1942, it was taken over by De Beers Consolidated Mines Ltd. I have analyzed those processes in some detail, not simply to record the events of the time but to illustrate and emphasize the immense power wielded by Oppenheimer's empire in Namaqualand, and how it was acquired.

Having noted the close relationship between Cape Coast and Anglo American, it is crucial to understand the close relationship between Anglo American and De Beers. Anglo American is a diverse investment company with holdings in gold, diamond, platinum, and coal mining, other industrial concerns, and in commercial enterprises such as banking, insurance, and real estate. It is the largest industrial and financial group in South Africa and a world leader in gold and platinum production. In 1993, Anglo American controlled an international empire of more than thirteen hundred subsidiaries and a wilderness of cross-holdings of stock.

The company was formed in 1917 by the Oppenheimers, a German family, who had acquired a major interest in Premier Diamond Mining Company of South Africa and control of Consolidated Mines Selection holdings that were used to buy up some of the richest gold-producing land in South Africa.

Under Ernest Oppenheimer's chairmanship, Anglo American acquired the rich diamond fields in South-West Africa (Namibia), a transaction that broke the De Beers hegemony in diamond production. But the De Beers company (which had been formed by Cecil Rhodes in 1888) continued to reap enormous profits because of its prominent position and use of cheap black labor. It diversified into cattle ranching, agriculture, wine production, railways, explosives, and other basic industries. In 1921, Oppenheimer was knighted. And in 1929, monopoly of the diamond industry was reestablished, albeit in a different form, with Anglo American now in control of De Beers and Oppenheimer chairman of both companies.[12]

In part II of the book (chapters 9 to 14), I examine the phenomenal industrial expansion by De Beers (successor to Cape Coast) of the alluvial diamond mining operations in Namaqualand after 1956, the year when the payable ore on the Kleinzee property south of the Buffels River was exhausted. There were enormous changes in most aspects of the community, involving considerable increases in the size and diversity of the workforce, elaborate diversification of all levels of technology, and the transformation of most of the existing infrastructure.

I have also attempted to highlight some of the complex effects that company-mining-town culture has on people's lives; I try to understand why many employees seem to remain loyal to the company, even when they feel disgruntled and hostile toward their immediate bosses and to the town itself.

Company towns tend to be portrayed as if they were totally closed communities. But even towns like Kleinzee, despite their barbed-wire fences, and where all residents are under the full control of the company, can never be treated as if they were totally closed socioeconomic systems. I have, therefore, drawn attention to some of the ties that employees maintain, albeit in different ways, with the outside world. Most unskilled and semiskilled workers have, over the years, been migrant workers from the Namaqualand region and other parts of Southern Africa. Neither they nor anybody else, regardless of occupation, have ever been able to become permanent residents of the town. As contracts terminate, so formal "membership" in the company-directed community ceases, and it is essential for most employees to retain some social affiliation elsewhere, in their home communities.

In order to avoid using the phrase *closed community*, I find it helpful to speak of differing degrees of closedness to reflect the extent to which people are encapsulated behind the barbed-wire entanglement that encircles the town. Moreover, since so few communities ever have totally fixed boundaries, even in a symbolic sense, in this book I use an alternative term, *threshold*, to describe the portal procedures of coming and going.

In chapter 14, I attempt a brief comparison of some of the common features company towns share with certain other social formations such as asylums, monasteries, convents, military bases, expatriate communities, and native reserves, with particular reference to the effects these kinds of organizations have on people's lives. (See also chapter 13.)

Mining in Namaqualand

The Namaqualand region was one of the lesser-known areas of the Cape Colony when the Union of South Africa was constituted in 1910, despite its copper, which had been commercially mined since the 1840s.[13] The Nama Khoi (the so-called Namaqualand Hottentots) had worked surface deposits of virgin copper long before 1652, when the first European settlement was established at the southern tip of the continent; then in 1685, the governor led a prospecting expedition to Namaqualand to pioneer European involvement in the industry.[14] In the nineteenth century, Namaqualand was, in fact, renowned for its high-grade copper ore, and many of its thirty-six mines had grand names, such as Wheal Julia and Victoria. Copper mining had an enormous influence on people's lives, giving rise to secondary industries and the growth of transportation systems, including the narrow-gauge railway connecting O'okiep and other copper mines with Port Nolloth. Improvements were made to the appalling roads in various parts of the region, the postal services were expanded and a crude telegraphic system was established.

Most important of all, though not necessarily the most beneficial to the local people, was the advent of wage labor in the area, which transformed the largely subsistence-level population of mixed farmers into part-time farmers and migrant laborers. More accurately, a system of mutual dependence developed, whereby local households exchanged their labor for the wages offered by the mines and secondary industry. The system was mediated by shopkeepers and *smouse* (peddlers), who accelerated the process of accommodation to the region. Often the copper companies themselves operated shops and trading posts, thus enjoying additional profit from the wages they paid (a practice well-known in company towns all over the world), but also that they might have better control over the workforce.

The system of wage labor—which, more often than not, had a migratory component—did not develop spontaneously as a voluntary movement of people from the rural areas to the mining towns in response to the demand for labor. As elsewhere, throughout South Africa the supply of labor was stimulated by the shopkeepers who introduced new commodities, which appealed to the new wage laborers and changed the local economy. The missionaries and other frontier ministers of the Christian religion took advantage of their new congregations, requiring members to pledge money; the cash then went toward paying the clerics' stipends, the cost of building churches and schools, and the general running costs of the Christian institutions. For example, by 1870, the members of the mission stations of Steinkopf and Concordia were paying the salaries of both their missionaries and their local schoolteachers. The newly converted were also obliged to clothe themselves according to missionary requirements and expectations.

Wagons and other Western commodities and trade goods could now be purchased with cash rather than by barter. And while the marketing of grain and livestock (in good seasons) provided another source of income for local people, involvement in the copper industry was the main source of cash income for the majority of rural Namaqualanders in the nineteenth and early twentieth centuries, as Smalberger has shown.[15] The necessity of having ready cash increased enormously after the formation of the Union of South Africa in 1910. White farmers were required to pay additional taxes, and the Coloured people living on the reserves were now obliged to pay various specified additional taxes in terms of the Mission Stations and Communal Reserves Act of 1909.

Diamonds

Diamonds were discovered in Namaqualand in August 1925, at about the time the copper mines were closing following the slump in copper prices after World War I. The subsequent development of the diamond industry largely filled the economic vacuum created by those closures. By the time the demand for copper increased again, in 1937, the old Cape Copper Company had been taken over by the O'okiep Copper Company, a consortium controlled by Canadian and U.S. capital.

While nearly all of the copper mining in Namaqualand involved underground operations, with their attendant dangers, alluvial strip mining on the diamond diggings provided fewer hazards for workers. At both the copper and diamond mines, the job of mineworker was an exclusively male occupation in the early days. Even today, few women at Kleinzee work in the actual mining area; exceptions are in the near-sacred diamond-sorting chambers and the security department. Only very recently have a few determined women found employment at bedrock level.[16]

When the mining operations at Kleinzee were being expanded after 1960, new technology replaced the old washing plant and pulsator, the pick-and-shovel excavation, and the loading of cocopans.[17] Bulldozers and draglines then denuded the land, stripping millions of tonnes (metric ton, equal to 1,000 kilograms) of overburden so that the "cleaning" of the bedrock, with its diamond-rich potholes and crevices, could take place. Varieties of specially designed dump trucks shipped the diamondiferous gravels to new washing plants and to a central sorting plant. Prospect pits were no longer dug by pick and shovel: the diggers were replaced by enormous, efficient, auger drills.

The romantic associations of gem-quality diamonds are well known. Diamonds adorn moneyed people everywhere, and the De Beers advertising campaigns are famous in Europe, America, and Japan. Although rubies and emeralds were once more greatly prized, today diamonds have triumphed: their status as the property of kings marked the beginning of a unique commercial history.

Diamonds come in all shapes and sizes, in many colors and shades. Some are almost priceless; others have only industrial value. Black boart diamonds do not excite the senses any more than a fragment of coal does, but many octahedral, blue-white gemstones, for which the Kleinzee mine is famous, can appear to the untutored eye to have come directly from a diamond cutter's hands.

In this book, I have taken it for granted that gem diamonds have great value and that their value varies with the vagaries of politics and the market. Colin Newbury has dealt with this subject so admirably in his study of business, politics, and precious stones in South Africa that I will steal his marvelous quotation from Adam Smith:[18] "[Gem diamonds] are of no use, but as ornaments; and the merit of their beauty is greatly enhanced by their scarcity, or by the difficulty of getting them from the mine. Wages and profit accordingly make up, upon most occasions, almost the whole of their high price."

My concern here is neither with the beauty of diamonds nor with their price—except indirectly—but with the hierarchical social system designed by the powerful corporate world to undertake the mining of diamonds for enormous profit. Hence my persistent, if at times covert, preoccupation throughout this book with the various courses of action taken by mining companies to acquire and maintain power over their property and the people they employ.

Part I

◆

Early Years
From Prospector to Company

The first discoveries of diamonds in South Africa occurred in the late 1860s and early 1870s, many hundreds of miles to the east of Namaqualand. One of the diamonds, known later as the Star of South Africa, weighed 83.5 carats. By 1870, thousands of prospectors and diggers had flocked to the banks of the Orange and Vaal Rivers. The well-known Kimberley mine was discovered in 1871. Other Kimberlite pipes were located later, and what was to become the giant of the diamond industry, De Beers Consolidated Mines Limited, was registered in 1888.[1] Premier Mine, famous for the 3,106 carat Cullinan diamond, was discovered in 1902.

The first discovery of diamonds in the semidesert of the Namaqualand region took place many years later at a location about six-and-a-half miles to the south of Port Nolloth, near the dry riverbed of the Kamma River, close to the boundary of Oubeep Farm.[2] That discovery, on 15 August 1925, was less dramatic than those at Premier Mine or Kimberley. The first stone weighed only one-half of a carat, but it was a near perfect, blue-white gemstone. Prospector Jack Carstens made his discovery using very primitive equipment—picks and shovels, a small sieve, and half an oil drum filled with water. Other gem-quality diamonds from the same site were registered during the ensuing weeks. Discoveries by other prospectors followed. Those north of Port Nolloth, at the Cliffs, Buchuberg, and around Alexander Bay, were associated with Solomon Rabinowitz, Israel Gordon, Robert "Sonny" Kennedy, the Coetzee brothers, a man named Gelb, and a few others. Then, late in 1926, Dr. Ernst Reuning, one of the geologists employed by Dr. Hans Merensky, discovered the fringe of the rich deposits of gemstones at Alexander Bay that were to make the latter famous when he unearthed an Aladdin's Cave of diamonds in 1927 (see appendix 1 for an account of Merensky's work and holdings at Alexander Bay). Two new discoveries south of Port Nolloth occurred in 1926: one, near the hamlet of Grootmis, was associated with a small Springbok-based syndicate; the other, near the mouth of the Buffels River, was Carstens's second discovery at Kleinzee.

As news of the 1925 discovery spread, a medley of visitors arrived at the diggings; each had his own agenda. Among the first was a digger from Kimberley, Robert "Sonny" Kennedy, who was well-known in diamond circles. Kennedy was intrigued by the alluvial deposits and was a regular visitor for several weeks, riding in from Port Nolloth on horseback. An excellent gravitater, he generously shared his knowledge with Carstens. Earlier, Kennedy had traveled as far north as Alexander Bay and seen promising diamond indicators in the gravel. After a week or so at Carstens's diggings, he suggested that the two

1.1. The First Discovery of Diamonds in Namaqualand, August 15, 1925
The site is six-and-a-half miles south of Port Nolloth on Oubeep Farm. Photo taken soon after the discovery: from left to right, Harry Jacobs (cook), William Carstens, Jack Carstens, the gravitater, and two workers.

1.2. Visitors to the Carstens Diggings after the 1925 Discovery
Pictured some months after Carstens's 1925 discovery are (left to right) Cullis Relly, Casperuthis, Vernie Carstens, and Dr. Humphrey.

of them join forces and leave someone in charge of the claims while they went to Alexander Bay to seek their fortunes there. Carstens turned down the idea, but Kennedy stuck to his plan, formed a partnership with the special justice of the peace at Port Nolloth, found diamonds, and was later able to sell his claims to Hans Merensky for £12,500.[3] Kennedy later made a small fortune in Tanganyika with Dr. John Williamson, a Canadian geologist.[4]

Another visitor to the diggings was Solomon Rabinowitz, owner of a trading store on the Steinkopf reserve, who spent his profits and spare time on various prospecting missions for copper and gold in that part of the country. Rabinowitz had a hunch that there were diamonds at the Buchuberg, some sixty kilometers north of Port Nolloth, and he went to look at the gravels and the wash. In less than a month he had declared 334 small diamonds having a total weight of 74.5 carats.[5]

Two unusual guests were Dr. W. A. Humphrey, a former government geologist, and Cullis Relly, his employer and successful Stellenbosch farmer. Relly worried whether the stones were perhaps not zircons, and whether the gravel had been salted with diamonds brought from India. Eventually, Dr. Humphrey declared the discovery to be a freak of nature and the party went back to Cape Town with no further interest.[6]

All of these visitors were prospectors in their own right; none of them had any connection with De Beers or any other mining or financial corporation, and certainly they had no access to the kind of capital needed to undertake large-scale prospecting and development. Then, toward the end of 1925, a man by the name of Henry James Saunders arrived at the diggings, ceremoniously perched "on top of a donkey cart." Harry Saunders turned out to be a Kimberley man who, before his retirement, had been a chief valuator for the Diamond Detective Department in Kimberley. He was, indeed, an expert on diamonds, and, at the time of his visit he was employed by the Diamond Protection Board, a public organization designed to combat illicit diamond buying and trading (IDB). The board, although not officially part of De Beers, was controlled by the directors of that company, and Saunders was considered to be one of its paid servants.

Saunders was enormously impressed with the diggings. Recognizing a good wash, and unable to mask his enthusiasm when two gem-quality diamonds showed up in one sieve, he asked if he could take a sample of the concentrates away with him. Later in the day, over a cup of tea, Saunders invited Carstens to accompany him to Cape Town to meet his principal, "Scottie" Ronaldson, to discuss the possibility of obtaining support to develop the diggings. George Scott Ronaldson was said by Saunders to be a well-respected Kimberley businessman, diamond buyer, and speculator. He was a member of the prestigious Kimberley Club, but at that time had no connection with De Beers. A meeting was arranged at the Civil Service Club in Cape Town, and fifteen gem-quality diamonds extracted from the diggings made an impressive parcel for Ronaldson to examine. The meeting was an enormous success. Formation of a syndicate was discussed, and in the cordial agreement that was worked out it was agreed that Ronaldson, on the one side, and Jack Carstens and William Carstens (Jack's father), on the other, would operate as partners on a fifty-fifty basis: Ronaldson would finance the venture, and Jack Carstens would carry out all the prospecting and other operations on the spot, with the help of an experienced digger whom Ronaldson would send from Kimberley. The partners would try to take options to buy all the coastal farms from Oubeep south to Hondeklip Bay, and beyond if necessary. Hein Becker, a solicitor in Springbok, would represent the syndicate in the option-to-buy-the-farms scheme.

When discussion turned to drawing up a formal legal contract, Ronaldson declared it was unnecessary to have one. "My word is my bond," he said, and he was adamant that neither party needed a solicitor. The agreement was sealed with a handshake. After the meeting, Saunders (who had been present, but had played no active part in it) assured Carstens that he had no need to question the absence of a formal written contract. "Ronaldson is the whitest man in Africa—he'll never let you down," he said. The next day Saunders and Ronaldson returned to Kimberley. Carstens returned to Port Nolloth.

Ronaldson did make funds available and he sent an old digger, named Benson, from Kimberley to help with the gravitating and general supervision at the claims. Benson knew how to operate a rotary pan and, in general, his experience added a great deal to the operation. The number of pick-and-shovel workers was increased. Harry Jacobs, from a well-known Saint Helenan, Port Nolloth, family, was hired as cook; a tent was purchased; and a horse was bought from a nearby farmer, making Port Nolloth more accessible.

As soon as Benson had learned the ropes, Carstens and Becker, the solicitor named by Ronaldson, set off to obtain options to purchase all the farms between Port Nolloth and Hondeklip Bay; they said they would pay the impoverished white owners four shillings and sixpence (4s. 6d.) for each morgen (just over two acres) in the event that diamonds were found on those farms. Although above the going price for farmland, it was a meager sum. The contracts stated that the owners could stay on their farms and carry on with their farming, but they would be required to act as caretakers for the syndicate and keep an eye open for illegal activities by IDB poachers and agents. Securing the signatures was not an easy task, because the agreement of all the sons, and often daughters, too, had to be obtained if their names appeared on the title deed to the farm. When Becker recorded the option-to-buy documents, he did so, unknown to Carstens, in Ronaldson's name only. The farm question was extremely important because without total access to the land productive mining would be impossible.

The last of the recorded early visitors to the diggings was Pieter de Villiers, the village schoolmaster at Grootmis, near Kleinzee, on the Buffels River, some fifty kilometers to the south. De Villiers, on one of his frequent visits on horseback to Port Nolloth, was curious about the rumor that diamonds had been brought from India. He was given the opportunity to observe the gravitating process, and after a few washes from a pile of gravel, he was amazed to see a magnificent diamond, sized at one carat, shining in the middle of the sieve.

Early in 1926, a passing farmer stopped by with the news that a diamond had been discovered at Grootmis. Carstens telegraphed Ronaldson immediately. The matter needed quick attention if they were to prevent the properties in the area from falling into the hands of other syndicates and companies, now active in southern Namaqualand. Ronaldson agreed, his man Benson went back to Kimberley, and Carstens hired a lorry and set off for Kleinzee, taking his equipment and provisions for three weeks. If alluvial diamonds occurred at Grootmis, on the Buffels River, he figured that they ought also to occur on Kleinzee Farm, which was about four kilometers closer to the sea. (Kleinzee Farm has enjoyed a variety of spellings over the years. Mid-nineteenth-century records use *Kleyne Zee*, which later became *Kleine Zee*. In the early twentieth century, *Kleinzee* was adopted as the official spelling, only to give way to *Kleinsee*. I have avoided the modern spelling because it seems to be at variance with the historical dimension of this book.)

The Special Significance of the Kleinzee Discovery

On his arrival at Kleinzee, Carstens met with Jan Kotze (Oom Jan), the principal owner of the farm. Kotze, his wife, two sons, and two daughters lived in a small, sturdy, stone house a mile from the river mouth. Although poor, the Kotzes were better off than the majority of the Buffels River people, who were almost destitute after a long drought. The Kotzes lived close to the small lagoon (the "Kleyne zee") at the mouth of the river, which was well-stocked with small fish. The riverbed itself provided good water near the surface, and there was also some limited grazing for stock.

Before any prospecting could begin, it was crucial to determine where the so-called Grootmis discovery had taken place. The site turned out not to be at Grootmis after all, but at the "crater" on the farm known as Annex Kleinzee, one of the properties previously secured by Becker. When confronted, the diggers argued that their claims were located on another farm, Vishoek, and it took a surveyor to prove to them that they were trespassing on a farm under option to Carstens and Ronaldson.[7]

The main task now was to prospect Kleinzee Farm, most of which lay on the south bank of the Buffels River. There were no visible surface boulders or clear indications as to where the ancient watercourses of the Buffels River might have been. Prospect pits sunk at random on one of the lower terraces near the sea produced small boulders and gravels, but the wash was "young," with no concentrates, or any of the other indicators associated with alluvial diamondiferous—the epidote, corundum, jasper, and so on.[8]

This discouraging experience continued for two weeks and Carstens was on the verge of leaving the area. Oom Jan was especially disturbed by the gloomy news because he, his family, and neighbors had started to pin their hopes on finding employment on the new diggings.

Meanwhile, Oom Jan had been combing the surface of his property for diamond indicators, which had been explained to him. One evening, he reported that at a dried-up pan at the southwest corner of his farm he had seen some large, surface garnets, but no boulders. It did not take Carstens more than a superficial examination of the site to make a confident decision to test the pan. The next day, they inspanned four donkeys to Oom Jan's little cart, filled a half drum with water from a well in the riverbed, and set off to the southwest corner of Kleinzee Farm. On arrival, a sieve was filled with gravels and conglomerate, and with the professional expertise of gravitating he had learned from Kennedy, Carstens was soon ready to turn over the first sieve, which displayed "a lovely wash." The second sieve was even better, and in the center of the third was a beautiful, blue-white, 2 ½-carat diamond.[9]

"My God!" said Oom Jan. "Ek het nou net die stukkie grond vir twee-honderd-en-vyftig pond verkoop" ("And I have just sold this bit of my farm for £250"). And so he had, for he needed cash urgently and, after all, what good was a dried mud pan to him where neither sheep nor goats would graze?

Although only a small property of 1,058 morgen, Kleinzee, when at a later date it was acquired, along with other Namaqualand properties, was to be an enormous asset to De Beers.[10] This was because, in the nineteenth century, Kleinzee had a unique history. It was first granted under Government Notice No. 1844, of September 1, 1852, as a perpetual quitrent to the estate of Robert Ripp, for 7s. 6d., paid annually.[11] Then on December 7, 1853, the following

1.3. Jack Carstens and Workers at Kleinzee
This photo was taken shortly after Carstens's second discovery in 1926. Note the rotary pan on the lorry.

1.4. Workers from Steinkopf Sampling Gravels
The four workers were pictured at Kleinzee in 1927.

1.5. High-grade Diggings at Kleinzee, November 1927
Looking south from the northwest face. Note the rotary pan at the left.

1.6. Kleinzee Camp, 1927
The picture shows three tin huts and a Khoi mathouse, with a large tent in the background.

year, it was converted by Charles Bell, the surveyor general of the Cape Colony, from a quitrent to a freehold tenure. Seventy-five years later, the freehold status of Kleinzee became one of its several assets in the diamond era, because its owners were legally exempt from the ban on prospecting and digging imposed by Section 2(1) of the Precious Stones Act No. 44, 1927. This exemption applied to Kleinzee on the grounds that prospecting and digging operations had already been in progress prior to April 1, 1927, the day that the act was promulgated.

Thus, the owners of Kleinzee had the unfettered right to exploit its diamond deposits without interference from the state. It was mined and prospected for thirty years, from 1926 to 1956, producing enormous profits at low cost.

2

The Struggle for Kleinzee and the Coastal Farms

T he verbal agreement into which Carstens and Ronaldson entered was a simple one: it involved partnership and reciprocity in their joint mining ventures, including the process of obtaining options on the coastal farms south of Port Nolloth as far as Hondeklip Bay and beyond. With the discovery of diamonds at Kleinzee in 1926, the terms of the agreement were crucial to the interests of both parties.

Meanwhile, Ronaldson had clandestinely formed a partnership with another Kimberley diamond buyer, Joseph Van Praagh; together, they started the search for capital to develop the Kleinzee enterprise.[1] They bypassed De Beers and Anglo American and went to London, believing that they would find financial support without difficulty. The London visit produced no funding, but they did meet another diamond merchant, Jacques (or Jack) Jolis, and they invited him to join their partnership.

Consolidated African Selection Trust

Returning to South Africa aboard a Union Castle liner, Ronaldson and Van Praagh by chance met two mining men, G. R. Nicolaus and J. A. Dunn, who were employed by the London-based Consolidated African Selection Trust (CAST).[2] Nicolaus had been general manager of CAST's Gold Coast diamond mine since 1924, and he and Dunn were on their way to Northern Rhodesia (Zambia), to the Roan Antelope Claim, a copper operation in which their company had a major interest. In the course of conversation, Ronaldson told Nicolaus and Dunn that he and his partners had, for a very modest outlay, obtained rights for the mining of alluvial diamonds over an extensive area of farms in Namaqualand. He described the prospecting work and the quality of the gemstones already recovered, adding that "the partnership [now] needed finance, and technical expertise to help them develop their claims. . . . On being told of the work of Selection Trust in opening up the Gold Coast [diamond] deposits, Ronaldson and Van Praagh enquired if they could look for aid from that quarter."[3]

On arrival in Cape Town, Nicolaus cabled Chester Beatty, chairman of CAST in London, in support of Ronaldson's proposal, and received an enthusiastic reply. Van Praagh and Nicolaus both journeyed to Port Nolloth and Kleinzee, where Nicolaus saw the results of a few months' work using a hand-operated rotary pan and gravitating sieves. Nicolaus, greatly impressed, invited R. J. Parker, a young American engineer working for Selection Trust, to evaluate the diamond potentials of the region. Later, another American, J. B. Wilmarth, was asked to make a more detailed examination based on his Gold Coast experience.

Wilmarth's arrival in Namaqualand, early in January 1927, coincided with Merensky's finds at Alexander Bay, and Wilmarth was able to visit the latter's claims and make comparisons between Alexander Bay and Kleinzee. He wrote two enthusiastic letters to the secretary of CAST regarding the value of both Ronaldson's property and the rich finds at Alexander Bay, where the diamonds were only a few inches below the surface: at Alexander Bay, all that was necessary was to turn over the gravel with a shovel and pick out the stones by hand. Following Wilmarth's first letter, the company moved rapidly, and by February 14, 1927, had quietly purchased a 50 percent interest for £30,000 in the rights over twenty-seven farms that Ronaldson had already acquired.[4] It was agreed that the management of the properties should be exercised jointly for the account of CAST and the Ronaldson partnership, probably by the incorporation of a joint stock company.[5] As soon as the transaction had been completed, a 40 percent interest in the farms was transferred into CAST's name, and, as though ignorant of Wilmarth's favorable reports, CAST sold its remaining 10 percent to Oppenheimer's Anglo American Corporation of South Africa at cost. The reason for this sale may have been a gesture of goodwill stemming from an agreement between CAST chairman Beatty and Oppenheimer, in which the latter promised to arrange for the Diamond Syndicate (which he controlled) to buy CAST's Gold Coast diamonds. In truth, Oppenheimer had no interest in industrial-quality diamonds such as those produced in Gold Coast, and the concession was simply one of his strategies to get a foothold in

Namaqualand diamonds, particularly at Kleinzee; this was his first holding there.[6] Oppenheimer had been watching the events south of Port Nolloth very carefully since the Kleinzee discovery.[7]

Having acquired its interest in the Namaqualand properties, in June 1927 CAST sent a team of prospectors to Kleinzee to evaluate the mining area more thoroughly. The group was under the direction of A. C. Clarke, with Wilmarth also on the team; two others, Dermody and Dumbleton, were added later. A preliminary report was soon prepared for Beatty, and a copy was sent to Oppenheimer.

Oppenheimer Negotiates with Ronaldson

Oppenheimer now realized that if he wished to acquire the Namaqualand properties, he had to move quickly. Entering into negotiations with Ronaldson, by July 1927 he had purchased, with considerable difficulty, Ronaldson's 50 percent interest in the properties. This immediately gave Oppenheimer the upper hand. Having already obtained 10 percent of the venture from CAST's Beatty, he now had a 60 percent interest, which he divided equally between Anglo American and a company directed by the Barnato Brothers. CAST retained its 40 percent. It did not take Oppenheimer long to oust CAST from involvement in the administration of Kleinzee. Clark and his team were recalled before they had completed their survey of the other farms, and Oppenheimer was free to begin making preparations for the formal establishment of his new company, to be named Cape Coast Exploration Ltd.[8]

Why did Ronaldson sell to Oppenheimer? And why did he sell for as little as £30,000? One view is that he and his partners J. Van Praagh and J. Jolis realized that they could never compete with Oppenheimer. There was, however, another very specific reason. Three months earlier, Oppenheimer had threatened to take legal action against Ronaldson with regard to another of Ronaldson's "partnerships" (one with the Harry Saunders mentioned in chapter 1). Had Ronaldson waited until the end of 1927, the tune might have been different because, that November and December, Carstens struck rich potholes of gemstones, equivalent in many ways to Merensky's diamonds at Alexander Bay. Production at Kleinzee for those two months was approximately 65,176 carats.[9]

Ronaldson and Oppenheimer: The Dawn of Cape Coast

In November 1927, two weeks after producing a 30,000-carat diamond harvest at Kleinzee, Carstens learned (probably from Harry Saunders's wife) that

2.1. 30,000-carat Diamond Harvest, November 1927
Two weeks after producing these diamonds, Carstens learned that Ronaldson had sold to Cape Coast for a paltry £30,000. Ronaldson sold not only Kleinzee but all the other properties over which options had been obtained.

Ronaldson had sold not only Kleinzee but all the other properties over which options had been obtained, for the paltry £30,000. It was only then that he discovered that his verbal agreement with Ronaldson had never been honored and that Saunders had been working for Ronaldson in November 1925, when he lured him into association with the "whitest man in Africa."

There must be hundreds of hard-luck stories of prospectors who, because they have nothing in writing or because they signed invalid documents, lose everything to crooked speculators. Our Kleinzee prospector, Carstens, who made the error of entering into a gentleman's agreement with a complete stranger, does not deserve much sympathy. In his defense, though, one can argue that the isolation of Kleinzee diggings from the muckraking commercial world of the late 1920s contributed to his inattention to his own welfare. Carstens himself writes: "From Kleinzee in those days it was extremely difficult to know what was going on in the outside world. The post, for instance, was delivered only once a week and a telephone had not yet been installed. I was literally stuck in the place without any opportunity of hearing or knowing what might have been happening behind my back."

Given the absence of any written agreement, all forms of restitution were out of the question. When confronted on the matter, Ronaldson argued that he had given Carstens a good bonus of £750 for two years of work and, according to Rudd and Watson, both company-appointed "historians," Ronaldson had asked that the latter be given a job by the new company when it was formed in 1928.[10] A job was indeed forthcoming—but, to say the least, a precarious one, especially after both Ronaldson and Van Praagh had become directors. The company, for its part, acquired the man best-qualified at that time for the job of mine pit superintendent.

Oppenheimer is said to have "had difficulty with Ronaldson." What is meant by this is that Ronaldson did not allow Oppenheimer to get his own way immediately. Other members of the board must surely have found this "difficulty" an embarrassment when various complaints and threats of litigation against Ronaldson were tabled at meetings. For his part, Ronaldson acted on the assumption that Cape Coast, having taken over his assets in Namaqualand, was now legally responsible for all his past actions, and the company did come close to being involved in legal proceedings for Ronaldson's previous derelictions. For example, an action was brought against Ronaldson and Van Praagh by Solomon Rabinowitz, the prospector mentioned in chapter 1. This matter concerned the fifty claims in the Alexander Bay area pegged by Rabinowitz while he was in partnership with Ronaldson and Van Praagh in 1927. At the Cape Coast board meeting on January 17, 1930, Van Praagh, in Ronaldson's absence, tabled correspondence, between Coulter & Co., a legal firm in Cape Town, and Ronaldson's solicitors in Kimberley, that dealt with the action. Van Praagh argued that "all the interests of himself and Mr. Ronaldson in Namaqualand were for account of the company." The board, objecting on the grounds that no documentary evidence had been produced for this partnership, put its collective foot down: Van Praagh was told that the company could not hold itself responsible for claims by third parties. Rabinowitz seems to have dropped the case soon afterwards.[11]

Another legal problem for the company related to the rights at "the crater" on Annex Kleinzee. Again Ronaldson's failure to tie things up created a worrisome situation, and steps had to be taken to protect the company's interests.[12] Ronaldson, it seems, had earlier taken unspecified steps to escape liability in the matter.[13]

Another action involved Carstens, who during the Kleinzee closures in 1936 had been kept on by the company as one of its caretakers of the property at a salary of £25 a month. Carstens decided that he had nothing to lose by instituting legal proceedings against Ronaldson for the recovery of £3,000, legally due to him in connection with nine claims he had pegged on Oubeep Farm in December 1925. The matter went before the Cape Coast board, where it was noted that Ronaldson had sold his interests "to a combine consisting of Consolidated African Selection Trust, Anglo American Corporation, Barnato Brothers, and A. Dunkelsbuhler and Company, who in turn sold their interests to the Cape Coast Company, the company undertaking to pay all costs and expenses in connection therewith, and to assume liability for all the existing bonds over property sold, and for all rates and taxes as from 1st July, 1927." The board agreed that Ronaldson had never paid the £3,000, and it was decided to offer £2,250, plus taxed costs, in settlement. This offer was accepted.[14] Ronaldson was a director of Cape Coast at that time.

After Ronaldson's death at age sixty-nine on June 27, 1947, an obituary in the *Diamond News* extolled his virtues. The writer mentioned his "kindly and generous disposition," "his constant thoughtfulness of others," and said "he certainly was the digger's true friend." Referring to Ronaldson's relationship with "Mr. Jack Carstens in his discovery and original development of the Kleinzee diamond field in Namaqualand," the obituary speaks of the "considerable sums of money spent [*sic*] by Ronaldson in search of new diamond deposits."

Ronaldson does seem to have been well thought of in his hometown of Kimberley. He belonged to clubs, founded the Kimberley branch of the Automobile Association, served on the Kimberley City Council, the Kimberley School Board, and other bodies. But he remained an outsider in more prestigious circles, and never became part of the De Beers establishment, which to many was synonymous with Kimberley proper. This latter virtue seems to have endeared him to the digger community, which respected his attempt to operate independently of Oppenheimer and De Beers. Oppenheimer operated on the assumption that common diamond buyers like Ronaldson should serve capital, not control it, and Ronaldson was made to toe the line in all his dealings with Anglo American and its sister company De Beers, which had come fully under Oppenheimer's control.[15] With the formation of Cape Coast, Ronaldson had no choice but to serve Oppenheimer's interests and pay the price of Oppenheimer's disdain for him.

Saunders and the De Beers Connection

Roughly seven years after the formation of Cape Coast, when Harry Saunders had been dead for as many years, his widow, Clara Saunders, wrote to Oppenheimer asking for her husband's share in the "Namaqualand Diamond Venture of Ronaldson, Van Praagh and Jolis." She claimed that, as his widow, £10,000 was owed to her by Cape Coast.[16] That letter of December 6, 1934, seems to have remained unanswered.

It is no surprise to learn that Saunders was part of Ronaldson's syndicate. He had, after all, been responsible for luring prospector Carstens into a bogus partnership with Ronaldson in 1925; and on a later occasion, in January 1927, he had been sent by Ronaldson to "check up" on the Kleinzee diggings. Saunders had retired from the Diamond Detective Department on pension in 1917. Later he accepted another position for £25 a month on the intelligence staff of the Diamond Protection Board (constituted under the Diamond Trade Act No. 48 of 1882). De Beers controlled the Protection Board, electing all eight of its members. Alpheus F. Williams, general manager of De Beers, was the chairman, and I. R. Grimmer, another official of the company, was secretary. The other six members were all directors of De Beers. The sole function of the board was to assist in the suppression of illicit diamond buying and trading, the board working in close cooperation with the Diamond Detective Department.

Saunders was never on the official payroll of De Beers "but on many occasions his services were borrowed by De Beers from the Protection Board for the purpose of inspecting new discoveries and gathering information about them and in such cases his expenses [and other remuneration] were paid by De Beers." He also did "a great deal of secret service work" for the company.[17] When Saunders first turned up at the Carstens diggings in November 1925, he was in Ronaldson's employ; this was without the knowledge of the Protection Board or De Beers. On his second visit to the Namaqualand area, in 1926, he was sent by De Beers (not by Ronaldson) to investigate the new diamond discoveries.

On his return to Kimberley in February, Saunders gave a verbal report to the general manager of De Beers. He also reported on "the quarter-interest that had definitely been promised him by Ronaldson." On February 11, 1926, he submitted a handwritten report that gives a detailed and very accurate account of the location and terrain where the first diamonds were discovered the preceding August.[18] He also supplied personal information about the prospectors in the area.

Neither the written report nor the informal discussion aroused interest in the general manager's office, and nothing further happened for a year, when Oppenheimer heard the details of Saunders's involvement with Ronaldson. Oppenheimer was outraged. Did he now have to waste his time with another of Ronaldson's partners—one who was not even a small-time business man? Saunders had to be eliminated, even at the cost of an indictment.[19] On February 11, 1927, Oppenheimer summoned general manager Alpheus Williams to his office: Williams, he said, had to inform Saunders that, as an employee of De Beers, he must cede all his rights to title and interest in Ronaldson's properties to the company.

Immediately afterwards, Williams sent for Saunders and said to him: "Saunders, you might put down on paper exactly what interest the De Beers company is entitled to." To which Saunders replied: "You put it down on paper that I was given a quarter interest in the syndicate formed by Ronaldson, and I will sign it." Williams instructed the company's lawyers to prepare a document of cession, and that same morning Saunders was asked to come and sign it. Williams writes: "He agreed [to sign] without the slightest hesitation. . . . [When he arrived] he read the document and then, in the presence of two witnesses, Mr. Burke and Mr. Selling and myself, he signed it and handed it back to me."

> I, Henry James Saunders of Kimberley, do hereby cede, assign, transfer and make over all my right, title and interest in and to the one-quarter share or interest which I hold and possess in and to a Syndicate floated by Messrs G. Scott Ronaldson, J. Van Praagh, Jacques Jolis and myself for the purpose of acquiring certain alluvial areas in the neighbourhood of Port Nolloth which areas have been acquired and are now held by and on behalf of the said Syndicate, unto and on behalf of De Beers Consolidated Mines, Limited for value received.

Later that day, "just after half past two," Saunders and his wife called at the general manager's office asking to have the document back so that they could record it against their joint will. When they did not return, the general manager, "sometime after five o'clock" that same day called on Saunders's lawyer, hoping to retrieve the document, only to be told that he "had been instructed by Saunders . . . [to repudiate] the whole thing." Williams continued to harass the family, repeating over and over that he had to have the document "because it . . . [gives us, De Beers] the one quarter share in the Syndicate." Meanwhile, Saunders repeatedly threatened to commit suicide, and Williams was terrified Saunders would take his life before the issue was legally settled.

Nothing much seems to have happened until March 15, 1927. Oppenheimer was in Cape Town, lobbying in connection with a new Precious Stones bill, which was about to be tabled. Winning in the Saunders affair was now crucial, and he wired Kimberley advising the company that legal opinion favored doing "nothing for the moment as cession is defeatable."[20] A month had passed when a senior director of De Beers, Sir David Harris, decided to get tough with Saunders, and the company's attorney recommended that they "should now write demanding return of document lent to [Saunders]"; if it was not handed back within twenty-four hours, legal proceedings would be initiated.[21]

Saunders's legal counsel replied six days later, returning the prized document—but it was franked with H. J. Saunders's repudiation. The rest of the letter deals with the way in which Saunders was being bullied by Williams;

it pointed out that verbal notice of repudiation had already been given to Williams on the afternoon of February 14, 1927. On March 29, 1927, the company's legal counsel replied, stating that De Beers Consolidated Mines did not accept Saunders's repudiation of the cession; they would insist upon a declaration of rights being obtained through legal process unless Saunders admitted in writing that he held a quarter-interest in Ronaldson's syndicate, and that such holding was, and is, the property of De Beers. The letter added that unless the matter was straightened out thus, legal proceedings would be instituted against Saunders and, if necessary, the other members of the syndicate. Oppenheimer knew that Saunders and Ronaldson shared legal counsel, and he proposed to serve notices to each member of Ronaldson's syndicate, informing them that Saunders's share was the property of De Beers; they would be warned against dealing with Saunders's share in any way.[22]

Meanwhile, the directors of the De Beers office in London began to voice their opinion on the matter, insisting that, despite the weakness of the company's case, "something should be done if possible to prevent H. J. Saunders getting away with the quarter interest in the syndicate."[23] Writing again a week later, they asserted "that legal proceedings against Saunders must not, on any account, be allowed to drop but must be fought to the finish. . . . In the interest of our shareholders [the directors] cannot sit down and allow the company to be bluffed out of its rights."

Back in Kimberley, manager Williams seems to have had second thoughts about the ethics and possible repercussions of the Saunders affair. In a three-page memorandum, a copy of which he sent to the London office, he states that the case against Saunders was a weak one. If the matter went to court, he said, Saunders was bound to bring in the name of the Protection Board, "and there will be the risk of odium being cast on the company if it is believed . . . that the company has used the machinery and funds of the Board not strictly for the suppression of I.D.B."[24] It took two weeks by mail boat for Williams's memo to reach London, where it arrived about the same time as De Beers telegram no. 75, conveying the following:

WE ARE ADVISED THAT WE SHOULD NOT BE SUCCESSFUL IN ANY ACTION AGAINST SAUNDERS AS WE CANNOT ESTABLISH THAT HE WAS OUR AGENT (FULL STOP) WE ARE ADVISED HE WAS MERELY AN INFORMANT

The telegram did not impress the London directors. They simply ignored it. But they did offer a blunt comment on the spirit of general manager Williams's memorandum, expressing surprise that Kimberley had selected a person with Saunders's professional connections for espionage.[25]

Harry Saunders died on March 22, 1928, aged sixty-one years, about a month after the Cape Coast company was formed. The firm took over Ronaldson's properties, and Oppenheimer achieved what he had set out to get. My attempts to obtain a copy of Saunders's death certificate failed, but in some circles it is firmly believed that he did carry out his suicide threat. An obituary in the *Diamond Fields Advertiser* of March 23, 1928, simply says he died of "heart trouble." Whatever the cause of Saunders's demise, it came in time for Cape Coast to proceed with its negotiations with Ronaldson unhampered by the "Saunders factor." Although Cape Coast Exploration Ltd. was officially registered on January 12, 1928, formal transfer of property from the Ronaldson syndicate to the new company did not take place until much later. Whatever the full reasons, these transfers took place after Saunders died.[26]

3

The Founding of Cape Coast

T he day-to-day lives of prospectors and diggers are a far cry from those who occupy the boardrooms of Johannesburg, Kimberley, and London. Equally different is the nature and quality of the social contracts by which they live their lives. Prospectors, diggers, and their casual workers are accountable to each other on highly individual terms. The prospector who cannot pay his men is answerable to them at a very basic, personal level, and the casual laborer who is too sick or too old to dig has to negotiate sick leave or a different kind of work. The company director, on the other hand, is a member of a corporation, which means that from a legal—and to a certain extent moral—point of view, when acting as a director he loses his individual identity. Thus, a cluster of directors is authorized by law to act as a corporation and the corporation exists independently of its members. It controls property and has powers and liabilities separate from those of its members. In the preceding chapter we saw how Ronaldson, once he had sold his holdings to Cape Coast, ceased to have any powers of his own in the company, while the latter was held responsible for certain of his liabilities. We saw how Alpheus Williams, although general manager of De Beers, was answerable to his directors in much the same way as an ordinary employee, such as Harry Saunders; both were servants of the company.

Although it is important to stress the differences between company directors and their employees, and especially the differences between directors and prospectors, it would be a serious miscalculation to overlook the networks that connect them. We have seen, for example, how well-informed the De Beers company was about the new diamond ventures in Namaqualand through its informer-spy network, whose job it was to appraise the value of the new discoveries and make observations that might prove profitable to the company.

Cape Coast Exploration Ltd. (Cape Coast) was registered in Pretoria on January 12, 1928, under the Companies Act of 1926.[1] Its first meeting after incorporation took place in the boardroom of Americosa House, Johannesburg, on January 27, 1928: "Mr. A. F. Lyall was voted to the chair and appointed chairman of the meeting."[2] The other directors present were R. B. Hagart, F. S. Langerman, J. Boyd, and J. van Praagh. All, with the notable exception of Ronaldson's partner Joseph van Praagh, were affiliated with Anglo American. The secretary then laid on the table a copy of an agreement, signed by all the directors of the company, whereby they agreed to take up, and pay for in cash, five hundred shares each in the capital of the company, this being the number of qualification shares required by them in terms of article 93 of the articles of association. Other routine matters were carried out, and the session closed. Apart from Oppenheimer's absence, the first meeting of Cape Coast's board had contained nothing remarkable.

However, it was not until February 17, 1928, that Oppenheimer informed the board of Anglo American Corporation at its 117th meeting that "a new Company called the Cape Coast Exploration Limited had been formed to take over the diamond interests of the Scott Ronaldson Syndicate . . . [and that] the initial Capital of the new Company would be £405,000 in £1 shares of which £400,000 would be issued as Vendors consideration, and 5,000 working capital shares, and the Anglo American Corporation would receive a certain number of shares for its interest in the syndicate." The original capital was subsequently increased to £565,000.[3]

Oppenheimer's statement, as recorded in the minutes just quoted from, although accurate, did not convey the complexity of Cape Coast's relationship with the Ronaldson syndicate; nor did they mention his personal involvement with Ronaldson or the nature of Ronaldson's dealings with prospectors, discoverers, other syndicates, and corporations. As far as Oppenheimer was concerned, those complexities were peripheral to his plan to control the diamond industry. Even the detail that CAST still held a 40 percent interest in the properties was irrelevant to him since he was in control of the remaining 60 percent.[4]

The Ronaldson Agreement of October 30, 1927

When the Cape Coast board convened for its second meeting, on April 14, 1928, Harry Saunders (mentioned in chapters 1 and 2) was conveniently dead and buried. The first item of business was to elect a chairman for the meeting. The duty was accepted by Van Praagh; again, Oppenheimer was not present. The secretary reminded the board that a complex resolution, tabled at the February meeting, needed to be dealt with. The resolution was designed to settle, once and for all, the transfer to Cape Coast of Ronaldson's Namaqualand properties, including Kleinzee, and those other properties Ronaldson had already transferred to other parties. The resolution reflected the principles and complexities on which the Ronaldson Agreement of October 30, 1927, was based. Neither Van Praagh's nor Jolis's name appears in the resolution— absences that are consistent with the detail that their names never appeared on any document dealing with Ronaldson's original claim to the Namaqualand properties. It was essentially

> an Agreement between Mr. G. S. Ronaldson of the first part, The Consolidated African Selection Trust Company, Limited, the Anglo American Corporation of South Africa, Limited, Barnato Brothers and Messrs. A. Dunkelsbuhler & Company of the second part, and Cape Coast Exploration, Limited, of the third part, providing for the sale to the party of the third part of certain properties described in the said Agreement, and registered in the name of the party of the first part, and of which the parties of the second part were the beneficial owners.[5]

The secretary then reported that various new assets had been acquired by the company: those from the Grootmist Diamond Syndicate, consisting of certain freeholds and mineral rights in Namaqualand, estimated at 58,930 morgen, together with options over certain other properties in the same district in return for 32,000 shares at £1 per share; those from the Green River (Namaqualand) Diamond Syndicate Ltd., consisting of 10,158 morgen plus options over other properties, in exchange for a similar number of shares; and assets acquired (for a cash consideration of £1,000) through Oppenheimer's negotiations with the H.M. Association (see appendix 2).

Toward the end of the April meeting, Van Praagh announced that the company was in the process of purchasing a holding in Consolidated Diamond Mines of South-West Africa Ltd. (CDM) by acquiring 4,100 shares at about 17s. 3d. He asked that approval be granted to acquire up to 50,000 shares in CDM. Both matters were authorized.

A financial statement, incomplete but dated as of April 10, 1928, was submitted at the meeting, reflecting the cash position of the company, with its total dependence on Anglo American. Among the omissions was the absence of any details of the proceeds of diamonds recovered during the six months ending December 31, 1927; another omission was that of expenditure for the same period. Both omissions relate to operations at Kleinzee.

However, the register of diamonds for that period indicates that approximately 38,060 carats (38,504 diamonds), valued then at about £266,484, were exported from Kleinzee to Ronaldson between July and December 1927.[6] The operating costs, including wages and salaries, for the same period were £6,410 19s. 1d., excluding "any of the overhead expenditure," details that reflect more than a prospecting operation.[7] The records do not answer questions that I have regarding receipt of those diamonds, or which parties benefitted from the sales. My original hunch was that Ronaldson and Van Praagh received, and sold, the eight parcels they received from Kleinzee during the six months from July to December 1927, but given Oppenheimer's control over the Central Selling Organisation (structured around De Beers and Anglo American) this is unlikely.[8] Another possibility is that the London partner, Jacques Jolis, claimed his portion, and that Van Praagh took some diamonds to England for appraisal and sale. There is no mention of the sale of these diamonds in CAST's files.

By June 1928, however, Cape Coast's minutes record that diamond sales from Kleinzee for the second six months of 1927 were £211,755, and for the first three months of 1928, £18,280. If we compare the above amounts with the Kleinzee register of diamonds, there is a shortfall of £54,729.75 for 1927. It is impossible to explain these discrepancies without Ronaldson's and Van Praagh's records. There are many inconsistencies, some of which suggest that the new company had lost some of its profits during this period. Nevertheless, there was cash in the bank for Cape Coast—a net credit of £121,928 13s. 11d. on July 20, 1928, and £12,075 2s. 6d. still to be received from the diamond output at Kleinzee for April and May. The company had also bought 5,125 CDM shares in London for £4,612. At the same June meeting, Ronaldson was nominated and elected as alternate director to Van Praagh, subject to the share qualification called for by the company's articles of association. Van Praagh was in England, and Ronaldson took his place on the board.

Oppenheimer, who continued to absent himself from meetings, was at this time working in the wings to strengthen Cape Coast's mining operations at Kleinzee. He negotiated with De Beers, and seconded the appointment of H. T. Dickinson, a young American go-getter, to replace F. A. Unger as the consulting engineer. Dickinson was given full authority over the operations at Kleinzee: mining, the mechanical, electrical, and metallurgical responsibilities, security, salaries, and housing. Provision was also made for a department in Cape Town to carry on secretarial, buying, and related tasks, and Dickinson involved himself even in the administration of these. Dickinson had boundless energy and a brazen personality, personifying Oppenheimer's attitude toward "managing," labor efficiency, and work in general. He was feared by everyone at Kleinzee—workers and staff alike. Although Dickinson's appointment signaled that Cape Coast Exploration had taken over the full administration of Kleinzee, the board continued to wrestle with the problems of share allotments, diamond output, the hidden agendas of the Ronaldson Agreement, and negotiations with the state.

Oppenheimer Takes Over

Cape Coast's lawyers actually took title of all the properties, including those held by CAST, on August 30, 1928. A complex transfer occurred on that day, involving Ronaldson, Van Praagh, Jolis, CAST, Barnato Brothers, A. Dunklesbuhlers & Company, and Anglo American Corporation. What at first sight resembled a mega-transaction of land between two parties turned out to be an elaborate network of buying and selling in which everyone seems to have been involved in several transactions with everyone else at the same time. At the end of the day, though, Cape Coast was sole property owner. That, after all, was the purpose of the exercise. The company now owned a total of twenty-seven properties, comprising some 166,000 acres and extending, with a few breaks only, for about 145 miles southward from Port Nolloth. Cape Coast had prepared the way for De Beers Consolidated Mines: De Beers took control of the diamond industry in the area in 1941, at which time it held 94 percent of Cape Coast's capital, ready for the total takeover the following year.

The most important meeting of the Cape Coast board in its first year of existence was on September 21, 1928, when Oppenheimer entered the boardroom as a director of his new company for the first time. During his absence, he had reduced Ronaldson and Van Praagh to common board members, as distinct from owners of property; he had put Dickinson, his consulting engineer, in full charge of every aspect of operations at the Kleinzee mine; he had secured the support and service of his Anglo American friends—Sir Reginald Blankenberg, L. A. Pollak, and G. A. E. Becker (not to be confused with Hein Becker, the Springbok solicitor).

The first item of business at the meeting was the formal appointments of Oppenheimer and Becker as directors of the company. The second was to appoint Oppenheimer as chairman of the company. It was then resolved that "Mr. G. S. Ronaldson, Sir R. Blankenberg and Mr. A. Chester Beatty be appointed Directors of the Company subject to the qualifications called for [in the articles]." Oppenheimer now had total control of the board and all its members.

The meeting finalized the Ronaldson Agreement, enabling the company

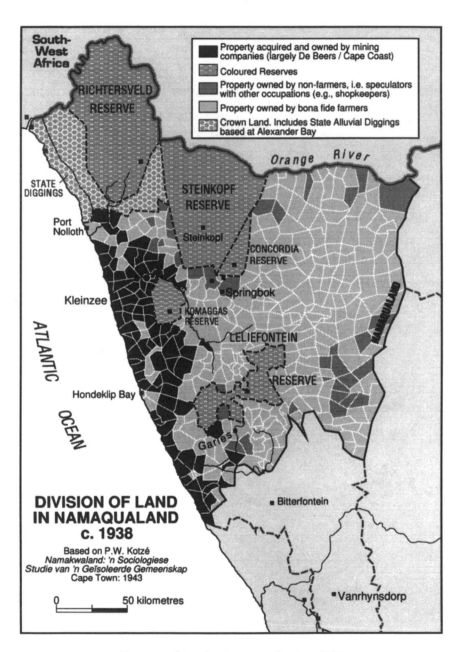

Division of Land in Namaqualand, c. 1938

to involve itself fully in mining operations and diamond production. R. H. Adamson (Ronaldson's manager at Kleinzee) was fired to make way for Herman Behrmann, Cape Coast's appointment. Dickinson's reign of terror and penny-pinching policies began; plans were drawn up to construct a washing plant and pulsator; Major D. Munro was appointed protection officer; A Dr. Steenkamp, of Springbok, was engaged as part-time medical officer; and new plans were created for the housing of staff and workers in a fenced-in mining town.

As to CAST's shareholdings in Cape Coast, a former employee of CAST, who understood Oppenheimer's motives very well, has recorded his insight into that part of the story. In a document now lodged in a company archive in England, C. A. Kidd writes: "In early 1939 Oppenheimer suggested to Beatty that CAST should exchange its holding in Cape Coast Exploration for shares in ANAMIT [Anglo American Investment Trust Ltd.] on the basis of three shares for two—i.e. its £164,000 of shares in Cape Coast to be exchanged for £246,000 in ANAMIT. These were extremely valuable terms and one may imagine that they were pitched so high as Oppenheimer was by then anxious to bring Cape Coast completely under his own control."[9]

The relationship between the growing Oppenheimer and Beatty empires was complex at this time. Oppenheimer feared the growth of American influence represented by Beatty (especially on the Rhodesian Copperbelt) because it challenged not only his territorial monopoly in Southern Africa but his commercial and financial power generally.[10]

4

Kleinzee Mining Town, 1928–1956

In October 1928, the Cape Coast board decided, probably reluctantly, to upgrade Kleinzee's mining technology and improve the living conditions of its workforce. The board would be reluctant to do so because the old Heath Robinson system of mining with its tent-and-shack housing was producing highly profitable numbers of superior-quality gem diamonds at very low cost. Cape Coast soon became notorious for its penny-pinching policy, and the board's decision to upgrade the infrastructure was prompted by considerations other than concern for its employees. For one thing, the company had to satisfy the state's minimum working conditions. It also wanted to reduce diamond theft, both by employees and by bandits who often raided the rich high ground at night: the construction of a plant and a pulsator and the establishment of a permanent workforce over which the company would have full control were ways of accomplishing this. A third factor was the board's anticipation of future expansion, when a change in state law would permit the company to mine its properties north and south of Kleinzee; in that sense, the building of the town in the late 1920s proclaimed Oppenheimer's control of the diamond fields south of Port Nolloth.

The new town cost the company a little more than £100,000, a mere fraction of the value of the gemstones produced in two months in 1927 using antediluvian methods of mining. Cape Coast paid the Ronaldson syndicate £3,422 6s. 11d. for the existing infrastructure—machinery, water pumps, and buildings—an amount included in the cost of the new town.[1] Construction did not begin until the following year (March 15, 1929), and it proved to be a difficult undertaking. Except for the mud bricks that were made locally and the stone for the foundations, all material and supplies had to be shipped by steamer from Cape Town to Port Nolloth and then loaded on lorries for a forty-mile sand-track passage to Kleinzee.[2] The alternative route from Cape Town was by railway to Bitterfontein and then by road via Springbok over the hazardous Spektakel mountain pass and along the dry watercourse of the Buffels River to Kleinzee.

The site chosen for the town was a mile and a half from the ocean and a quarter of a mile from the south bank of the Buffels River, on a piece of ground declared by the company's geologists to be devoid of diamonds. To give the town a tidy look, the vegetation (such as it was) was stripped from the entire site; as a result, when the prevailing southwesterly winds blew strongly in summer, they carried large quantities of fine sand, in suspension, which pitted windows and car and lorry windshields; and the dry east winds were even worse. Fogs also blew in from the sea in the evening and early morning. Rainfall was scarce—seldom more, and generally less, than five inches per year. However, good winter rains produced fields of wildflowers in the spring; for six weeks the desert blossomed.

A poorly constructed system of roads, drains, and culverts was laid out, and the entire town and mining area were encircled by an elaborate system of barbed-wire fences that diverted all noncompany traffic to the east side of the town. But the first major construction job was to update the water-supply system, which was crucial to everything else. In that region of low rainfall, where the river flowed only once every five or six years, there was complete reliance on subterranean water. Two wells were sunk in the sandy bed of the Buffels River, and water was pumped up to a large storage tank near the southeast boundary of the town site. The water was brackish—drinkable but not particularly palatable; to the company, this was an irrelevant consideration because the main purpose was to supply the reduction-plant system. The plant was fed by cocopans that were hooked on to an endless, steel haulage rope; the rope pulled the pans on tracks from the mining area up the ramp to the crusher, where they were tipped and then returned to the mining area.

The washing plant, pulsator, and haulage were powered by electricity generated from the power station's diesel engine, which also provided enough current for domestic use and for the searchlights used to spot IDB thieves entering the mining area at night. A blacksmith's shop and other workshops were built close to the plant, equipped for fitting and turning, electrical work, and carpentry. A service garage was established for company vehicles, and the mine store (not the company store) also formed part of this cluster of buildings.

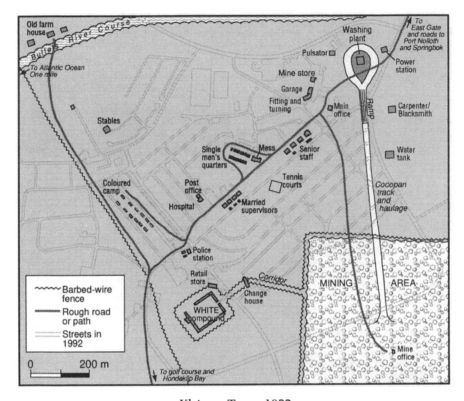

Kleinzee Town, 1932

A hundred yards or so to the south was the office building (administration block), which was occupied by the manager, engineer, mine secretary, the protection officer, and an office clerk.

The actual mining area (the diggings) was very close to the town; it was linked to the white laborers' barracks (compound) by a barbed-wire security corridor about two hundred meters long, through which white workers had to pass to get to the pit. To the north of the compound lay the Coloured camp, a collection of tin huts erected to house workingmen of color, who were required by law and custom to be segregated from the white workers.[3] Close by were the police station, company store, and hospital. To the east were the houses reserved for the employees known as "staff": sixteen single-men's quarters were assigned to supervisors and artisans; a row of four small houses was for married supervisors; and, at the furthest point east, were four larger houses for senior staff ("management"). Close to the single-men's quarters was the mess, a relatively large building that doubled as the town's recreation center for dances and other social events. The newly built company town of Kleinzee had few recreational facilities. Later, a tennis court was built, and workers found they could play golf and cricket on remote salt pans outside the town.

Most of the housing was completed by November 30, 1929. It provided, as well as shelter, running water, and electricity for the majority of workers, "luxuries" the likes of which were unknown in the area. The Coloured workers were less fortunate; they had to wait twenty years for their living conditions to be significantly improved.

When mining operations got into full swing toward the middle of 1930, roughly 235 men were employed by the company. A high proportion were married, but housing was available for only 11 wives and a handful of young children. Three old farmhouses on the north side of the Buffels River were allocated to guards and their families. The company always made a hierarchical distinction between the 19 staff members (5 senior staff, 14 supervisors, or foremen, and assistants), the 6 artisans (craftsmen), the 10 guards, the 165 white laborers, and the 35 Coloured laborers. Those regarded as staff were English-speaking (with two exceptions) and represented the South African English establishment. All the laborers and guards were Afrikaans-speaking, and most of them held political attitudes that were very different from those of the staff.[4]

Thus, the new town was quite small, designed to accommodate only employees of the company and, in the case of a select few, their wives, children, and domestic servants. Even at its peak, between 1928 and 1932, there were never more than about 260 people altogether.

Like other company towns, Kleinzee was not built for the people who lived in it. It was the rational result of the decision by a board of directors whose chief goal, while obeying basic rules that had been laid down by the state, was unhindered production at the lowest cost.[5] The people were as much part of the machinery as were the washing plant, the haulage system, and the fences. The system was expected to operate smoothly and, as far as the company was concerned, harmony could be achieved only if there was loyalty to Cape Coast and obedience to the system. It was logical, therefore, that the town could have no outsiders. Everyone worked for the company, either directly or, in the case of the women, indirectly. The few wives at the mine were there to make their husbands better servants of the company. Similarly, Coloured women in domestic service were allowed to live on the mine only to work for the white families, thereby helping the wife to get her husband to work in the morning and make the home more comfortable. If a wife (or, for that matter, a domestic servant) brought discredit to the company (as did a painter's wife who was found guilty by a mail-order store of fraudulent conduct) her husband was dismissed. The company always regarded "deviant" or

4.1. De Beers Board and Officials, 1937
Standing, left to right: Solicitor C. E. Hertog, L. J. Parkinson (formerly manager of Kleinzee under Cape Coast), an unidentified man, secretary H. F. Lardner Burke, and general manager D. Mc Hardy. Sitting are seven directors of De Beers Consolidated Mines, left to right: G. J. Joel, H. T. Dickinson (former consulting engineer for Cape Coast), H. P. Rudd, chairman Sir Ernest Oppenheimer, A. G. W. Compton, Sir Robert Kotzé, and Harry Oppenheimer.

4.2. Kleinzee Staff, late 1930
The senior staff, seated on chairs, are, left to right: Jack Carstens (mine pit superintendent), V.L.M. Wilson (mine secretary), L. J. Parkinson (manager), Frank Humphreys (manager elect), C. G. Trevett (engineer), and Redmond Orpen (protection officer). Chapter 4, note 4, lists names of other staff members.

4.3. Mine Staff Women (above)
Photo probably taken in 1931. Back row, left to right: Mrs. Mackintosh, Mrs. Pringle, Mrs. Schneider, Mrs. Mostert, Mrs. Witt, and Miss Ruby Humphreys. Wives of the senior staff are seated: Mrs. Carstens, Mrs. Wilson, Mrs. Humphreys, and Mrs. Trevett.

4.4. "A Girl's Best Friend" (right)
Mrs. Pifer, the manager's wife who loved diamonds, in 1939.

"disruptive" behavior with grave suspicion—a sure indicator of IDB tendencies. Thus, when management learned that a new assistant protection officer and his wife were not legally married, both were given twenty-four hours to be "out of the gate."

The only male resident not employed by the company was the owner-manager of the retail store. However, a few years after De Beers had acquired Cape Coast's interests, the store, which had started to make enormous profits, was taken over by the new company, with the previous owner employed as manager; he was required to conform to all company rules and regulations. With the store under company control, there was an immediate rise in prices, which sparked off a wave of discontent. The mine manager was so outraged at the reaction that he sent out a circular telling people to cut out "the whispering campaign in the Camp."[6]

There was no resident doctor during the early years at Kleinzee; all routine medical treatment was carried out by an orderly. The company did, however, have an arrangement with local doctors in Springbok and Port Nolloth to make monthly visits to the mine, and to be on call for emergencies. Most such doctors were quite unsuitable. A Dr. Cowan was blind and had to be accompanied by his wife, who was a nurse; another was dismissed because he was suspected of IDB. In 1931, a mercy flight arrived from Kimberley to take a man who was seriously ill to hospital because no doctor was available to treat a bite from the venomous puff adder *(Bitis arietans)*. The plane had to land in the open space behind the married quarters.[7]

Other doctors were appointed from time to time. Some did not stay long enough to leave any impression, and most were barely competent to practice medicine. One was deranged and had to be fired, while another, an alcoholic, would beg for brandy when his supply ran out. Yet another, after having his contract terminated, missed his train at Bitterfontein and spent a month in an alcoholic haze in the local hotel.

A Dr. Jackson, who was said to be a good doctor, decided, after a week in town, to launch a general attack on the standards of health. The water supply, he said, was not purified; it presented a serious problem. He reported on the state of the sewage and refuse system, stating that the latrine buckets were being emptied in the wrong place, doubling the stench from the large households where "buckets overflowed by the end of each week-end." Doing laundry on the premises at the "lower houses," where domestic washing was done in the kitchen or bathroom, was said to pose another health problem, whether done in the kitchen or bathroom. There was an "athlete's foot hazard" in compound washrooms; the diet for the workers was poor because it contained too little fruit and vegetables; and the pigpens were filthy. The hospital, said the doctor, noting that there was no ambulance for the injured and acutely ill, in general was inadequate. Dr. Jackson soon lost interest and left after a couple of months. No one challenged his allegations.[8]

Fences

In the 1940s, the popular song "Don't Fence Me In" was adopted by the white employees as a theme song to depict their feelings of "fenced-in-ness" that developed with the increase in security measures associated with checkpoints, X-raying, and barbed-wire fences. The first barbed-wire fence in Kleinzee extended around the whole property, excluding the western boundary, the assumption being that entry from the sea was unlikely. There were four locked gates: east, north, south, and west, and it was a violation of company rules to enter or depart from any of these without approval of the manager or one of the senior staff, all of whom had keys to the gates. Within this wide encirclement were a number of other fences. In the 1930s, one marked off the town; another—made of double barbed-wire on the south and east sides—marked off the mining area; and an elaborate, double fence enclosed the compound. The pulsator had its own fence to prevent thieves from making off with unsorted diamondiferous concentrates. The police station, too, had its own fence, as did each of the eight houses for married people.

To most employees, the fence that imposed the greatest restriction was the company's boundary fence—because it prevented contact with the outside world. In fact, the east gate became the only point of departure and entry for the town, resembling a border-crossing point between two countries. Today, the main checkpoint is situated at precisely the same place, but the movement of people in and out of the town is controlled by an elaborate, computerized system managed by six security guards.

In the 1930s, in theory all employees had to have their persons and their belongings searched before leaving the town. In practice, the main targets were the white contract laborers who lived in the compound, and when compulsory X-raying was introduced in 1932, only the white contract workers were "put through the X-ray." Later, X-raying was extended to others, but never to senior staff. White women seem also to have escaped the ordeal, as did the Coloured workers. In the 1930s, the company treated the Coloureds as a sort of specially reserved and protected low-paid "caste," separate from the white contract workers; thus, although they often did the same job as the whites, most other aspects of their lives on the mine were inferior: worse living conditions, lower wages, and little protection from the state. The company expounded the view that the Coloureds were inscrutably honest by nature, devotedly loyal to the company at all times, and this made X-raying unnecessary—a privilege that cost the Coloureds twenty years labor without a wage increase.[9]

Closures

The 1932 Closure

Early in 1932, barely two years after the town was completed, the effects of the Great Depression on the diamond market forced the company to announce the suspension of all mining operations at Kleinzee. There were many lay-offs: the white contract workers, most of the Coloureds, and many other employees were let go. By July 23, the workforce had been reduced to twenty-nine men, whose job it was to maintain the property, guard the mining area, and prevent illicit mining on the company's properties along the coast. Salaries were drastically reduced, but members of the skeleton staff had relatively secure jobs and little to do. An acting manager was appointed. There were occasional visits from the consulting engineer and directors, and Oppenheimer one time came to inspect the property. Oppenheimer's son Harry, recently down from Oxford, also graced the straggling community of watchdogs with his presence. These sporadic inspections were treated with both apprehension and excitement, and the senior staff, such as they were, went to great lengths to impress the distinguished visitors that they were doing good work for the company, overindulging the guests with lavish hospitality.

The company had no cause to complain about the cost of maintaining the property. Running costs during closure never exceeded £675 a month, an amount that included salaries, wages, and the cost of acquiring options on new properties. The shareholders, moreover, continued to receive handsome dividends, despite the closure, at rates of between 7½ percent and 20 percent for the next four years.[10] During the five years of closure, the small labor force kept the buildings and plant in good repair, maintained the water and electricity supply, guarded the diamond deposits at Kleinzee, and kept in constant touch with the lessees of the various other Namaqualand farms owned by the company.[11] Those in the retained workforce were cut off from the rest of the world for five years, and they led a very isolated and restrictive existence. Two families had automobiles and so were able to drive to Cape Town for their annual leaves, but the others had to rely on local lorry transport to reach bus and train terminals.[12] Manager Humphreys's report to head office on the mine's closure was brief and cold. It read, in part:

The last truck of ground was washed on Saturday, May 6th and on Sunday we commenced the discharge of the Namaqualanders [white contract workers]. We are examining them [for the possibility of diamond theft] at the rate of about 18 to 29 per day and up to date the X-ray and process of retrenchment are working smoothly. We shall have completely retrenched by the 23rd inst., although it is essential that a few of the old guards remain over till the month end, whilst for the necessary returns, a couple of the office men will be retained for a few days. The filling in of the richer areas at the Mine Pit is practically complete, and the remaining men are engaged upon cleaning up the trucks and painting them. The pipes are also being attended to. As regards the plant, the rope has already been removed from the Haulage, greased and stored away, whilst all the exposed iron work, etc., is also being cleaned and painted, throughout the Washing Plant. Several of the discharged employees including the Engineer, Washing Plant Superintendent, and others, are being allowed to proceed in the Chevrolet car and a lorry to the rail [head] after the 23rd inst. [Six others] will receive their fares, etc.[13]

Humphreys also forwarded the engineer's report regarding the condition of the infrastructure—the plant, pulsator, haulage system, power and pump stations, water tank, garage, workshops, all unoccupied buildings, X-ray, search light, automatic telephones, and so forth.[14] The report described the plans to preserve these now-to-be-idle items. But there was no comparable report on the employees and workers, who were required to vacate their living quarters immediately after receiving their final pay. The white contract workers were given official notice of termination on July 16, as were the Coloured workers. The staff, excluding senior staff, were informed by the manager on 1 June that their contracts would terminate at the end of the month. Dr. Cowan, the blind doctor, informed on May 28 that work at Kleinzee would end on July 23, was told: "Your contract expires on that day."[15]

On May 1, the manager issued a memorandum detailing the routine for X-ray examinations as people left Kleinzee:

All discharged Whites are in future to be examined by X-rays. The procedure will be as follows: Men leaving will be assembled in the waiting room under guard. All kit will be stored on the opposite side of the waiting room. One man will then pace forward with his kit to the physical examination room, where he himself and his kit will be thoroughly searched. His kit will be passed through the X-ray room and examined if necessary. The man will then enter the X-ray laboratory and a photograph will be taken of the abdomen. He will remain in the X-ray room until the film is developed. If all is clear, he will then be permitted to leave through the laboratory door with his kit, straight into the Police Station Enclosure. If the film reveals anything of a suspicious character a second photograph is to be taken and if the presence of a diamond is confirmed, he will be handed over to the Police and charged. In the event of the Rays disclosing a diamond in his kit, he is to be called to view it himself, and he and his kit will be handed over to the Police. All admittance into the laboratory, except by members of the Protection Staff or Police, is strictly prohibited.[16]

Some employees reacted strongly to the company's retrenchment methods. The resident mine engineer felt that the least the company could have done, in his case, was to pay his (and his family's) return expenses to Johannesburg. He wrote a long, complaining letter to the manager asking for special consideration on the grounds that he was appointed from Johannesburg and had been given expenses from Johannesburg to Kleinzee.[17] Another letter to the manager came from a white contract worker from nearby Grootmis, who had been permanently disabled in an accident at the mine. He wrote:

> I understand that the work of the company is stopping on the 23rd. I wish to inform you respectfully that I have been in the service of the company for the full five years, and that I have in such service lost the use of my leg which is now permanently disabled and I can do no hard work with it. As I am dependent upon the mercy of the manager, I ask that you will not discharge me from your service. It is certain that you will retain the services of a few men for sundry duties. . . . Trusting you will understand since I am poor and cannot do any heavier work.[18]

The plant superintendent wrote:

> I was engaged in Kimberley in April 1930 for service with the company at Kleinzee, and my travelling expenses from Kimberley were borne by the company. By the time the mining operations cease here, I shall have been in the employ of the company for over two years, my service is being terminated through no fault of my own, and it seems to me but fair that the company should bear the expense of my transportation to the place in which I was engaged, and should return me free of cost to my home in Kimberley.[19]

Others asked the manager to use his influence to find them new jobs with the company. A few received testimonials, but not much more. Four men argued, as the plant superintendent had done, that, because they had been let go through no fault of their own, the company was morally, if not legally, responsible for finding them other jobs.

The trauma of being laid off in 1932 was devastating. The most immediate problem was getting home from an isolated place where there was no public transport. The company paid travel expenses for some people, but generally these were the better-paid employees. Even for them, the arrangements were inadequate. The Coloured workers suffered most. Being underpaid, they were accustomed to surviving on monthly credit, a system that enabled them to send money home each month and feed themselves in the Coloured camp. When they were laid off, literally penniless, they were unable to hire a lorry to take them to their homes.[20]

As to "severance pay," everyone received "leave-pay"—that is, pay in lieu of any accumulated leave. The staff fared better than other employees. They, as salaried people, were members of the Provident Fund, to which they had contributed 5 percent of their earnings and to which the company had contributed a like amount. According to the rules of the fund, both amounts, with accumulated interest, were paid out on retrenchment.[21]

The process of getting people off the premises, following the X-raying described above, involved escorting them through the gate and, having gotten them out of town, making sure that they left the entire company precincts. Only a select few received free transportation to the railhead. It is surprising that the company did not, in the interest of security, pay for everyone's transport, given its concern that individuals might return at night to dig up buried parcels of diamonds. But Cape Coast specialized in cutting costs, and once a decision to trim the budget had been approved, it was near impossible to alter it. At the time of the closure, the company was trying to recoup some of the £1,808 17s.10d. it had spent on its new X-ray machine.[22]

Watchmen (Some of Them Women)

As already noted, a small staff was retained to guard the diamondiferous gravel at Kleinzee, to oversee the company's other properties along the coast, and to maintain the town's infrastructure. A team of twenty-two watchmen was appointed. Seventeen were white: the manager, mine secretary, protection officer and assistant protection officer, the company farms supervisor (to look after properties in the south), a mechanic-cum-electrician, a motor mechanic/driver, a painter, eight guards, and a lorry driver. Five Coloured workers were also retained. The white people (who had all been laid off on June 23) were immediately rehired under new contracts at greatly reduced salaries.[23] After the mine closed, Humphreys asked the state to allocate extra police to assist his guards to protect the "un-mined" diamonds, including "all richer faces of the property [which had] all been very adequately covered with boulders."[24]

The reinforcements arrived in August, at which time there were two sergeants and eleven men in the police barracks. Three of the eleven were assigned to guard the pit, three to mounted-patrol work, two to regular foot patroling, mainly at the eastern fence, and three to keep an eye on the empty compound buildings and grounds to ensure that no one returned to dig up diamonds that had been buried before the mine closed.[25]

In August 1932, C. H. Beck, the secretary of Cape Coast, and an Anglo American pilot landed on the airstrip at Geelpan, five miles southeast of Kleinzee, to inspect the newly closed town.[26] Living conditions continued to be much the same as when the mine was open, although there was no electricity during the day. At night, a Benz semi-diesel produced sufficient electricity for the residents and the searchlight, which for the first few years after closure scanned the nighttime mining area and surrounding fences. Residents had lights until 10 P.M. on weekdays, 11 P.M. on Saturdays, and midnight at Christmas and New Year's, when there were dances.

Company vehicles and the two private cars were serviced by the manager's driver. Another driver operated the "tip lorry," or garbage truck, and drove the post lorry to Port Nolloth every Tuesday, Thursday, and Saturday to send out and collect mail. The senior staff had standing weekly orders for fruit and vegetables from the Wellington Fruit Grower's Retail Store in Cape Town. Packages mailed from Cape Town on Thursdays arrived in Kleinzee just before noon on Saturdays. The post lorry performed an important service and for most people was the only link with the outside world. On post days, everyone waited for the lorry to appear. First seen in a cloud of dust to the north, it then descended into the Buffels River valley before driving up to the Kleinzee post office. As well as ferrying mail, the driver ran errands for people, such as collecting "off-sales" orders from the Port Nolloth Hotel—a case of beer for one, a bottle of Old Brown sherry for another, a half-jack of brandy for someone else.

In maintenance of the infrastructure, the most important assignment was that of the painter. To prevent destructive rust, caused by the salty fogs that developed nearly every night, his job was to paint with red oxide everything from the steel girders of the plant to the corrugated iron roofs of the houses. It was a Herculean task. A Coloured assistant did most of the scraping and wire-brushing in preparation for the paint. Two other Coloured men worked with the lorry driver, loading the lavatory buckets on Mondays and Fridays, collecting garbage on Wednesdays, and traveling on the Port Nolloth post lorry on the other three days. Another Coloured man worked in the power station, and another did odd jobs. The fifth, a cobbler and saddler, did all the shoe repairs in town and maintained saddles and bridles. He also skinned and butchered small game when the senior staff bagged something when out hunting.

Security was a major task. The protection officer was assisted by the former pit superintendent, and both supervised the six guards, who were now armed with automatic pistols. Four were always on duty in the mining area, and two were at "the crater." One guard did full-time mounted-patrol work. Another continued to live with his family at Dreyer's Pan, where he guarded the northern farms on regular mounted patrols. The farms' supervisor kept in touch with all the tenants on the company's southern properties. Detailed monthly reports on every aspect of security were submitted to head office.

Closure and Community

When the mine closed in 1932, a total of fifty people lived at Kleinzee. In addition to the twenty-two employed men, there were eleven wives, twelve young children, and five female domestic servants. The population did not interact equally on a regular personal basis; in fact, the opposite occurred. Despite their reduced salaries, the "senior staff," with little work to do, preserved a pretentious exclusiveness, holding select dinner parties, picnics on the beach and in the veld, and ostentatiously displaying the cars that they could barely afford to run. They consciously set themselves and their children apart from the other ranks. Their standing in the company allowed them to come and go freely from the town, make occasional trips to Port Nolloth and Springbok, and enjoy annual holidays in Cape Town, where their children were later sent to boarding schools. At the other end of the socioeconomic scale, the five Coloured workers and the five domestic servants formed another tightly knit group. They had shared home ties, having come from the same towns and villages, but it was their color and low status that set them apart, not their clannishness. Another group, the guards and their families, also kept very much to themselves.

Paradoxically, although the patterns of social interaction during closures (other closures followed that of 1932) resembled, on a small scale, those when the mine was in full swing, the reduced number of people and greater isolation produced even greater social distance. For their dinner parties (sometimes combined with a game of bridge), the rump of the old senior staff dressed in suits and cocktail dresses—a culture of exclusiveness that reflected the narrowness of their lives. Their motives were surely similar to those at colonial outposts in other parts of the world, where people emulated their home culture, dressing for dinner to reassure themselves that they still lived in the real world. At Kleinzee, people in a lower social strata dressed up on Sundays, some parading down the main street, for no apparent reason other than to re-mind themselves that they, too, were part of the other world—customs of per-sonal adornment not unlike those of the Owambo contract workers, who dressed up on Sundays for their own personal satisfaction while they lived in an artificial and alien world.

At Christmas, a semblance of communality emerged. A large kameel-doorn (camelthorn) tree *(Acacia giraffae),* cut from the upper reaches of the Buffels River, was placed in the mess dining room, and the whole camp (ex-cluding people of color) was invited to parties; some neighboring white chil-dren from Grootmis were also allowed to attend. One of the senior staff dressed up as Father Christmas and had to be "found" by a search party on a sand dune. Each New Year's Eve (sometimes at Christmas, too), a dance was held in the mess. The company provided food and large quantities of beer and sherry, much-needed lubrication to blur the status distinctions among the white employees for a few hours once a year. There was always live music—concertina, guitar, and violin, playing largely *boeremusiek,* but also some popu-lar, old-fashioned "English" tunes. On such occasions, all the white employees and their wives celebrated their collective isolation on this southernmost tip of the Namib desert.

The Mine Reopens

The official role of this watchman crew (and their families and domestic ser-vants) during the closure was looking after property and preventing illicit dia-mond digging. But the team of retainees also served to maintain the local culture, so that when other workers returned after the closure and the hooter announced the beginning of the first shift, when the endless haulage rope began to move again, it was almost as if nothing had changed during the years of closure.

There was both uncertainty and relief when news reached Kleinzee that the mine would reopen on October 1, 1937. What would salaries and wages be after the wheels began to turn again? Would their services still be needed? Outside the company's fences, the news of the mine's reopening spread quickly, and hundreds of white Namaqualanders again applied for pick-and-shovel work; former supervisors were asked to return, and soon things re-turned to "normal"—almost exactly as they had been in 1932. It could hardly have been any different, with 80 percent of the original workforce filling the same slots they occupied five years earlier. All the old problems reappeared. Married men asked for houses that did not exist and had no choice but to continue living in the single quarters. Poverty continued in the region, with many local people still out of work. Disputes arose between farm tenants and the company over their status on the farms, and IDB resumed everywhere.

But there were changes. Among those with which Cape Coast had to deal was the fact that the wages it paid to its white contract workers were far below those paid by the State Alluvial Diggings and the copper companies for similar work. Thus, while the size of the rest of the workforce remained constant, the number of contract workers declined by at least 10 percent. The state continued to insist that only white labor be employed "in the diggings," but it was unable to control wage levels. As before, Cape Coast opted for low wages, to maintain the cost per load, based on mine expenditure, below 3/9.06 (three shillings and 9.06 pence).[27]

At the same time that the board was attempting to curb wages and cut costs, it was asking that production be stepped up. In June 1938, the consulting engineer, in anticipation of a shutdown at the end of the year, wrote demanding that an average monthly production of from 5,500 to 6,000 carats be achieved.[28] The new manager, Drury Pifer, who always enjoyed a challenge and wished to impress his superiors, informed the consulting engineer that the total production would be met in two months, adding that workers would be laid off by November 30, rather than December 31. "But [I will] keep workers on 24 hours notice in case we need them longer."[29] Pifer was not a particularly popular manager, but he did his job efficiently, and was always concerned that the contract workers be treated fairly according to company rules. He also had academic leanings and was an American, factors that seem to have counted against him in the managerial role. He later became a highly successful and well-respected professor at the University of Washington, Seattle.[30]

The company's insistence on cutting costs and reducing staff had disastrous consequences on mine safety. A power station engine that had not been serviced seized up and part of the cylinder head flew off, nearly killing James Agenbag. Gus Gottsiff (Gottseif?), the electrician, was electrocuted and killed by the high-tension wires leading to the X-ray equipment because there was no one to turn off the current; his assistant, Van Zyl, was badly shocked and burned when he attempted to rescue him. There was no resident physician at the time. Dr. Palmer-Field, the new doctor, had been sacked by Pifer on the grounds that he was irresponsible and psychotic.[31]

Closed Again, but Small-scale Prospecting Continues

As the mine prepared to lay off workers in 1938 for its second closure, the X-ray machine was again tuned up for an exodus. Almost everyone left: the drillers and blasters, trackmen, blacksmiths, diggers (loaders and bedrock cleaners), trammers, haulage men, the trommel workers and feeders from the washing plant, jig operators, and gravitaters from the pulsator. Some lorry drivers also left, as did cooks, washermen, and cleaners. A small contingent remained in much the same way as in 1932. On December 17, 1938, the complement of employees at Kleinzee was forty-seven (seven staff, one artisan, nine white laborers, eight guards, and twenty-two Coloured workers).[32]

Although production was suspended, a prospecting and development plan was initiated, and seventeen of the Coloured laborers were assigned to the job. They dug three-foot-wide trenches, cleaned the bedrock, loaded gravel into the mobile crushing plant, operated the rotary pan, removed the tailings, tapped the concentrates from the rotary pan, and did the gravitating. The diamond sorting, measuring of trenches, stratigraphy recording, and writing of reports was done by the mine superintendent and a geologist—responsibilities later given to untrained employees.[33]

In September 1939, when World War II began, all Namaqualand was a blaze of color after exceptional rains had brought to life a myriad wildflowers. The Buffels River, in full flood in early August, had swept tonnes of muddy tailings into the sea. A Coloured man was drowned in the strong current while attempting to cross the river at Grootmis.[34] The pump house was nearly swept away, although on August 21, when the river was still flowing, the flood level was down six feet. In June 1939, the company's aerodrome at Geelpan was licensed by the state, and in July 1940 the director of air services asked the company to keep the runway in a fit state for emergency use during the war. Although Geelpan did not become a military base, the company regarded the small expense and inconvenience to be part of its war effort.[35] (In 1948, a landing strip made from mine tailings was built on the west side of the town for the exclusive use of the company.)

Security was again an issue during the war years. In 1940, it was decided to move the police station to the east gate, at an estimated cost of £2,400. It was also decided to X-ray the Coloured workers and increase the range of staff to be X-rayed. Soon everyone but senior officials was required to be X-rayed. The inclusion of Coloured workers in the X-ray net created a political problem. There was only one entrance to the X-ray laboratory, and separate entrances for each ethnic group had to be built.[36] There was some resentment on the part of the Coloured workers when they heard that they had to go through the X-ray—*"onder die ligte gaan"* (literally, "under the lights"). The Coloureds had always regarded themselves as being above suspicion and in a different moral street from many Namaqualand whites. Later, they acquiesced, for which they were rewarded by the acting manager: he obtained permission from head office to give them the "customary Christmas present of foodstuffs and tobacco averaging 10/- per head"—a gift they had received when the mine was open. That Christmas, they received 2 pounds meat (valued at 1s.), 12 ½ pounds of sifted meal (3s. 3d.), 6 pounds of sugar (2s.), ½ pound of tea (1s. 4d.), two tins of sweetened condensed milk (1s. 3d.), and two bags of tobacco (1s. 2d.). [37]

De Beers Takes Over

On December 15, 1941, De Beers bought the entire capital share of Cape Coast, which had gone into voluntary liquidation. V. L. M. Wilson, the acting manager, was appointed "the accredited agent of the De Beers Company in Namaqualand."[38] The news caused a stir throughout Namaqualand because it signaled the possibility of new jobs. At Kleinzee, the "retainers" looked forward to better wages and salaries under their new employer, some of them saying they were proud to be working for De Beers because of its fine heritage (it included Cecil John Rhodes and L. S. Jameson). What they had not taken into account was that the connection to De Beers also meant a connection to Kimberley, and that in time the lives of everyone in the little Kleinzee community would be affected by the arrival of Kimberley people, notably the artisans and apprentices.

Mining operations under the new company did not begin until August 1943, and not much happened during the next year. No one in the little company town had expected the war to affect their lives very much, but then enemy submarine activity was reported off the coast. The possibility of attack prompted the South African Air Force to consider building a new aerodrome at Sandkop to accommodate bigger planes, and also the establishment of an air force camp. For a while, company management decided to "black out" Kleinzee after mounted patrolman Jan Goosen (a renowned tracker) reported that he had seen "Snapsnees" (Japanese) footprints on the beach near Elandsklip. Goosen had concluded that the small footprints he had observed there must have been those of sailors disembarking from a Japanese submarine.[39]

New People with New Ways

From mid June 1943 onward, a steady flow of new employees, many from Kimberley, started to arrive. Some were qualified, others seemed never to have used a hammer, spanner, or screwdriver before. Fitters and turners, electricians, boilermakers, carpenters, and other tradesmen, plus apprentices and handymen, worked day and night so that operations could begin by August 1. Some of the white contract workers arrived during June and July to repair the cocopan tracks and reinstall the haulage system.[40]

Reg Turner, the new engineer and manager, arrived early in June, bringing with him three senior, skilled artisans from Kimberley (a workshop foreman, a construction foreman, a carpenter, and nine apprentices). His job included building seven new houses, increasing the size of the company store, repairing and painting all the existing buildings, improving the workshops, extending and modifying the washing plant, pulsator, and tailings disposal system, improving the roads, digging a new well in the riverbed, renewing the old pipelines, and replacing the rusty barbed-wire fences. A guest house was built for visiting consultants and other VIPs, several new vehicles were purchased, a library was opened, a billiard table was set up, and a teacher was employed to educate the growing number of children up to second grade. The expansion, limited though it was by present standards, proclaimed the superiority of De Beers and allayed any fears that another shutdown was imminent.[41]

On May 10, 1944, twenty-four wooden crates containing sections of the mine's first excavator diesel shovel arrived from English firm Ruston Bucyrus Ltd. to be assembled at the site by an engineer. The assembled machine cost £4,686. Dragline equipment was added later at an additional cost of £535.[42] The first operator was Corneels Goosen, a white Namaqualander from Dikgat Farm. He (plus machine) soon became the hero of the pick-and-shovel workers because it was now possible to load a cocopan with one scoop, rather than a hundred shovelsful. There is an oral tradition that on cold mornings when the diesel engine refused to start, Pieter Brand, an eccentric handyman, was invited to demonstrate his technique of priming the carburetor with a high-octane gasoline.

Brand and other old-timer employees attempted to modernize their skills without formal training, but the artisans and their apprentices from Kimberley had brought their skills with them, together with new attitudes toward management and authority that had never before been encountered at Kleinzee. The newcomers held wild parties and irreverently livened up mine dances with their frolics. They sang bawdy verses to traditional songs, introduced new ways of dancing, drank heavily, complained about the absence of formal entertainment, and made few concessions to others. For them, Kimberley, the headquarters of De Beers, was home, and the locals had that reality impressed upon them in the Kimberley song:

> Kimberley, Kimberley, Kimberley
> You diamond digging boys
> We'll all go back to

Kimberley when we can
You may think we're lousy
But you have never seen us scratch
We'll all go back to
Kimberley when we can.

Although there was resentment in some circles, especially after the Kimberley set, with antimanagement intentions, temporarily took over the running the newly established Rec Club, the artisans and their apprentices endeared themselves to many. In April 1945, the boilermaker married the new postmistress, soon after her arrival.[43] And a year or two later, a mine official's daughter started dating an apprentice electrician; the couple married a few years later, against the wishes of her family.

The labor force of white contract workers failed to stabilize in the 1940s, and by the middle of 1945 the company was desperate. Even the Coloureds were finding jobs elsewhere; many had signed up for military service. It was well known to De Beers that black labor (largely Owambo) had proved both cheap and satisfactory at their sister establishment of Consolidated Diamond Mines at Oranjemund. A successful application was made to the administrator for South-West Africa for permission to recruit approximately three hundred workers from Owamboland. The majority of the white workers were paid off at the end of 1945 as the first lorryload of Owambos arrived to work for 8d. (eight pence) a day (the lot of the Owambo worker is discussed in chapter 7).

Meanwhile, the Coloured workers, who had hitherto lived in corrugated iron shacks, were being moved into a newly constructed compound. The manager stated that the site of the compound had a "natural advantage . . . [it was sheltered] from the prevailing wind, [remote] from the hospital and European quarters and [near] to work." Twelve workers would share rooms that were 27 feet by 12 feet, built on the opposite side to the kitchen and mess.[44] Toward the end of 1949, the Owambo workers were repatriated at the insistence of the South-West African Administration. De Beers, anticipating this move, had decided to recruit workers from the Namaqualand Coloured population; thus, as the last of the Owambos left in January 1950, they were replaced by Coloured labor at the wage rate of 3s. 6d. per shift—the same wage they had been paid for more than twenty years (see chapter 8).

The late 1940s and 1950s were unsettling years for many regular employees. Everything seemed out of character with their experience: they had seen the changes involving contract workers and other unskilled laborers and the influx of new people from outside of Namaqualand (notably the various Kimberley contingents); even the addition of a few postwar luxury goods to the stock in the company store seemed to be part of a new world. Management, too, was confronted with the dilemmas of change, especially in the area of security. Once again, questions as to who should be X-rayed and searched loomed large. Toward the end of 1952, the De Beers chief protection officer, I. M. Van Rooyen, visited Kleinzee for two days. Van Rooyen claimed to have found a number of loopholes in the security system, ranging from inadequate fencing to the "undesirable" practice of laborers bunking out at night "to visit female domestic Coloured servants." He recommended that the compound be sealed off completely, as it had been in the days of the white Namaqualanders and Owambos. Other recommendations included permitting only leather handles on suitcases (hollow metal handles were being used to smuggle out diamonds) and adopting "a policy whereby any employee [or family member] could be searched and X-rayed whenever required." Dogs would not be allowed in the mining area without permission, and firearms and private tools were banned because they could not be X-rayed.[45]

In a broader perspective, these changes are insignificant, involving little more than trivial shifts in lifestyle. They bespeak attempts by management to revamp the existing security system to satisfy head office. Company towns everywhere are organized on similar structural principles, with clear distinctions between managers, senior staff, foremen (supervisors, guards, etc.), and laborers (contract workers). The workforce in Kleinzee between 1928 and 1956 was recruited from three ethnic groups and at three different times: first came the white Namaqualanders, second, the Owambos—black peasants from South-West Africa, and, third, the Coloureds from the Namaqualand reserves. The enormous discrepancies between the wages paid to each of these ethnic groups are an exclusively South African phenomenon, but elsewhere in the world there are many examples of recruiting mineworkers from the ranks of specific ethnic populations, and paying them minimum wages.[46] In chapters 5, 6, 7, and 8, I discuss the roles and employment experiences of the various ranks of employees, including the lot in life of the groups of contract workers—the men who did the heavy work over the years.

By the early 1950s, the population of Kleinzee had increased to about 380. Thirty-two white men and their wives were now housed in the town; among them they had fifty children, and they employed twenty-nine Coloured, female domestic servants. There were twenty white men and three single white women (a teacher, a nurse, and a postmistress) in single quarters. The compound housed two hundred Coloured, male workers, many of whom had wives on the reserves. And seven Coloured men and their wives had quarters in the old Coloured camp. Some of the Coloured wives seem to have been in domestic service.[47]

5

The Manager and His Staff, 1928-1956

The enormous profits made by the company over the years depended, to a large extent, on the availability of low-paid laborers who, like mineworkers everywhere, were prepared to place themselves at the disposal of the employer with little opportunity to negotiate wage levels or resist the authority of their bosses.[1] However, the company's hierarchical power system extended beyond the laboring class: all employees were involved. In this chapter I want to analyze the various occupational levels between the laboring class and the mine manager. The company made very clear distinctions between its employees, and paid them accordingly, as part of a system of socioeconomic differentiation designed to maintain the status quo.

If the *mine manager* was characterized by the authority vested in him by head office, his *senior staff*—sometimes called *officials*—occupied the next level in the hierarchy: the mine secretary, the engineer, the protection officer, and the pit superintendent. Below them were *regular staff*: the compound manager, the medical orderly, the storeman, the office clerk, and the supervisors (foremen). Then came the *artisans*, whose numbers varied from time to time; they ranked above the *guards*, who, except for the laboring class of *contract workers*, occupied the lowest position in the hierarchy.

Senior Staff

In December 1930, all the staff, both senior and regular, posed for a photograph on the front steps of the mine office to mark the completion of the town.[2] All wore suits for the occasion. Senior staff, or management, sat in chairs: these were the acting manager, the manager-elect, the secretary, the engineer, the pit superintendent, and the protection officer. The photograph captured the spirit of the occasion: in the company's eyes, it represented their respectful servants doing a job of work for the directors in a remote part of the world; for those posing, it illustrated their feelings of importance as employees in one of Oppenheimer's companies.

Although the mine manager enjoyed near total authority over all employees, he depended enormously on the support he received from his senior staff to maintain that authority and to assist him in carrying out the company's mandate efficiently. The secretary was his right-hand man, being at once bookkeeper, paymaster, the one in charge of stores, provisions, and requisitions, and coordinator of labor recruitment, among other duties. At the end of each working day, he weighed and counted the diamonds in the presence of the manager and the pit superintendent. Each of the three men had a different key to the safe, ensuring that the door could be opened only when all three were present.

The engineer was responsible for the maintenance of the plant, pulsator, power station, and pump house, the construction of roads and buildings, and the fencing of the property. The pit superintendent's job was to mobilize the pick-and-shovel workers in all phases of open strip-mining and to coordinate activities at the pit with those at the washing plant and pulsator. The protection officer was responsible for the prevention of diamond thefts at the mine, the plant, and the company's other farms; he supervised all security checks, including the searching of employees leaving town. Later, when X-raying became standard procedure, he and his staff ran the new procedures for detecting diamonds hidden in body orifices.

The manager and his senior staff were rewarded for their service to the company through not only their incomes but also the quality of the houses their families lived in. Each house had a living room, dining room, kitchen with pantry, three bedrooms, and a three-piece bathroom. By Namaqualand standards in the 1930s, these houses, with their hot-and-cold running water, flush toilets, and electric lights, were luxurious. They were also furnished, adequately, if not fashionably. The manager's house was a little larger than the other three, having four bedrooms and bigger carpets—a detail that everyone was expected to notice. All these houses had servants' quarters and washhouses separate from the main building. The properties were fenced off and the grounds covered with four inches of washed pebbles from the pulsator tailings—the latter to keep down the dust.

The senior staff also enjoyed other privileges. They were the only ones permitted to bring their own furniture and appliances with them, if they wished: as trusted employees, they were not searched when they left the town and could take their belongings with them if they left the company's employ. All four families had radios and cars. Their houses were connected to the company's local telephone system, which enabled wives to phone each other, their husbands at work, and the company store, ordering goods for delivery. The protection officer, being separated from his wife, was content to live in single quarters facing the Atlantic Ocean, have his meals in the mess with the supervisors, and cadge whatever invitations he could to dine with the four families.

The Manager

When Herman Behrmann was appointed manager on July 23, 1928, he looked forward to moving into the new manager's house, after the discomforts of the £100 tin house in which he had been living. It came as a tremendous blow to him when, without warning in February 1930, he was fired to make way for Lute James Parkinson, an Anglo American Corporation mine manager and part of the new order. Parkinson, a young American, had been selected by consulting engineer H. T. Dickinson (also an American) to give class and efficiency to the new mining community, under Dickinson's jurisdiction. The appointment was temporary and Parkinson held office as acting manager. The family arrived in March 1930 and stayed for eleven months, when Parkinson was appointed to a senior position in Angola. Parkinson's salary at Kleinzee was £100 per month, plus a £5 housing allowance for his free house. His successor Frank Humphreys, another Anglo American employee, was appointed manager at a salary of £75. The company paid his fare from Johannesburg to Kleinzee and he was entitled to "such medical attention and hospital treatment as was available" free of charge. The appointment, as was the case with all other salaried employees, was subject to termination, with three months' notice on either side. He was entitled to thirty days leave a year, which could be accumulated to ninety days after three years service, and he agreed not to carry on any private work without written consent of the company.

Humphreys was a demanding manager, but his obligations to the company ceased at 4:30 P.M. when the final hooter sounded. As long as the tally for the day was a thousand loads or better and the running costs were low, he was satisfied. He sent monthly reports and a weekly letter to Dickinson, all of which reflect his dutiful compliance with the orders he received. When problems arose, whether it was a failure in the plant's alarm system, the notorious Bitterfontein robbery,[3] work stoppage because of rain, the flooding of the Buffels River, or a rude, complaining letter from his engineer, he simply reported them in a matter of fact way, indicating that all had been taken care of efficiently.

This is not to say that Humphreys ever shirked his responsibilities or that he neglected to promote the company's beneficent image on appropriate occasions. As long as he was fully in charge of operations, he did what was expected of him. When Sister Madeleine of the Roman Catholic mission in Port Nolloth, asked for old clothes for the poor, he immediately arranged for a collection and sent them to her.[4] At Christmas and New Year's, he wired greetings to the Kimberley office of Cape Coast, De Beers, Souwesfin, Anglo American, Consolidated Diamond Mines (Luderitz), and the Cape Copper Company.[5] He obtained Dickinson's approval to give £50 to the Dutch Reformed Church in Springbok and £25 to Saint Andrew's Anglican church in Port Nolloth.[6] When Dickinson told him to cut costs, he said it was impossible as long as he had to go on employing white Namaqualand labor at high wages.[7] When the haulage system lost eight hours and twenty-three minutes of hauling time in two days owing to electrical problems, he immediately ordered all his staff to attend an enquiry after work the following Saturday to find out "who the culpable parties might be."[8] He did, however, have two anxieties about the future. Were there, in fact, any buried parcels of diamonds in town for which people might return after the mine closed? And what effect would the salty mist have on the steel girders and other structures of the reduction plant.[9]

Humphreys enjoyed sport and felt that everyone else should, too, although there were limits to his benevolence. He did what he thought best for the white contract workers, encouraging rugby, boxing, and regular sports days on which teams competed in tug-o'-war, loading-the-cocopan, sprinting, and other events. But he did not like the Coloured workers and did nothing for them. In fact Humphreys wanted the company to have all the inhabitants of the Komaggas Reserve removed from their land, believing that their being so close to rich diamond deposits made them a nuisance.

Humphreys directed most of his sports energy to the needs and interests of the senior staff, which coincided with his personal preferences for better-established games such as tennis, cricket, and golf. His predecessor Parkinson had built the first tennis court, and Humphreys saw to it that the surface was properly maintained. But, where, in this dry, windblown semidesert, would one play cricket? Following the long-standing tradition of salt-pan cricket and soccer established in neighboring Port Nolloth, he selected Blaaupan, a convenient locality about three miles from town, because of its smooth surface. Cricket matches were great social occasions, especially the matches against neighboring towns. Blaaupan, being outside the fenced area, was accessible to visitors without their having to enter the town.

Humphreys describes the 1930 Boxing Day (December 26) staff cricket match against Port Nolloth in his June report of that year. A canvas marquee was erected to serve as clubhouse and bar and benches were provided for spectators. Some visitors sat in the comfort of their cars. Two Union Jack flags flapped in the southwest gale, the women prepared food and served drinks, and two local musicians played country music over the lunch break. A marvelous photograph taken at the match shows couples dancing—some of the men still with their cricketer's leg pads on. Kleinzee won the match and both teams returned to town for a formal supper and dance. No contract worker, white or Coloured, was ever permitted to participate in such events.[10]

Golf, too, flourished while Humphreys was manager. Dissatisfied with the three-hole, makeshift, sandy practice course, he instructed his engineer to map out a regular nine-hole course at Geelpan, a dry, yellow pan surrounded by sandy yellow oxide deposits, several miles out of town. The course proved to be a tremendous success. The surface of each "green" was covered with a three-inch layer of coarse, pulsator-washed sand, and each player was equipped with a folding T-scraper to level a path from the ball to the hole. The tees were made of salt-pan clay. Red golf balls, which could be seen more easily on the fairways, were favored. As is the golfing custom, some holes were named to express their particular character: the third hole was called the punchbowl because the green was located at the bottom of a hundred-foot sandy hill; the fourth green, perched on top of a hillock of yellow oxidized soil and brown boulders, was known as the pimple.

Score cards were deposited with the secretary at the end of each round and handicaps were accurately assessed. Trophies included a variety of silver-spoon awards for both ladies' and men's events. The engineering department presented a home-made trophy for annual competition. The bowl—the Captain's Bowl—was inscribed: "May the same spirit which has prompted the making of this Bowl ever preserve the following of the Royal & Ancient Game of Golf for Kleinzee."[11] Ironically, the presentation of the Captain's Bowl coincided with the mine's first closure; another hand-made trophy, the Dikkop, for cricket, was presented at the same time. Golf was played by the senior staff, two of the senior staff wives, and some other staff members, and matches were sometimes arranged with Port Nolloth golfers. There was no clubhouse, but an automobile sufficed: it doubled for a tea booth after the first nine holes and as the nineteenth hole at the end of the day.

Rock angling was a burning passion with Humphreys—an obsession that often determined his movements the moment the hooter blew at the end of the shift. With the ocean close by and company vehicles at his disposal, he was able, together with the secretary and the pit superintendent, to fish along most of the rugged coastline, including beaches closed to other people for security reasons. This freedom to go where others could not set the manager and his senior staff apart from the rest of the community, thereby widening the gap between them still further.

The rigidity of the occupational hierarchy permeated personal lives throughout the town. The senior staff found themselves predestined to belong, socially, to one impenetrable clutch, whether they liked each other or not. So they gave their exclusive, formal-dress dinner parties (they had their maids wait at table in black dresses, white aprons, and starched caps; the secretary's wife had her husband install a hidden bell under her chair so that the maid could be alerted to clear the plates between courses), which when consultants such as H. T. Dickinson visited became even more elaborate. Families quarreled as to who should have to the honor of having "Dickie" to dinner, even though everyone was terrified by these formal visits. Dickinson, however, had a reputation for arrogant abruptness, which made the challenge seem even more worthwhile. Apart from their bridge and dinner parties, the four senior families together took trips to the sea whenever the howling southwest winds let up for a few days (the fishing expeditions were nearly always undertaken by the men alone). Only tennis, cricket when someone was needed to make up a team, and (as noted above) golf and holidaytime dances provided "acceptable" occasions to meet and mix with the "other ranks."

That snobbish attitudes and behaviors would be cultivated in this back-of-beyond place may seem extraordinary. However, in addition to their status positions in the company's hierarchy, the senior staff shared the distinction of military service. The mine secretary had held the rank of major in World War I and was awarded the Military Cross (a British Empire medal) for bravery in Mesopotamia. The engineer had also served in the war with the rank of major. The pit superintendent had been with the South African Forces in France during the war and had spent six years in the Indian Army, retiring with the rank of captain. The protection officer, Major Orpen, C.M.G., had given his name to the famous Orpen's Horse, of which he was in command during the South African (Boer) War. His father had been surveyor-general of Griqualand West and was closely associated with Cecil Rhodes.[12] This British colonial military identity was as important in determining rank at Kleinzee in the early 1930s as it had been at De Beers long before. Management at Kleinzee has always been "English," in the sense I have used it here. The ethnic rift between English and Afrikaner employees, so marked sixty years ago, persists despite enormous socioeconomic change; management remains "English," albeit in a greatly modified form.

Other Staff

If the senior staff and their families were in the manager's clique, how did the rest of the staff fit into the picture? Their occupations (see appendix 2, table

2.1) were diverse: medical orderly, plant superintendent, office clerk, compound manager, pulsator superintendent, assistant protection officer, supervisors (foremen). In general, they shared the same income range, an average of about £30 a month, although supervisors earned less than the others. Occupationally, a loose-knit group, this pattern carried over into leisure hours. They had minimal interaction with the senior staff after the shift, although a few ventured onto the tennis court and golf course, and those who played cricket were welcomed when needed. The majority of these employees were recruited from other parts of South Africa and were English-speakers or Afrikaners who upheld the political values of the British Empire. Only four houses were available for married men, and the majority were housed in single quarters—small, mud-brick bungalows—but these were in short supply and two people sometimes had to share a unit. Each bungalow was supplied with electricity and sparsely furnished with bed and mattress, table and chair, chest of drawers, washstand, water jug and basin, and slop bucket. There was one communal ablution block. Residents of the single-quarter complex had their meals in the mess, where Karl Marks, the Abyssinian cook, served three meals a day (and lunch packs for the foremen who worked in the mining area). Accommodation was free, but everyone paid a mess fee, which included laundry.

To the southwest of the single quarters was a row of four small houses, originally built for married supervisors. But such was the demand for this accommodation that their allocation depended on which four people, in the manager's opinion, provided the most essential services. So the first house was allocated to the painter; the second to the only married qualified artisan; the third to the medical orderly (an important position because there was no regular doctor at that time); and the fourth to the manager's driver and motor mechanic.

Artisans

Artisans always play an important part in construction and maintenance of mining infrastructure.[13] At Kleinzee, their numbers have always tended to fluctuate according to the amount of expansion being undertaken. In January 1932, there were seven artisans: four fitters, one electrician, one power-station operator, and a carpenter. Only one, a fitter, appears to have possessed a recognized ticket, and wages varied accordingly. The qualified fitter's wage was £35 a month; all the other artisans, except for the painter, were treated as handymen and paid a set wage of £18 a month. The painter, although paid less (£15 a month), was given a free house. The driver-cum-mechanic received a handyman's wage.

Guards

Six guards patrolled the mining areas at night, and the mounted patrol did a routine round of the main fences every day. All guards were poorly paid (about £14 a month). Guards did not qualify for the company's married housing, although the head guard was assigned a tin building that had housed the shop in the prospecting days and three others lived with their wives in old farm housing on the north bank of the Buffels River. One guard was based at Dreyer's Pan, where he and his wife lived in a tin house. This man was part of the mounted patrol that covered the farms between Dreyer's Pan and Oubeep. He was paid £2 more than any other guard as compensation for his isolation in the sand dunes. His Coloured helper lived in a shack, earning the lowest wage of all workers—£5 a month.

The duties of a guard were always arduous and sometimes dangerous, especially at night when they were expected to protect the company's property from raids by IDB bandits in the high-grade area. Most were recruited from among the poor Namaqualanders who had lived in the vicinity of Kleinzee before the discovery of diamonds. They remained poor on the low wages they received, but they were acclaimed by the company for their honesty and loyalty. Sometimes they were mildly ridiculed by management for their naive view of reality and danger:

> Every evening in 1930 . . . the crooks, as we called them, would arrive the moment the sun went down. Half the night we would be fighting them with pick handles as our truncheons. Our guards—the simple Namaqualanders—were furnished with electric torches [flashlights], wizard devices to them. They had an

5.1. Senior Staff Houses, 1930
The larger house, left, is the manager's.

5.2. Compound, 1930
Housing for contract workers.

5.3. Change house and Barbed-wire Corridor
Photo of the change house shows the corridor through which workers passed to and from the compound and the mining area (1930).

5.4. Single Quarters and Mess, 1930
This was the accommodation for white employees who were not provided with houses.

5.5. Space for Race, 1932 (above)
Shifting the Coloured camp away from the "White" compound in March 1932.

5.6. On Guard (left)
Guard Jan "Pampoen" Goosen, a former contract worker, dressed for mounted patrol. As head guard he wore riding britches, leggings, Sam Browne belt (with .45 revolver), and a pith helmet.

idea that to shine a torch on a man [would] paralyse him, and he would be incapable of movement while the light held him.

After one of the raids I listened to the cross-examination of one of the guards
by a security officer.

"Well, Jan, What happened last night?"

"There were a lot of crooks in the Main Area last night, at least thirty."

"Yes, Jan. Tell me what happened."

"Well, I got very close to these chaps and I torched them."

"And what happened then?"

"I torched them again and they didn't fall over so I went quite close to them
and they ran away and I couldn't catch them."

But Jan, for all his simplicity, was a faithful stalwart and, when he came one
day to report catching a crook red-handed as he crawled through the fence, I told
him that for the sterling work he had done I had decided to promote him to Captain of the Guards.

Handing him six soda water bottle tops [crown corks] I told him to pierce a
couple of holes through each and get his sister to sew three on each shoulder.
Never for a moment did I think I would be taken seriously, but next morning,
there was Jan mounted on his horse with top boots, riding trousers, khaki shirt,
the Sam Browne belt which I had given him—and the bottle tops on his shoulders
glinting in the sun. . . . "Nou sal ek die crooks opdonder, meneer!" [Now I will be
able to bugger up the crooks, sir] said Jan as he rode away on patrol. He wore
those "stars" for many months afterwards and became the envy of all the farmers
far and wide. From then onwards he was known as Kaptein.[14]

These white Buffels River people were deemed by the company to be decent
simple folk with few material needs and interests—which inevitably worked
against them, for it made them easy prey to a devious form of patronage. After
acquiring their farms, the company took them over, as it were, "for their own
good." Management incorporated them as if they, together with their farms,
were part of the company's assets. They could now be treated like poor relations, and paid as if they were common laborers.

The Socioeconomic Hierarchy, 1930–1956

A number of changes occurred at Kleinzee between 1930 and 1956—that is,
between the building of the town and the mammoth development plan of the
post-1956 decade. Several new houses and buildings were added; sporting facilities were improved; security was upgraded with the wider use of X ray; a

resident physician lived in town; and a qualified compound manager was installed. Women were now being employed for the first time—a nursing sister, a teacher, a postmistress, a mess cook, a bookkeeper in the company store, and a typist in the office. But in the overall social and economic picture, nothing had really changed since the 1930s. True, senior staff salaries had increased over the years: by 1948, the mine secretary was earning £83 10s. 0d. a month, compared with the earlier £65; the mine pit superintendent got £70 16s. 8d., increased from £45; and the compound manager (now part of the senior staff hierarchy) earned £55 a month. But, to cite an example from the other staff, supervisors earned only £4 more than they did in 1932.[15]

In chapters 6, 7, and 8 I turn to discussions of the three ethnic groups who, at different times in the early days, did pick-and-shovel and other hard labor. As already noted, the first of these contract workers were white men recruited mainly from the Namaqualand region; the second group were black Owambos from South-West Africa (Namibia); the third group were Coloured Namaqualanders from the local reserves. In chapter 12, I review the entire system of stratification designed by the company to facilitate control over workers and employees so as to generate maximum profit for its shareholders.

6

White Man as Contract Worker

T he first generation of contract workers employed at Kleinzee under Cape Coast were white men, recruited mainly from Namaqualand, but also the neighboring districts of Vanrhynsdorp, Calvinia, and Kenhardt. Many were impoverished farmers, and all had suffered from the effects of protracted droughts in the 1920s and the depression of the 1930s. They were recruited to do all the pick-and-shovel work in the pit as well as other manual labor. They were housed in the compound, which segregated them from the rest of the mining community, in much the same way black contract workers are on other Southern African mines.[1] Cape Coast would have preferred to have employed cheap black labor, which would have cost less than half the wage they paid these poor whites, but, as already noted, the company had to conform to state labor regulations (an early form of job reservation that favored whites) and toe the line with regard to the Precious Stones Act of 1927. The employment of local Coloured labor (above a specified quota) was also out of the question, for similar reasons.

In South African English, the word *compound* (derived from the Malay *kampong*, village) originally referred to the enclosure in which workers were housed on diamond mines for the duration of their contracts.[2] As early as 1889, "all 10,000 African mineworkers [in the Kimberley area] were accommodated in what came to be called *closed* compounds."[3] Kleinzee's barracks-style worker housing epitomized the compound. Four separate, linear buildings were constructed to enclose a quadrangle. Three of the buildings were subdivided into dormitories, which provided sleeping space for roughly two hundred workers. The dormitories were sparsely furnished: iron bedsteads, coir mattresses, blankets, and separate lockers for clothes and personal possessions. The fourth building, on the west side, housed the kitchen, dining hall, showers and washbasins, and a reading room-cum-library. The *kak balie* (shit bucket) lavatories were outside the quadrangle; emptied twice a week, they were disinfected with *dip* (a commercial disinfectant). The complex also contained the guards' quarters and later a small office for the newly appointed compound manager, Osborne N. Pringle, an Englishman who had once worked in the Port Nolloth branch office of the Copper Company.

The grounds of the compound were surrounded by a barbed-wire security fence. A double fence spanned the west side (which bordered a public road) to prevent parcels of diamonds being tossed over to anyone on the outside. No worker was permitted to leave the fenced-in area unless accompanied by a guard. Even the relatively short walk to and from work involved several guards each shift.

Recalling the early days of the Kleinzee compound, people say, "Ons was almal tweemal in daardie plek toegekamp" ("We were all doubly fenced in inside that place"); that is, they were locked inside two security fences—the main fence, which they shared with everyone else, and the compound fence. Throughout the 1930s, 1940s, and into the 1950s, many people at Kleinzee referred to the town as "the camp," "the mine camp," or, in Afrikaans, "*die kamp.*" This idea of a camp was associated with the fact that the whole of Kleinzee farm had been fenced in as company property to keep insiders in and outsiders out. It goes without saying that being doubly fenced in had an enormous impact on their lives. Compound life, in its expression as physical space, imposed a new identity on them as workers completely subordinate to management for as long as their contracts lasted.[4]

The Shift

The Kleinzee day began at 5:30 A.M., with the wailing of "the hooter," the siren that everyone awoke to, Monday to Saturday. The compound breakfast was served at 6 A.M., after which everyone working in the pit was escorted to the change house, located about one hundred yards to the east of the compound. Here they stripped in a room at the north end of the building and marched naked along the passage to another room at the south end, where they dressed in work clothes and *velskoens* (hide shoes, like heavy moccasins) provided by the company. They left via a door on the southeast side that opened onto a barbed-wire corridor that guided them to the mining area—a walk of only five hundred yards. At 6.55 A.M., the hooter blew again, exactly five minutes before the shift started, and the steel haulage cable was set in motion by the powered wheels of the washing plant.

At noon, the hooter blew again, and the plant and haulage stopped for the lunch hour. All the mineworkers now marched to the "Crystal Palace," as management called the large, twelve-window, corrugated-iron construction, built at the workers' insistence to shelter them from the wind. Here they drank their coffee and ate their *onsies*—the workers' name for sandwiches made from wholemeal sourdough bread and thinly smeared with an *onsie* (literally, a little ounce) of butter. At 12:55, a warning blast of the hooter alerted employees to the 1 P.M. start-up.

At 4:30, the final hooter blew, and the workers now retraced their morning route through the corridor to the change house, where they shed work clothes, showered, and returned naked down the passage to dress in their own clothes before being escorted back to the compound. Workers were supposed to be under constant surveillance, and the change house routine was theoretically supposed to prevent workers from taking *blink klippies* (shiny stones) back to the compound at the end of the day. Diamonds were sometimes carried in the nose, ears, mouth, or anus, but complete body searches were rarely carried out. There were always two guards on duty in the compound, as well as a number of unofficial informers, who reported any suspicious IDB activity to the chief protection officer. How many informers there were is not recorded, but they were expected to report any suggestion of subversive activity in the compound; the company had to be at all times in full control of the workforce.[5]

By May 1930, construction of the washing plant and pulsator was completed, and the first cocopan ascended the ramp to tip gravel from the mining area into the jaws of a powerful crusher. Thus began the process of mechanically extracting diamonds.

The plant was designed to process an average of 1,000 loads a day, and management expected the monthly tally to be at least 26,000 loads. As the day's tally accumulated, the count was recorded on a large notice board for the whole town to see. It was considered important for workers to know the tally because, when the town was set out, the thousand-loads-a-day requirement was the basis on which "housing accommodation had been provided for staff and employees."[6] (Actually the number of carats produced depended more on the quality of the gravel than on the number of loads supplied.)

When the new technology was tested that May, the tally for the month was only 6,867 loads, due to start-up problems. In June, the number had nearly doubled, to 13,574, and by October it had reached 25,572 loads, producing 5,826 diamonds, weighing a little more than 7,008 carats. By the mid 1940s, after the plant had been expanded, more than 30,000 loads a month produced up to 158,687 carats.[7]

Recruitment and Contract

On February 1, 1932, there were 165 white contract workers at Kleinzee. Most worked in the pit, but 10 men worked on the plant, 3 in the power station and pump house, 1 in the shop, 3 in the garage, 9 in the compound, doing cooking, cleaning, and laundry, and 2 in hospital and sanitation.[8] The turnover was relatively high. The manager reported that in the first two months of operation, 11 were discharged and 37 resigned. Between May 1930 and July 1932, a total of 551 white laborers, largely from Namaqualand and adjacent districts, had worked at Kleinzee. From time to time a few people from the Transvaal and South-West Africa managed to slip into the recruiting net.[9] There was, however, no shortage of white labor at that time: there were 850 names on the waiting list in June 1930, a figure that excluded those disqualified by the South African Police for security reasons. High unemployment at the time among all groups in the region suited the company. In November 1930, the manager said so in writing: "[We like] to have a surplus of labor so that [we] can pick and choose and eliminate weaklings."[10]

Recruitment was thus never a problem and much of the selection was left to the chief protection officer, Redmond Orpen. Orpen said he was always on the lookout for "good honest type workers who would not get involved in IDB and who would prove to be loyal employees of the Company, and would stay permanently and reduce the rate of wastage."[11] It was part of Orpen's job to visit the farms in the district, especially those owned by the company but run by caretaker tenants. He would urge farmers and farmer-tenants "to employ a native," to harvest and to look after stock, so that the farmer could work full-time for the company; the practice, he said, would be "more economical for them." And in fact, many desperate, impoverished, black and Coloured workers were prepared to work for farmers at that time for as little as ten shillings a month plus basic rations.[12]

All contract workers at Kleinzee signed a six-month contract. Among other clauses, one required that they remain for the full period in order to qualify for a week's leave or the equivalent in cash. Somehow, not everyone stayed for the full six months, thereby forfeiting their leave privileges. Why did they leave? There must have been many reasons, but some men simply could not stand the confinement and lack of freedom—the feeling of *toegekampheid* (closed-in-ness). Others went to look for better-paying jobs and better working conditions (for example, at Alexander Bay), while some went home to claim inheritances—often no more than a small portion of a drought-stricken farm.

It has been suggested, erroneously, that all workers went to Kleinzee in anticipation of making their fortunes from IDB. Certainly some believed they could become rich by diamond snatching, imagining that every spadeful of gravel or sand sparkled with diamonds. True, men cleaning the bedrock in the rich ground were often tempted to pocket a parcel of gemstones from a pot-hole, but they rarely did so. Every worker in the mine area was under the eye of a supervisor-cum-foreman whose main job was to prevent workers from taking diamonds.

Contract workers were employed under the same general conditions as other employees. When they signed on, they had to agree to devote all their time and energy to the service of the company, not to absent themselves from work or town without written consent, and to carry out all lawful instructions from management; instant dismissal was the price of noncompliance. They agreed to submit to search or X ray at any time, with instant dismissal for possession of diamonds. The company accepted no responsibility for loss of personal effects, regardless of the cause.

We have already noted that Cape Coast always attempted to run the mine on a shoestring budget, keeping all wages as low as possible. In May 1930, "the Company was offering 6/- per day minimum, less deduction of £3 per month for food, plus free housing, working clothes and medical attention." Increases were recommended from time to time, and wages went up by 6d. a shift to a maximum of 7s. 6d. for pick-and-shovel laborers. They also had the opportunity to work overtime on occasion, for which they received time-and-a-half. In May and June 1930, contract workers averaged £11 18s. 10d. and £13 2s. 0d., respectively, including overtime. In October 1931, the average wage was £15 4s. 2d.[13] Wage increases of 6d. a shift did little to improve the monthly wage, and pick-and-shovel workers had no other choice but to work overtime if they wanted to increase their income significantly.

The South African government continued to put pressure on the company to increase wages and improve working conditions for white labor, based on the model it had adopted on the State Alluvial Diggings at Alexander Bay, where the state itself was under pressure from the workers. But Cape Coast listened to the state under duress only, and it resented the proposal by the minister of mines to establish a minimum wage of 7s. 6d. per day for white workers, rising to 10s. per day after six months work, plus free food and quarters.[14] At the May meeting of the Cape Coast board, L. A. Pollak (Oppenheimer's alternate director) stated that "it was out of deference to the wishes of the Government [that] white men were being employed exclusively, though the work could quite easily be done by natives, who would only be paid 3/- per day."[15] By January 1932, the minimum wage paid was still 6s.[16]

Company policy was intolerant both of workers making demands or any hint of opposition to its policies. When the manager at Kleinzee mentioned in his report that there had been a minor confrontation with white workers, it did not take long for head office to ask for more details regarding "an allusion to [what they thought must have been] an uprising on the part of the Namaqualanders employed at Kleinzee."[17] Manager Parkinson replied immediately to allay any fears head office might have had regarding worker demands or state interference in its wage policies.

> At the end of June a certain number of workmen who had been engaged in May, and whose work had been satisfactory, received an increase of their daily wage from 6/- to 6/6, and a few to 7/6 per day. The morning after the list stating the names of these employees, was posted up, all the men, upon arrival near the pit, lined up, and, through their spokesman, informed [the pit superintendent] that none of them would go to work unless an assurance was given them, at once, that the daily wage of every man employed would be immediately increased to 7/6, and that food and provisions would be supplied free. [The pit superintendent] told the spokesman to go to work at once, and when he refused, instructed him to go to the change house and turn in his uniform as he was discharged under clause 10 of his contract. When the spokesman turned round to tell the others, he found that they were all on their way to work. Together with the spokesman, who was immediately dismissed, one or two others, whom we regarded as being in earnest about the matter and as probable inciters, were dismissed, and the matter was dropped as far as the others were concerned.[18]

The free issue of work clothes was an important benefit as far as the workers were concerned. The standard issue was a wide-brimmed cowboy-style hat, heavy cotton khaki trousers and shirt, and velskoens; a laundry operated at the change house, where also repairs were done to both work clothes and velskoens. The change-house security system was abolished after a new X-ray machine was installed in 1932, and subsequently all workers were X-rayed whenever they left the town, their personal effects also being thoroughly searched.

Work

Most white contract workers were employed in the mining area, doing the strenuous, back-breaking, pick-and-shovel work. A typical alluvial strip face contained six to twelve inches of sand, a two-inch layer of hard calcrete, followed by twenty-four inches of softer limestone and light gravel. Once the diamondiferous gravel was reached, large boulders had sometimes to be moved as workers dug down to bedrock—a total of six to eight feet or more. To get to the gravel, workers had to hack their way down through the calcrete capping with carefully tempered picks, a job requiring both stamina and skill.

Before being loaded and taken away, large slabs of capping often had to be broken with sledgehammers. Dynamite was introduced later, but blasting could be done only at the end of the shift, and the picks, sledgehammers, and crowbars remained in use as important tools of the trade. Hand loading of cocopans was a strenuous task, and especially unpleasant when the loading was into the prevailing southwest winds in summer or the scorching easterly blasts of April and May. Loading continued regardless of the weather; except for lunch breaks and at the end of the shift, the haulage system stopped only for accidents. In "deep ground," when the bedrock lay thirty to forty feet below the surface, tiers had to be created in the face so that the gravel could be moved from one level to another. Sometimes it would take five levels to reach the cocopan track.

The pick-and-shovel operation was done under careful supervision. Each gang of ten or twelve laborers worked under the watchful eye of a foreman-supervisor, who directed operations according to instructions from the pit superintendent and the head supervisor. Foremen also had to keep all workers, especially bedrock cleaners, under surveillance to prevent theft. Most diamonds are located in the crevices and potholes in the bedrock, and workers loading sand, calcrete, and low-grade gravel seldom saw a diamond, let alone an opportunity to steal one.

Other workers included jackhammer operators and a blacksmith and his assistant. The blacksmith's job was to sharpen and temper picks and jackhammer drills and repair other equipment. There were also mule drivers and trammers, "donkey haulage" operators, and track layers. These men had to get the loaded cocopans to junctions where hook-on men could take over. The hook-on men hammered the steel haulage rope into the retaining brackets on the cocopans, a reverse process taking place when the empty cocopans returned from the washing plant. Some work had to be done after hours. The greasers, for example, had to lubricate the cocopan axles and wheels over which the haulage rope traveled. For this they were paid overtime. Greasers, with assistance from the hook-on and hook-off workers, were also responsible for reporting frayed sections of cable that needed replacement.

After the Shift

Workers who lived in the compound had few contacts with townspeople: they saw only the compound manager, the guards, the doctor, and those they met in the workplace. Their main contact with the outside world was the dominee (pastor) of the Nederduitse Gereformeerde Kerk (NGK), who visited Klein-zee every four months.

Although the company encouraged recreation among all its employees, it did not allow the contract workers to participate in sport outside the compound: the workers boxed among themselves and played rugby on the rough, stony surface of the grounds allocated to them. Occasionally, townspeople watched the rugby games on weekends, peering through the barbed-wire fences. Some of the workers played musical instruments—concertinas and guitars—and, like the Kimberley diggers in the 1870s, before women arrived, they danced with each other: the "men" wore work clothes and the "women" paraded in their best after-work finery. Some workers played cards; some enjoyed reading. The library was so poorly stocked that in December 1930 the contract workers contributed £15 to the library out of their own pockets; an additional £10 was collected from the staff, and the company donated £5.[19] Then there was the Workers' Dramatic Society: when the mine closed in 1932, seven members wrote to the manager informing him that each had pocketed £1 4s. 1d. of the society's donated funds. "When the mine opens again," they wrote, "we will give it back."[20]

Another form of "entertainment" was the once-a-week shopping day at the retail store. When the doors were opened to the contract workers, they were closed to the rest of the town. Workers also shopped via mail-order catalogs, a commercial medium well known at that time. No details of actual purchases, either at the store or via mail order, are available; however, in 1950 the Namaqualand Coloured workers (who enjoyed similar practices but earned half the wage of the earlier, white Namaqualanders) spent an average of £1 a month each on mail-ordered goods and about £1.7 each at the retail store. A major portion of the Coloureds' wages was, however, sent to their families. A few people saved substantial amounts of money in post office accounts.

Shopping sprees and mail orders for the white Namaqualanders focused mainly on clothing. Blazers and badges were important items. Orders to the

Bond Badge and Blazer Company were placed for blazers and individual badges that the customers designed themselves. No details of the designs and mottos survive, but the State Alluvial Diggings museum at Alexander Bay has an exhibit of digger culture that includes a mannequin dressed in a stylish blazer (with badge), said to depict a contract worker on a Sunday in the 1930s.

The official philosophy of mine compounds in general at that time was: Keep the men fit, happy, and well fed.[21] Reporting on the Christmas program for 1931, manager Humphreys wrote:

> Sports on Christmas day in the Compound were very successful and were entered into most enthusiastically by the men—the most popular event being the "Bun & Treacle Race"! The Tug-of-War and Prize distribution took place in the afternoon. The Company donated £5 for the prizes. At one o'clock the men were provided with quite an excellent feed of roast fowl, plum pudding etc., which they much appreciated.[22]

Detailed records of compound diet outside of the Christmas season do not exist. There do not appear to have been serious complaints—other than about the lunchtime onsies. Porridge, milk, and coffee was the standard breakfast. After work, the men were served meat and potatoes (sometimes rice). The manager reported in June 1930 that the men were "eating regularly, probably for the first time in the lives of so many of them. The appetites of the new men are tremendous for the first two weeks after their arrival."[23] In another report to head office, the same manager explains how happy the workers must be.

> The food supplied is ample and there is an average gain [in weight] of 4.7 lbs after 6 weeks. There are facilities for football, boxing, and quoits for the men's amusement. And each Sunday they are permitted to go to the sea in the charge of two or three supervisors. The company orders films for the whole town from time to time, and these were shown at separate viewings to white workers, coloured workers, and the staff. At the pre-Christmas sports meet in 1930, the white workers were shown a Charlie Chaplin film which they enjoyed.[24]

The next order for "cartoons and comedies," chosen by the manager, included a request for *Felix Tries for Treasure* and *The Misfit*. Perhaps he thought these were specially suitable for compound dwellers on a diamond mine.[25]

The NGK was very active among these workers. Members of the church elected deacons and elders who, in the absence of a dominee, held services on Sundays. In 1930, the company donated £50 to the congregation. One dominee, W. L. Steenkamp, guarded his position as visiting minister with great tenacity. In a letter to the manager, he wrote: "Give us the right to do [all] spiritual work [at Kleinzee] and do not allow other denominations to work among the Dutch-speaking men, seeing that Kleinzee falls within my area."[26] The following year, he asked for another "£50 or a bigger denomination" from the company, adding that he planned "to conduct confirmation" on November 28 and 29.[27]

Reports on Steenkamp's preaching upset management. Diamonds, he is said to have preached, were God's gifts to the Namaqualanders, to discover and sell without interference from either the state or any mining company. "Where can you see the name of the company inscribed on the *blink klippies*," he is reputed to have said. The manager also took exception to his sabbatarianism, after discovering to his annoyance that he could not get the "religious workmen to work [overtime] on Sundays."[28] But Steenkamp was never denied entry to the compound and the company never withdrew its financial support for the congregation: management knew how important Steenkamp's influence was in maintaining morale among the labor force.

A few veterans of the era have recalled with some nostalgia the "Namaqualander's Sports Meeting" of New Year's Day, 1937, when one of the competitive events was cocopan loading. Six or seven pans and gravel to fill them were lined up at the compound's sport site. After the starting pistol, three-man teams competed to see which one could load a cocopan in the shortest time. Such reenaction for pleasure of the backbreaking work of the pit brings home the truth that contract laborers everywhere take pride in their work. In addition to the cultivation of the physical stamina and team work required to load a cocopan efficiently, there are other examples from the workplace such as meticulous bedrock sweeping and cleaning. A particularly prized skill was wielding a pick with such precision as to be able to hack holes in calcrete before applying a crowbar. Blacksmithing, too, required great precision, when at the end of every shift picks had to be resharpened and tempered.

When the question of improving leisure facilities was discussed, Drury Pifer, the manager, held the view that, although there were a few older men interested in recreation, it was mainly the young who should be catered for. "There is little desire for intellectual entertainment . . . [and in the compound one needs a] system to fit in with their natural [*sic*] background." Costs, he said, should be kept as low as possible, recommending at the same time a new wireless with loudspeakers (cost £20) and, to keep the young men physically fit and active, "a swimming bath in the barracks" (cost £150 for a pool six feet deep, thirty feet long, and fifteen feet wide). The manager also recommended a miniature rifle range, a recreation hall, motion pictures, writing and card tables, a wrestling and boxing ring, handball courts, and a new football field. This was in 1939. None of these suggestions was ever followed up, confirming once again the company's reluctance to spend money on its workforce.

Class, Status, and Race

If company towns are "closed" social formations, then compounds that house contract labor are doubly closed. Moreover, it is virtually impossible for a man to move up in the socioeconomic hierarchy and escape the constraints of compound life. At Kleinzee, a few better-paid jobs (such as cook, greaser, and jackhammer operator) were theoretically within every man's reach, but by and large all workers earned much the same wage and were subject to exactly the same restrictions and rules of the compound system. In this regard, there was nothing unique about the formal structure of the Kleinzee compound when it was occupied by white men.

There are, however, a few documented cases of men who crossed the class line that separated compound dwellers from others in the town. A prime example is Albertus P. (Ben) Engelbrecht. Hired on January 9, 1929 as laborer no. 13, in May 1930 he was offered a job as supervisor (foreman) at the salary (not wage) of £18 per month, and given a room in the single quarters in the main town. By January 1, 1931, Engelbrecht was earning £27 10s. 0d. and occupying the de facto position of assistant to the pit superintendent (head foreman). When the staff posed for their photograph in 1931, Engelbrecht was there, dressed in a suit like the others. He was laid off with other employees on June 30, 1932, but when the mine reopened in 1937, he was invited to return to his former position.[29]

Engelbrecht was not the only one to achieve barrier-breaking upward mobility. Contract worker James Agenbag was promoted to the position of manager's driver and later he was given the job of motor mechanic and diesel-engine operator. Jan Goosen, once a laborer, became the senior mounted patrol guard and later the farms' manager for the company at Groenriviermond. Earl Rich, too, was once registered as a contract worker; he became a senior guard in charge of the company's property at Dreyer's Pan. Another promotion was a pick-and-shovel man who was appointed to the important position of pit timekeeper.

How should we explain these promotions from the ranks of the contract workers? It is clear that they were all chosen by management because of their skills and presumed honesty and reliability, but it is also important to reflect on their other attributes. Engelbrecht was said to have been "a cut above the others." He was not, in fact, a Namaqualander at all, but a member of a respected, high-status Vredendal family. As an outsider, he was an appropriate choice to be put in authority over his former peers without inviting their resentment.

James Agenbag came from the upper reaches of the Buffels River, where his father was a farmer and a justice of the peace and his mother was the teacher in the little state school at Drierivier. The Agenbag family was important in the region, and James was a good driver with credentials of honesty. The position of manager's driver was as prestigious then as that of pilot today. Jan Goosen was one of the original pick-and-shovel workers before Cape Coast purchased the holdings of the Ronaldson syndicate. He had proved his honesty and reliability over the years. He also knew not only the terrain but all the people of the region, inside and outside the town, including their footprints—so it was said. Earl Rich, too, was renowned for his honesty and tracking skills. Moreover, his father was at that time a justice of the peace and related by marriage to Oom Jan Kotze, one of the original owners of Kleinzee Farm. The timekeeper was soon recognized as an exceptional person, and later he in fact went on to prove his excellence, passing the state matriculation examination by correspondence (while he was at Kleinzee) and going on to university to qualify as a doctor. It goes without saying that, in the context of South African society at that time, each of these "relocations" from the compound to better jobs would not have taken place had these contract workers been black or Coloured.

Whites, as we have already seen, also had the advantage of a higher wage scale, although the higher wages received by whites were determined not by the company but by pressure from the state.[30] In fact without pressure from the state, the company would have not paid whites more than 3s. 6d. a shift, which was the going rate for unskilled labor at the time. In the 1940s, when the state lifted its restrictions on the employment of cheap black labor at Kleinzee, the company laid off all its white workers and recruited foreign black Owambo from South-West Africa, paying them 8d. per shift—eleven times less than what whites had received and five times less than the minimum wage for black South African contract labor. (see figure 6.1).[31] The company rehired a few of the whites to fill semiskilled jobs, paid them more, and gave them equal standing with other whites in the town such as the blaster, the blacksmith, the excavator driver, and helpers for the electrician, the boilermaker, and the fitter and turner.

While there is much truth in Marx's idea that, once involved in a career of unskilled wage labor workers cannot expect to be able to change their standing, racial affiliation can change the situation. At Kleinzee, race came to

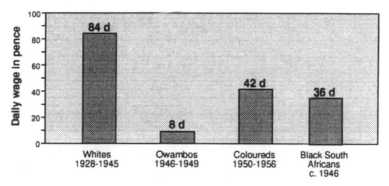

6.1. Same Work, Three Wages
Daily wage for same work paid to three different ethnic groups of workers employed on the Kleinzee diamond mine between 1928 and 1956: white Namaqualanders, black Owambo South-West Africans, and Coloured Namaqualanders. Also shown, for comparison, are wages paid to Black South Africans (e.g., Xhosa) on other mines.

the rescue of the white Namaqualand wage earners, enabling all of them to find better jobs, either through rehiring or elsewhere. Some moved to the cities, where they found work in the booming wartime economy; some found jobs on the local copper mines, where a semiskilled, self-trained carpenter, for example, received 10s. 6d. a shift; others were able to fill jobs formerly held by those who had volunteered for military service. And some benefitted from the weather: Namaqualand had by this time recovered from a long drought, and the continued good rains enabled some to return to farming.[32]

7

The Owambo Contract Worker, 1943–1949

The decision by De Beers to employ black South-West Africans at Klein-zee was made in the latter part of 1943, as a result of management's failure to recruit sufficient numbers of white workers after the preced-ing closure. Some of the groundwork to change the source (and ethnic affilia-tion) of contract workers had in fact been done a few months earlier by Donald McHardy, then general manager of De Beers. In a memorandum re-garding the reopening of Kleinzee, McHardy indicated that he was strongly in favor of switching to black contract labor because it was cheaper, specifying black Owambo labor because of its success at Consolidated Diamond Mines at Oranjemund (CDM) and because it was the cheapest of all. His calcula-tions indicated that it would cost the company £9,500 to improve living con-ditions in the compound sufficiently to attract white contract workers again, and wages would have to be in excess of 7s. 6d. (90 pence) a shift. If black Owambo contract workers were employed, no improvements, other than new kitchen equipment, would be needed, and the starting wage would be no more than 8d. a shift, the standard South-West African rate.[1]

Some background about South-West Africa will be useful here. South-West Africa (present-day Namibia) had been declared a German Protector-ate in 1890. Thirty years later, after World War I, the League of Nations conferred a mandate on South Africa to administer the former German ter-ritory. The terms of the mandate stipulated that South Africa could not profit from its rights of administration, but in 1922 it established "native reserves"

7.1. Washing Plant and Power Station, 1930s
The installation of a mechanical recovery plant and power station made it possible to process more than one thousand loads of gravel per day.

7.2. Cocopan Haulage
Looking north toward ramp and washing plant, 1930.

7.3. Owambo Trammers
Trammers are shown on the ramp, late 1940s.

7.4. White Pick-and-Shovel Workers
Excavating at the east face, 1930.

7.5. Surveillance, 1930s
Excavating near the pit superintendent's office. Note the searchlight and observation deck for nighttime surveillance of the town.

7.6. West Face, 1930
Loading cocopans.

7.7. Down to Bedrock, 1950

Coloured workers at bedrock level. Note Kleinzee's first excavator loading the cocopans on the left.

7.8. Taking Samples

Sampling the ground in the middle of the town. Mobile gasoline-powered prospecting "plant" operated by Coloured workers, late 1940s.

to facilitate control of the indigenous population. (After World War II, when the United Nations replaced the League, South Africa refused to relinquish the mandated territory, and it was not until 1990 that South-West Africa secured its independence under the name of Namibia.)

The enthusiasm of the De Beers general manager for employing the cheapest black labor in Southern Africa was tempered only by his concern to be politically expedient and avoid getting on the wrong side of the government by giving to blacks jobs that had hitherto been reserved for whites. But McHardy was an optimist. In September 1943, he wrote to the secretary for South-West Africa to explain his company's difficulty in obtaining local labor for the mining operations at Kleinzee:

> The Directors are greatly perturbed at the seriousness of the labour position, and a drastic curtailment of operations at Kleinzee is inevitable. . . . [This letter is] to inquire whether His Honour the Administrator [would] sanction the recruitment of 300 Ovambos for service at Kleinzee under the same conditions as those obtaining at the Consolidated Diamond Mines of South-West Africa, Limited.[2]

Within a week, the secretary telegraphed his assent, but stated conditions:

> APPROVAL HEREBY GRANTED FOR YOU TO RECRUIT 300 OVAMBOS FOR WORK AT KLEINZEE NAMAQUALAND SUBJECT TO FOLLOWING CONDITIONS STOP BOYS TO BE PAID AT SAME RATES AND BE PROVIDED WITH SAME CLOTHING AND FOOD AS CONSOLDIA [CDM] STOP MAXIMUM PERIOD OF CONTRACTS TWO YEARS STOP BOYS TO BE UNDER PROPER CONTROL OF LICENSED COMPOUND MANAGER AND NOT ALLOWED TO WANDER ABOUT STOP YOU MUST UNDERTAKE TO CONVEY BOYS TO PLACE OF EMPLOYMENT AND RETURN THEM TO PLACE OF RECRUITMENT FREE OF CHARGE STOP YOU MUST OBTAIN AUTHORITY FROM UNION IMMIGRATION FOR THE ENTRY OF THESE BOYS INTO THE UNION[3]

De Beers accepted all the conditions and immediately requested permission from the South African government in Pretoria to employ foreign blacks, giving an assurance that "the natives would be under strict control and supervision from the time they were recruited until they were finally repatriated upon expiration of their contracts."[4] Permission was immediately granted.

The first lorryload of Owambo contract workers arrived in Kleinzee at the end of December 1943. Others followed in the new year. The Owambos came from northern South-West Africa, having been recruited from various "tribal" areas by the South-West African Native Labour Association (Pty) Ltd. (SWANLA) in Grootfontein. In 1945, the company paid SWANLA £2,888 for 304 workers (£9 10s. 0d. per head).[5] The "tribal" composition of one of the first groups to arrive at Kleinzee was given as twenty-seven Ondonga, twenty Ukuanyama, two Ukuambi, and one [from] Zambesi.[6] The arrival of the Owambos evoked tremendous interest and curiosity from the residents of Kleinzee. Wives, children, and domestic servants came out of their houses to see the open cattle trucks packed with singing black workers as they traveled along the main street to the compound on the last leg of their long, dusty journey.

Doing Their Own Thing

The Owambo workers lived in their own world at Kleinzee, encapsulated and confined to their compound barracks in much the same way as the white workers had been. But the Owambos were much more spirited than the white Namaqualanders, showing much more initiative. They gained much better control over their personal and collective lives than the whites, quickly establishing their own rules, often in defiance of the company. They organized their own leisure, sporting, and religious activities, and they complained when the food was not what they wanted, insisting that it should be changed as soon as possible. They liked to sing. Sometimes they sang in a large ensemble, like Welsh miners, but generally they grouped in smaller choirs, each with its own repertoire, singing Christian hymns and their own work songs. Some groups got permission to go caroling on Christmas Day, visiting the homes of various bosses. They went on supervised trips to the sea—a phenomenon the majority had never seen before. One Sunday, two men drowned when they plunged into the cold waters and were swept out to sea by the current.

Soccer was their favorite sport, but they played it according to their own rules. Sometimes, without warning, and for reasons not apparent to white onlookers, spectators would join in the match. In short, they did their own thing, whether it was soccer, singing, or furthering their education. They persuaded a new compound manager to provide space for a small schoolroom and to furnish it with tables, chairs, and a blackboard, and those who had some formal schooling would teach their less fortunate brothers basic reading and writing skills. Two people from the town volunteered to teach night school for a short period, but association of that kind was not encouraged by management. The majority of the men were Christians, having been associated with mission stations in Owamboland. Often, church and school overlapped in the compound, as it had at home.

In leisure hours, all Owambos seemed preoccupied with personal adornment. Some made their own clothes. Sewing machines were made available to them in the compound, and the men spent hours sewing and stitching. Despite their low wages, they traded briskly at the company store, especially after the introduction of the sixpenny token—a reward they received for any diamonds picked up in the diggings. The Owambos bought all kinds of cheap jewelery, scented soaps, face creams, hair oils, clothing, needles and thread, and, especially, lengths of gay colored and printed material. These items were mainly for presents and/or brideprice when they returned to Owamboland, but they also used the prints in making patchwork pants—trousers. It was during this period that De Beers took full control of the retail store, erstwhile privately owned, in order to reap the full financial benefit of trade with the Owambos.

On Sundays, many of the workers decked themselves out in smart clothing, whether purchased from the store or made up of items they had brought with them or had made. This custom of personal adornment at weekends was similar to that practiced by the earlier white contract workers. For both sets of workers, it provided opportunity for self-expression according to individual sense of fashion, culture, and style. The idea seems to have been to dress as smartly and idiosyncratically as possible. Some of the outfits suggested interesting, often rebellious, attitudes and sentiments, like those of the compound headman Johannes, whose Sunday togs were riding breeches, top boots, Sam Browne belt, and a British officer's tunic, to which were pinned, like military ribbons, rows of colored brooches. The symbolism may have represented, unbeknown to his fellows, his resentment of being under South African authority and his identification with the Englishness of the company under whose instructions he carried out his duties.

Another, but different, manifestation of self-presentation was the popularity with the Owambos of pocket-size vanity mirrors. An individual Owambo might be seen using his mirror to reflect on his image while on the job, if a few minutes could be spared. The mine superintendent one time observed one of the trammers, while waiting for the next truck to reach him, examining his face, laughing and chatting to himself. On asking to be enlightened, the company official was informed by the senior "boss boy" that the trammer was saying over and over to himself that he had no idea he was so black and ugly. The trammer enjoyed the humor of his blackness in this new society, where whiteness ruled but collective worker blackness enjoyed the power.

Owambos at Work

In the days before the Owambos arrived, white laborers were earning 7s. 6d. per shift plus overtime—about £15 a month, when the demand for overtime was high. During the Owambo period, Coloured laborers were paid on the average 4s. a shift plus overtime—about £6 or £7 a month. The set rate of pay for Owambo labor was 8d. a shift. In June 1947, their average monthly income was £1 18s. 0d., including overtime—a tiny sum, less than a quarter of the wage paid to South African blacks for comparable work at that time.[7]

Contrary to management's belief that the Owambos were "simple tribal people," "unspoiled by civilization," "like children and expected to be treated as such," they knew exactly what their rights were and when they could expect action, of whatever sort, by the company. For example, when one group did not receive its issue of underpants en route at Grootfontein, they complained immediately: they knew that their contract stated that "every native must be supplied free of charge with a blanket and a pair of underpants when leaving Ondangua." On arrival at Grootfontein, they expected a shirt, one pair of goggles, and a mess tin. And after a year's service, they expected another free issue of a blanket, a pair of shorts, and a shirt.

At the end of their contract, they expected to be repatriated in batches of fifty, to receive provisions (bully beef and bread and jam) for the trip home, that they would stop, first, at Oranjemund on the way, then continue on to Kolmanskop, and so on. They were also very reluctant to part with their passes, even for inspection by the compound manager. In such matters they were generally a step ahead of the bosses. Their passes were their passports—the documents that would get them back to their homes. At Kleinzee, they insisted on immediately receiving their wrist badges. These good-quality, brass identification tags (which incidentally could be meticulously polished) had their employment numbers clearly engraved on them. They well knew that without such a clear identification, all kinds of confusion could occur, especially in the pit.

McHardy had believed that the Owambos could not work as well as the white contract workers—the earlier trammers, haulage men, and bedrock cleaners, but the work went on with little change. The optimum tally was maintained and the production of diamonds continued as planned. In short, they did pretty well everything the Namaqualanders had done—albeit a little differently. If they were temperamental at times, there was usually good reason. The only job they said they could not do was the harnessing and driving of the mules for drawing cocopans to the haulage at the pit. The mules had always been handled by Coloureds, whom the Owambos rudely regarded as "Bushmen." So the Coloureds continued to handle the mules, and the Owambos were satisfied.

They had respect for human skeletons, and when they came across burials —even Bushman remains—they tried to prevent the authorities from removing them. Sometimes they would debate both practical and philosophical issues while working. They had great contempt for white men who could not fathom what to them were simple, logical sequences. For example, they could not understand the white man's inability to understand why angry scorpions did not sting people who had been inoculated by traditional medicine men. Another credibility gap involved the sixpenny tokens mentioned above. The "pick-up" system had been introduced to prevent diamond theft. It provided a quick cash incentive to workers (particularly those involved in bedrock cleaning) every time they saw a diamond. The pick-up system was also practiced at CDM, and the general belief was that since the Owambos were "simple tribal people" knowing "nothing of the underhand ways of evil men there would be little temptation or opportunity to engage in smuggling."[8]

So many diamonds were being picked up by the Owambos in May 1944 that a new position, diamond collector, had to be created. The job was given to L. Fourie, and for security reasons he was deemed to be the only person allowed to exchange a 6d. token for each diamond handed in. When rich deposits were being worked, the number of pick-ups was spectacular. Between March 13 and 18, 1944, the Owambos handed in 3,182 diamonds, weighing 3,705 carats, which was equal to 58.5 percent of the total production for that period. The average pick-up during the whole of 1944 was 37.5 percent. The amount declined considerably after the first mechanical shovel went into action in 1944, but in 1945 10.8 percent of all the diamonds produced came from pick-ups.[9] The market value of diamonds picked up in 1944 was roughly £421,539.

The pick-up system inevitably generated some discord among the Owambos, who interpreted it as a method of distributing unequal "bonuses." Some jobs, such as tramming, provided little opportunity to pick up a diamond, while bedrock cleaners, especially those working in the deposits of high-grade gravel, were sometimes in the thick of the gemstones. In March 1944, one pothole alone yielded more than 1,000 carats in pick-ups to a handful of workers. In early October 1944, the men on the ramp and crusher hopper at the plant staged a go-slow strike. Acting manager Turner reports that "they . . . planned to work as leisurely as possible, and, though our tally for that day was 973 it should have been at least 1,200. . . . They say they don't get a chance to pick up diamonds." Turner suggested paying the trammers an extra 3s. 6d. per month to keep them quiet. Nothing further came of that incident, and the workers seem to have resolved the problem of pick-ups among themselves.[10]

Owambos and Compound Managers

The cause of the problems the company sometimes experienced with the Owambos was generally the actions (or inaction) of foremen, supervisors, and managers. Notorious among these were the compound managers. Major Brinton was appointed compound manager at Kleinzee on December 28, 1943, to be in charge of the new contract workers who were on their way from Owamboland. Brinton was an authoritarian former policeman who demanded obedience to all his commands, and those who did not fall in line were immediately branded as "insolent and disrespectful in their behaviour toward Europeans." As each lorryload of workers arrived, he ranked them according to his own criteria of what marked a potential troublemaker.

A year after Brinton's appointment, there was some minor trouble in the pit when twenty-seven workers struck work and, as a consequence, were sent back to the compound to "cool off," as was the custom in the absence of a union. The problem seems to have arisen after the group had refused to load cocopans from the north into a gale-force southwest wind. Brinton reported on the incident, as he saw it, in a letter to the manager:

> [On their return to the compound] . . . they immediately packed their Suit Cases, Blankets, etc., and walked up to the main gate where they demanded admission [*sic*] to proceed back to their homes in Ovamboland. This, of course, was refused and they then threatened to rush the gate. I was present and warned them. One said in a very defiant way "If the Police come blood will flow all over this gate and on the ground." I had anticipated something of the sort would happen and had phoned the Manager for assistance, but before assistance arrived quite ten minutes or more, I was alone inside the gate, and a European guard was outside the gate. One or two threatened to climb over the gate and were again warned by me. At that time it looked as if anything may have happened. Some hours later, they gathered their belongings and returned to Barracks.

Brinton's letter continues:

> During the past fortnight 52 weapons have been seized, and all these were found in Barrack Room No. 4. These weapons consisted of Pick Axe handles full length and half, strong long sticks, Iron Bars of various descriptions, thick pieces of wire, etc. The first two lots of weapons were destroyed. The workers are now being more or less searched at the Compound gate by the Native Police on their return from work. Since then no more weapons have been discovered. I must point out, however, that all the weapons referred to were found hidden in blankets, etc. in Barrack Room No. 4.
>
> The men . . . in the Compound have nothing to complain of. They have good quarters, electric light, good food, a plentiful supply of water and washing facilities. No complaints have yet been received from any of them. A well stocked store adjoining the compound buildings is opened to them for an hour and a half three times per week from 5.30 to 7 P.M.[11]

Brinton's letter provides insights into the character of compound managers of that ilk and their attitude toward workers under them. More important, though, are his remarks about the men in Barrack Room No. 4 and (although the strikers later returned to the pit) their determination to retain their independence in a foreign land. Brinton was incapable of accepting, in any way, the spirit of that determination, or any challenge to his authority. He resigned his position some weeks after writing to the manager—forced out by the Owambos.

After Brinton's departure, the manager wrote to the magistrate at Springbok, informing him that there were now 252 Owambos working at Kleinzee and that 50 more were expected any day from Grootfontein. He asked the magistrate to hold "periodical court at Kleinzee to try petty cases," believing that regular court sittings would help control the workers in a way his compound managers could not. The magistrate was not impressed with the apparent urgency of manager Turner's request, replying that "this is not possible at present."[12]

Brinton's replacement was an unstable bartender, E. Herridge (address, c/o Nababeep Hotel), whose only credential seems to have been that he was "interested in the Ovambos. I really love and understand [know how] to handle Ovambos," he wrote in a letter to the manager. Herridge arrived on June 1, 1944, but stayed only three hours before he was escorted out of the gate by the protection officer. In that short period of time, he had complained about the weather and the "sickly looking Ovambos" and had a fight with the manager. He returned to the Springbok-Nababeep area, where he was immediately offered a bartendership at another local hotel.[13] How a person like Herridge could be appointed becomes clearer if we consider the contents of a letter that, two weeks before Herridge was offered the job, the mine manager had received from the director of native labour. The government official informed the manager that the compound manager at Kleinzee did not need a compound manager's license in terms of the Native Labour Regulation Act No. 15 (1911); Kleinzee, he said, was not regarded as a labor district in terms of the act, and since the company was employing labor from South-West Africa, there were no rules to follow with regard to their employment of foreign blacks.[14]

Few compound managers were acceptable to the Owambo workers. Brinton's successor, Kloppers, also proved incompetent, and Crosbie, a well-intentioned older man from Kimberley, was an object of ridicule to the workers, and did not last long. His successor, Guthrie, was soon recalled by head office because "inspection of the compound reveals that [he] has not been discharging his duties with any degree of efficiency or zeal." Soon after that, while the compound was under the supervision of an unidentified manager, it was found to be dirty, and the medical officer discovered bed bugs in the buildings. The MO had unsuccessfully attempted to prevent the infestation with the "use of blue-butter freely applied at all possible breeding places in walls, floor, and ceiling." Later, DDT powder and liquid were recommended for use in both the compound and native hospital.[15]

In July 1947, head office sent James Sandilands, from Wesselton Mine, to take over the compound and to improve workers' living conditions. Sandilands seems to have earned the respect of the Owambos, and he held his job for several years. Qualified, well-intentioned compound managers such as Sandilands were especially valuable to the company because they kept the system running smoothly. They were responsible for the quality of food, the general health of the workers, sending the sick to the doctor, negotiating with management, and so forth. When Sandilands arrived he improved the cooking facilities and made the food more nutritious by adding to the diet powdered yeast, dehydrated vegetables, and orange juice. He also improved the quality of the bread (which had been made of 77 percent unsifted meal and 23 percent mealie-meal) by maintaining the standards required by law. "Compound bread" was required to contain 66 percent no. 1 unsifted meal, 16 percent maize germ meal, 15 percent mealie-meal, and 3 percent soya bean flour.

Sandilands worked closely with the new manager, A. H. Gyngell, and between them they arranged to repair and paint both the compound and the hospital. He also followed the general manager's instruction that each worker should have his own locker for storing personal belongings. There was also a storeroom with shelves, where workers could deposit their purchases from the company store.

In accordance with the provisions of its contract with the men, the company was responsible for transferring remittances to the workers' families in Owamboland, officially and safely. Cash transfers were complex, requiring elaborate documentation regarding kin relationships, the names and addresses of headmen and subheadmen in Owamboland, and registration numbers.[16] The Owambos sent home almost all of their earnings. One record states that "32 Ovambos (Nos. 31–62) remitted £104-4-6 from Kleinzee to [the Native Commissioner in] Ondonga" on October 4, 1944. Since each worker received a monthly wage of roughly £1 at that time, we might conclude that the figure given above was for a three-month period. When wages increased from 8d. to 1s. a day, the amount sent back home increased considerably.

Two General Strikes

The Compound Strike

In mid 1944, one of the workers (known only as Ovambo No. 100) fell seriously ill and was hospitalized.[17] His condition worsened and he was transferred to Springbok hospital, where "malignant dilation of the colon" was diagnosed. He refused surgery and was returned to Kleinzee as "a stretcher case." A week or so later, his brother, No. 254, approached the compound manager to ask whether No. 100 could be sent back to Owamboland. The matter was discussed with the manager, who interviewed the brother and promised to look into the case.

The next day, the whole of the Owambo workforce was on strike. Compound manager Klopper reported on the events in a letter to the manager:

> On 19/8/44 all boys drew their rations at 5.30 A.M. without anyone saying anything to me or the Head Foreman. At 7 A.M. when the gong was sounded for them to proceed to work, they all refused to go and demanded to see the Manager. I phoned the Manager who arrived about 10 minutes later. From him they demanded the immediate repatriation of No. 100. Through the interpreter it was explained to them that this could not be done immediately, as certain arrangements had to be made for his removal, and promised them that it would be done within 10 days. To that they objected and told the Manager that they would remain on strike until such time as No. 100 was repatriated. Nothing could induce them to go to work and they remained on strike until 21/8/44 when all went to work. On 29/8/44 No. 100 and the two ringleaders Nos 2 and 254 were repatriated. The former was a parson and I may mention that all trouble in the Compound prior to the strike was always caused by him in such a way as to shield himself and giving the blame to others and I got information after the strike that he, No. 2, actually incited the boys on 18/8/44 to go on strike on 19/8/44. He, however, was repatriated and I feel convinced that most of the trouble in the compound will come to an end.[18]

Rather than attempt any detailed interpretation of this strike, I can only observe that it was a compound matter and unrelated to the workplace. It would be easy to play armchair anthropologist and suggest a complex of witchcraft and sorcery, attributing "accused status" to No. 2 or No. 254 and "victim status" to the ailing No. 100. On the other hand, I suspect that co-workers simply felt it best for the sick man to be sent home to die, or at best be treated by someone other than the incompetent doctor at Kleinzee or the impulsive Springbok surgeon.

Striking for Ephraim: The November 1944 Strike

The Owambo workers understood the nature of their contracts with De Beers as well as others had done, and in some ways, they understood better. For the Owambos, the South African Police had absolutely no place in their lives, and they expected all negotiations regarding their work and leisure at Kleinzee to be carried out with the company. While the company understood this in general, individual employees, including certain managers, did not. The November strike concerned police involvement and interference in Owambo/company affairs, and the presumption by certain white employees that workers should obey every order and command without question.

On October 28, 1944, Willie Prosser, an engineer of sorts, complained to S. Harris, the acting pit superintendent, that "boy No. 257 [Ephraim] refused to work on the Machine." Harris told Ephraim that he had to obey Prosser. When Ephraim refused, Harris sent him to the compound, giving the compound manager orders to allow him to return only when "he was prepared to go on the Machine." Four days later, Ephraim returned to the pit, again refused orders, and was once more sent back to the compound. He returned to work on November 4.

Three days later Harris wrote to the manager:

> On the morning of the 7th Prosser sent word that boys 257 and 281 had left the machine and gone into the claims to work on bedrock. I again instructed these two boys to go to the machine or back to the compound. Boy No. 257 said he was remaining where he was and that if I worried him any more he would jump out of the claim [*sic*] and assault me; he being in possession of a shovel which he used in a threatening manner. I told him there was no such thing as fighting at work and that if he did not leave the Bedrock I would have to get him removed. I then asked Mr. Turner (the acting manager) to have him removed by force if necessary as his method of resistance had already spread, as now natives numbers 281 and 198 had also refused to leave the bedrock and continued to work wherever they wished to; but they were receiving no pay.[19]

The main issue, as far as the workers were concerned, seems to have been the question of diamond pick-ups. It was, in fact, the custom among them to rotate positions from time to time, particularly when working in rich gravel. Situations like this were not unusual and were generally solved in a few days by the workers themselves. But on this occasion, before they had the opportunity to reach a compromise, the acting manager arrived with two policemen. Ephraim was again told by Harris to leave the claims. He refused "so

[Harris] charged him with threatening to assault [him]." When the police tried to arrest him, all the workers closed ranks and prevented Ephraim from being arrested. The two policemen gave up and reported the matter to their seniors. Captain Jonker, of the South African Police, now took over. The protection officer explains the next move:

> In the meantime Mr. Turner and I tried to persuade these Ovambos to hand up Ephraim before the Police should come and effect his arrest by force. We were again unsuccessful. We stressed the point that if they don't hand up Ephraim, there is sure to be trouble, as the police [were] determined to have Ephraim. Nothing in the world would convince them. They all stated that if Ephraim is arrested all of them must be taken [en bloc].[20]

It is really quite remarkable how Ephraim was protected by his fellow workers. Neither the bosses nor the police ever discovered how they arrived at a consensus under these difficult circumstances. It is equally remarkable how badly the manager and his senior staff managed the matter. The workers had absolutely no intention of negotiating with the police, whether they were from the Kleinzee contingent or the twenty-four men who suddenly arrived, fully armed, from elsewhere, with the district commandant. Without police involvement, they would have negotiated with management for a couple of days until a solution was found. But that was not to be.

Security officer De la Rey writes:

> [The police and management] then decided to have Ephraim arrested in front of the Compound at knock off time. The Police lined up with fixed bayonets in front of the gate. When the Ovambos approached the compound, Mr. Turner again went forward to implore them to hand up Ephraim, before there was trouble. They were in an ugly mood, and were seen picking up stones and were in possession of empty bottles. They were allowed to file past, but owing to the crush Ephraim could not be spotted. The police went after them into the Compound, where there was a clash between police and the Ovambos inside the Compound. I remained at the gate. Ephraim was eventually arrested and another Ovambo was also arrested for obstructing the police. Twenty-one Ovambos and one policeman were injured, not seriously. The police were withdrawn and guards were placed on duty at various parts in case of further trouble. Nothing occurred during the night.[21]

The following day, the manager telegraphed head office in Kimberley:

ALL OVAMBOS RETURNED TO WORK EXCEPT TEN COMPRISING FOUR IN HOSPITAL

AND SIX OUT-PATIENTS ALL MINOR INJURIES (STOP) ALL QUIET AND WORK PRO-
CEEDING SMOOTHLY[22]

A few days later, another telegram was sent to justify management's action
and report on the functioning of the new rock crusher at the plant—the latter
seeming like a metaphor for police intervention and the injuries inflicted:

OVAMBOS ALL QUIET OBEDIENT AND BEHAVIOUR IMPROVED SINCE CLASH (STOP)
ONLY SIX INJURED NOT AT WORK WHO WILL RETURN IN A DAY OR TWO (STOP) NEW
CRUSHER WORKING SUCCESSFULLY[23]

In a letter to the manager, Dr. Archibald Gow, the medical officer, reported that between 5:30 P.M. and 6:00 P.M. on the day of the police attack,
"twenty one native Ovambo employees reported at the Native Hospital. Five
more reported the following morning. . . . Sixteen of them had small punc-
tured wounds from a quarter to half an inch in length, and up to half an inch
deep . . . two natives had superficial punctures of the chest wall, the remainder being confined entirely to the buttocks and legs."[24] Gow added that all
the injuries were the result of a clash between natives and the police, during
a bayonet charge by the latter.

After the De Beers general manager, Donald McHardy, had examined
the reports and considered the details, he wrote condemning both management and police for their individual and combined actions. He pointed out
that the incident could have been avoided if the acting manager and the acting
pit superintendent had exercised more discretion. And "it should have been
obvious to both those officials that any attempt by a member of the police
force to arrest a native in the pit would undoubtedly lead to trouble involving
all the other native employees." Of Captain Jonker's action, McHardy wrote
that his "using force to the extent he did . . . is inexplicable and . . . discloses
a grave error of judgement."[25]

A report of the incident in the *Cape Times* on November 9 stated that "a
police posse under the district commandant used bayonets to break the resistance of 250 Owambo mine laborers who refused to surrender one of their
number." At his trial in Springbok, Ephraim received a sentence of fourteen
days for resisting arrest and thirty days or a £7 10s. fine for failing to carry out
police orders. Eru Petrus (No. 301) received a fine of £2 or fourteen days for
obstructing the police.[26]

Captain Jonker and the commissioner of the South African Police obviously felt that much more should be done to quell the "unrest," recommending that both Ephraim and Eru Petrus be repatriated immediately and that

"management also get rid of the principal malcontents concerned in the strike."[27] The new manager at Kleinzee, Pieter Louwrens, disagreed. In his reply, he stated that "Ephraim and Eru have already been prosecuted and punished for their offence and . . . [should] not be penalised . . . further by cancelling their contracts."[28]

When the regular pit superintendent returned from leave of absence, he heard the Owambo workers' account of what had happened. As he recounted it later:

> An Ovambo refused to obey orders when detailed from one job to another. In-stead of bringing enlightened patience to bear, Harris [my replacement while I was away] stormed, raved and kicked up an unholy shindy. He demanded the po-lice; and, foolishly the Manager consented. In came a detachment of police from Port Nolloth and their arrival was a signal for all the Ovambos to down their tools and crowd back to the compound . . . the police then fixed bayonets and charged through the doors until they got hold of [Ephraim]. All this was most unnecessary . . . and could have been avoided with a little understanding and tact. As it was, when the fracas was over, the men refused to return to work unless [Harris] . . . left the property. Otherwise they threatened to kill him by night. Harris was off back to Kimberley before another sun rose.[29]

The details of the strike reflect some of the attitudes toward these black workers, as well as how they expected to be treated and their attitudes to-ward their various bosses. Perhaps the most significant detail was the strength of their resistance and their ability to mobilize themselves in a unified move-ment while events seem to be going against them. In the case of the strike I have described, not even the compound manager had any indication that it was imminent. Moreover, the Owambos always seemed to get their way de-spite the enormous odds they faced. They got rid of Harris, and Turner seems to have been sent back to Kimberley earlier than he had expected. Harris they especially disliked, having summed him up the first day he took over from the regular pit superintendent. Harris always carried a loaded revolver in his pocket and made a point of dropping live cartridges on the open bedrock to make quite sure that "these savages realised that he was armed." The workers had great contempt for him and it did not take long for them to get rid of him. The manager also got on the wrong side of the workers for bringing in the po-lice, and one day his car was pelted with bread and porridge.

The Owambo workers during their years at Kleinzee always resolved their labor disputes through their own initiatives. In the 1944 strike, it is noteworthy that all 277 workers—the whole body of Owambos—decided to resume work.[30]

Stress and Strain

Given the stress and strain of their confinement to the compound, it is remarkable how little "disruptive" behavior there generally was—even more remarkable considering the criminally low wages paid to the Owambos. The strikes cost the company very little. The only allegation of serious acts of vandalism to company property is recounted in an unsubstantiated report, probably from Harris, that "Owambo drillers wait for the opportunity to slip off the hoses [from the jackhammer] and insert sand and gravel into the machines." Judging from the date of the report, the alleged behavior was linked to the second strike, when the workers were gunning for Harris in the pit.[31]

I was not permitted to consult the detailed medical reports about these workers in the archives of Anglo American. However, the Kleinzee records report five Owambo deaths during their Kleinzee years. In April 1944, No. 176 died of malignant endocarditis, probably caused by meningitis. He ran a temperature of 105 degrees Fahrenheit and was placed in isolation in a tent. He was "buried one mile south of the Compound 200 yards from the sea, care being taken to ensure that the grave was not in diamondiferous ground."[32] When Shanyenga Kanghono died in Springbok Hospital on May 6, 1944 (cause unspecified), the main concern was what to do with his personal effects. He was buried at the same site as No. 176—a burial place that remains unmarked to this day. At about the same time there is mention of another "Ovambo dying in Springbok Hospital of acute appendicitis." Kleinzee doctors never attempted emergency surgery; all cases were sent to Springbok.[33]

Some Owambo workers occasionally felt (and not out of hypochondria) that they would benefit from a surgical procedure that had been performed on one of their friends in a local hospital. In January 1947, the mine doctor sent three men to Springbok for surgery because they insisted on having their appendixes removed. "Dr. Basson refused to operate," thereby preventing what might have been an "epidemic." There had, in fact, been a demand for this surgical procedure at Consolidated Diamond Mines (CDM) in 1945, when scores of appendix operations were performed on Owambo workers. Dr. McGregor, who did the surgery at CDM, was alleged to have grown tired of this unnecessary chore and ended up doing no more than skin incisions— a dangerous practice since at a later date another surgeon might dismiss a real, attack of acute appendicitis.[34]

The company seems always to have repatriated workers who arrived with "undesirable" or "untreatable" diseases. In June 1945, Haidua Kandje was repatriated because he suffered from dementia praecox, Dr. Gow saying "he was a danger to himself and others and had mental delusions which were worst at full moon." Another man was repatriated, in 1946, because he had a "contagious venereal disease."

There do not appear to have been many serious injuries among these Owambo workers. An exception was Indonga Timotheus, who is reported to have had his right leg torn off at the knee by the haulage wire. A few minor injuries resulted from assaults. When Shangengange No. 73, an Ukuanyama, was mildly stabbed on a Monday night during Owambo shopping hour by No. 205, the company laid a charge against No. 205 "as an example to others."[35]

General Exploitation

Between 1944 and 1949, more than five hundred black South-West African workers, largely from Owamboland, worked at Kleinzee for the lowest minimum wage in the history of the mine—8d. a day, rising to 12d. a day in 1946. The cost of recruiting each of these workers was about £9 10s., and the facilities provided for them in the compound were the minimum by South African standards. As we have already seen, some had the opportunity to work overtime, and for others there was the pick-up system. A few Owambos were also allowed to work after regular shift hours as gardeners and houseboys for senior officials. In combination, odd jobs, overtime, and shift work produced monthly earnings (excluding pick-up earnings) ranging from 17s. 6d. to 29s. 6d.— sometimes a little bit more. In June 1947, after wages had increased to 12d. a shift, the average monthly wage of all 301 Owambo workers was £1 18s. 6d. The most telling evidence of their exploitation is reflected in a comparison of their earnings with the other groups who did the same work—that is, the Coloureds and whites (see figure 6.1).

Regulation of Owambo welfare was almost nonexistent. Under South African law, a compound manager overseeing Owambos need be neither qualified nor licensed because Owambos were foreign contract laborers. The magistrate at Springbok informed the manager that the company did not even have to take out an employer's recruiting license provided the labor force "was confined to natives coming from South West Africa under contract." The government required only a monthly health return and a monthly labor return.[36] Some irony may be seen in the implications of this indifference on the part of the South African government: these temporary sojourners from a neighboring country that was under South African protection were not required to receive that protection—such as it was—when away from home. The Owambos at Kleinzee occupied the lowest possible point on every scale of social differentiation in South Africa. They received no protection from the state, they were totally isolated from the rest of the world, and, wards of the company for as long as their contracts lasted since they agreed to a contract of specific length, they were not at liberty to pack their bags and leave.

What is remarkable about these people was their ability to solve their own labor problems—problems that by and large were created by their employers. They got rid of incompetent compound managers, an acting pit superintendent for whom they had enormous contempt, and even a manager. Through all this they displayed covert loyalty toward the company, not by choice or preference, but because they knew that they were the wards of De Beers. In a foreign country, had the company turned against them they would have had no ally.

Actually, it was not so much the company they showed loyalty to, but key individual bosses. They approved of and liked some; others they regarded with contempt. As seen above, in November 1944, when they felt they had been betrayed by the manager who called the police, they found police intervention totally unacceptable. The Owambos expected the company to be on their side. Another, very specific, example comes from March 1946, when the company received a request from the magistrate's office in Vanrhynsdorp for an Owambo interpreter to assist the state in a trial in which a man from Owamboland was accused of raping a white woman. An interpreter was duly sent, only to be "threatened" by the police before the hearing and then dismissed by the prosecutor because he considered the interpreter's translation in court to be inaccurate and his Afrikaans too colloquial. When the interpreter returned to Kleinzee, he reported the discriminatory treatment he had received in Vanrhynsdorp. The manager, Toby Holland, supported him, complaining to both the magistrate and to the police about their insults and threats to the employee he had sent. The manager's supportive action was applauded by the man and his co-workers at Kleinzee, who in turn showed great loyalty and respect to Holland.[37]

The mobilization of Owambo solidarity was not based on *amakhaya* (home boy) principles—a form of mutual support that occurred among Xhosa and other contract workers (see chapter 11). Not all Owambos came from the same "tribe" or village. The origins of Owambo solidarity can more likely be found in the wider context of Owambo political movements in the preindependence years of South African control, beginning in the 1920s, when the pattern of strikes and walkouts parallels those described above at Kleinzee during the 1940s.[38]

The company employed Owambo contract workers for a little less than five years. Quite unexpectedly in 1949 they were recalled by the South-West African administration because white farmers there had complained that they were experiencing a shortage of cheap black labor.

8

The Coloured Namaqualand Worker

The Coloureds, as we have seen, were involved in the alluvial diamond industry from the very early prospecting days, when they were employed as pick-and-shovel laborers, water carriers, cooks, messengers, and so on. As prospecting ventures evolved into small-scale diggings, so the Coloureds began to take on semiskilled tasks that were highly valued. However, it was not until 1950 that the Coloureds were recruited in large numbers.[1] This chapter deals first with the status of the Coloured workers in the early days, then discusses their experience during the compound years.

Early Days, 1926–1949

The discovery of diamonds in Namaqualand coincided with local droughts and the Great Depression, a combination that did not augur well for good race relations between the Coloureds in the reserves and the neighboring white farmers. When competition for jobs developed, the state protected the whites by guaranteeing them a higher percentage of jobs as well as better wages on the alluvial diamond mines. Oppenheimer (who favored cheap labor) in March 1930 was consequently forced into a wage and quota agreement with the minister of mines.[2]

The quota system, which favored whites three to one, was rigidly applied from July 1930, when there were only forty-four Coloured workers at Kleinzee. They earned an average of £6 7s. 6d. per month. The 165 white workers earned an average of £11 18s. 10d. per month, including overtime.[3] Over the years, the ratio remained the same, but the Coloured wage decreased to an average of about £5 10s., including overtime. State policy and local management's implementation of the quota and the regulations related to it produced more segregation between the two groups than had ever existed before. Thus, when the manager wrote to the consulting engineer in April 1931, he reported that all the workers on the ramp were Coloured and all those working in the pit were white.[4] This caste-like practice spread into other areas: Coloured workers were assigned to "sanitary" (latrine) and "domestic work." The latter was flexibly interpreted to include the building trade (Steinkopf produced excellent masons and carpenters), road construction and repairs, fencing, and other important work on the plant and in the pulsator, the workshops, protection work, and shoemaking.

Whether they worked on the sanitary lorry or in the power station, the rate of pay was roughly the same. Masons seem to have received a better rate, but never received a wage equal to that paid to white artisans. When the white contract workers moved into the new compound in 1930, Coloureds continued to live in A-frame tin shacks, ten people to one unit, where they cooked for themselves on Primus (kerosene) stoves and outdoor wood fires.

The Coloureds had to wait for many years for better accommodation. In fact, they never benefited materially from the construction of the town, although in the town there were fewer restrictions on their movements. They had contact with the domestic servants and could visit them in their quarters attached to the staff houses. Some played musical instruments—concertinas, guitars, and banjos—and they held regular Saturday night dances. Some of the men found lovers. Weekend picnics at the seaside were organized occasionally, and these were well attended by the maids from the town.

At Christmas and New Year celebrations, many of the old-timers visited their bosses and were treated to a couple of drinks. For example, every Christmas, Piet Vries, Isaac Cloete, and George MacDonald visited the mine pit superintendent to get their Christmas boxes (gifts) and to sit with him round the kitchen table to celebrate the old pioneer days at the diggings and to reinforce old ties of patronage with tots of brandy. The use of the kitchen on these occasions marked their asymmetrical relationship in the "real" world of the company town and the wider society. Participation in these ritual occasions was always expected, and the libation of brandy obligatory. A teetotal manager who offered coffee and cookies never lived down his refusal to play the game. Management also customarily gave foodstuffs and tobacco as Christmas presents, which came to be regarded as part of the workers' rights.

The state gave Coloured workers little protection or assistance over wages and living conditions, and took minimal interest in their welfare. Right from the start, the Coloureds had to go it alone in their relations with the company. It took decades to get an increase in wages: the basic wage in 1950 was 3s. to 3s. 6d. per day, exactly what it had been in 1930. The few increases and extras they received during those years were attributed, correctly or not, to the efforts of their immediate bosses, rather than to the company. The Coloured workers knew they were on their own and that they had to work hard at maintaining good personal relations at lower levels of authority, right down to establishing amicable relationships with junior bosses. When compelled to deal with the company, they did so in small groups. This was not to protest but to negotiate in terms of their actual, and perceived, position in the socioeconomic and cultural hierarchy. Fourteen Coloured workers, who had served the company for many years, expressed some of their feelings in a shrewd letter, written in English, to the manager in June 1932, when most of the labor force had been laid off:

> We just take the opportunity to write you these few lines, that we are thanking you ever so much for all your Compensation so far and we get our notice yesterday which we are quite satisfaction with. But we thought that the Company are responsible to return us to Steinkopf, For the company brought us; Thats we are begging you to convey us if possable please, we are not unwilling to transfair ourselves, but you know that we poor, and that our wages are much less, And we had no credit this month, and now we got nothing less to hire a lorry, and in case that Company's lorry we be absent we would'ent mind to hire a [lorry?] on the Companys account; hoping and trusting that our temtations wont be in vain. Answer: please?
>
> Under Sgnd by yours faithfully boys.[5]

The letter had its intended effect: a lorry was provided to take them to Steinkopf.

Both Cape Coast and De Beers employed recruiting agents on the reserves. The agents bypassed the *raad* (council) and charged their own unspecified recruitment fees. One agent, Myer Caplan, a general merchant in Steinkopf, acquired three hundred shares in Cape Coast in 1935.[6] Caplan and the mine secretary, Wilson, had an arrangement whereby a telegram or letter would produce the desired results. For example, on December 10, 1929, Caplan wrote to the manager at Kleinzee.

> I am sending per to-day's train 10 Boys [from Steinkopf]. I have advanced 10/- to each of 8, with the exception of Freddie Davids and Felix Wessels, who have only

5/- advanced to them. Please deduct above from their salaries in due course. I shall forward more boys as soon as I can get them together.[7]

Another example of the recruitment system came on February 6, 1930, when the mine secretary telegraphed Caplan: "Send 30 boys @ 3/6 per day." On February 28 he told Caplan: "Send 15 boys immediately. 3/6 per day."[8] Many questions remain unanswered regarding Caplan's involvement in the recruiting business, and especially his close relationship with the Steinkopf people and his willingness to give credit to the poor, accepting payment later through his elaborate, and profitable, barter/credit system.

With the exception of two workers, no labor was recruited from the Komaggas Reserve in the early days despite its proximity to Kleinzee. The problem stemmed from the company's insensitivity and hostility toward the Komaggas people at that time. Cape Coast had gone as far as to suggest that they be resettled because of their propinquity to rich diamond deposits. In February 1932, manager Humphreys told his consulting engineer he thought much more needed to be done to prevent illicit digging in Namaqualand, especially in the Komaggas area:

> The police are still inadequate in strength . . . to deal [efficiently] with the menace, especially when the graduates of the Komaggas School of Mines thoroughly grasp what an enormous gravel run they possess at their very feet. In my opinion the Coloured community should be put off the "Reserve" and compensated, and Komaggas proclaimed a "prohibited area," but presumably the Powers that Be would be too fearful of losing a few votes by such action.[9]

There was, at this time, considerable confusion as to the status of the Namaqualand Coloured people—also known as "The Basters" (mixed descent)—with regard to the type and standard of accommodation they were legally entitled to receive. The company was interested only in minimum requirements, and after studying the law the consultants eventually ruled that "a Namaqualand Bastard [sic] is [not] an aboriginal" nor is Namaqualand a "labour district" in terms of the Native Labour Regulation Act of 1911. In other words, as long as only Namaqualand Coloureds were employed at Kleinzee, the act did not apply. As for housing, what was "laid down for natives [i.e. blacks] will be good enough for [the Coloureds]." The Department of Mines stipulated, however, that the Coloured and white compounds "must not be back to back."[10]

The Coloured worker thus stood in an ambiguous relationship to everyone in the town, particularly the white workers, with whom, despite their sharing a common culture, they had little contact. They earned 3s. 6d. per day, roughly half the white wage, but five times the Owambo wage, yet they did the same work, often involving more responsibility (e.g., gravitating, bricklaying, and carpentry). True, the Coloured workers had more freedom of movement than the white workers, not being totally confined to their barracks behind barbed wire at the end of the day, but in the final analysis, during the 1930s and early 1940s, they remained at the bottom of the socio-economic pyramid at Kleinzee because of the multifaceted dictates of South African law. The white workers, despite their confinement by the company for security reasons, were protected by the state in ways the Coloureds were not, and when they left the employ of the company their status reverted to the privileged position afforded to all whites in South Africa.

The attitudes of bosses in high places toward the complexities of ethnic labor at Kleinzee is captured in a letter from Dr. Beets (geologist for Anglo American) to the Kleinzee manager. He asks him to send photos of machinery in Kleinzee to Robert Hengherr, whose company supplied the diesel engines for the Kleinzee power station. He would "like [also] to have a photo with 'milieu' i.e. several niggers, palm trees, crocodiles and so [on]. I told him that the country round Kleinzee is not populated by 'Kaffirs' but by 'ons mense' [white Namaqualanders] and 'bastards' [brown Namaqualanders] and that these also make a splendid 'milieu.'"[11]

Compound Years, 1950–

In January 1950,[12] after all the Owambos had been repatriated, they were replaced by 264 new Coloured workers recruited from throughout Namaqualand. Almost three-quarters of them (74%) came from Steinkopf and its sister reserve Concordia. Only 9 percent came from the other reserves of Komaggas, Leliefontein, and Richtersveld. The remaining 17 percent were townsmen from O'okiep, Nababeep, Springbok, and Port Nolloth. World War II being over, Coloured veterans had returned to their homes; now, after five years of good rains, a new cycle of drought had signaled their need to look for work beyond the borders of the reserves. The state's quota system of the 1930s, favoring white labor, no longer applied, and the whites moved into new jobs in the towns and cities, reserved for them under new apartheid legislation.

The new Coloured workers were required to sign contracts for six months, after which they were entitled to two weeks of leave before signing on for a further six months. Some workers chose to accumulate leave, others took pay in lieu of leave. The turnover was high, and of the 264 men who began work in January 1950, only 74 were still employed two years later. New recruits replaced those who did not return after leave.

The conditions of the new contract reflected a change in attitude toward the Coloured workers. The contract now contained a clause making "compassionate" leave possible for a wide range of matters: harvesting and plowing were considered good reasons for leave, as were returning to help look after children if the worker's wife was seriously ill, attendance at a funeral, and, occasionally, rest that was needed after a long spell of strenuous labor. On the reserves, the *raad* now acted as the recruiting agent, and the company began to transport workers to and from the reserves.

The average age of single Coloured workers in the early 1950s, when single men comprised 73 percent of the total, was twenty-three; the average age of married men was forty. The latter, with their greater responsibility as breadwinners, stayed longer on the job, and some worked for the company for twenty years or more. In February 1951, the average monthly wage of an unskilled Coloured worker, including overtime, was £6 2s. 6d. a month. On entering employment, he was paid 3s. 6d. per shift. If he renewed his contract after six months, he received 4s. a shift. After his second six months of service, he would receive 4s. 8d., provided this was recommended by his overseer. Overtime was paid at the rate of time and a half. A clear distinction began now to be made between unskilled and semiskilled workers (the latter including those who did skilled work). Twelve men earned more than £15 a month, and 88 earned an average of £12 8s. a month, including overtime. In other words, roughly 36 percent of the total Coloured labor force—the skilled and semiskilled workers—now earned double the wage of a pick-and-shovel laborer.

Earnings were spent cautiously. According to a survey carried out in 1951, the total Coloured labor force spent about £325 a month on COD mail-order parcels; £550 went to the company store in cash sales. Coloured workers also sent £700 home each month. The mail-order purchases and the cash sales did not represent frivolous self-indulgent buying: most purchases were taken home when contracts expired. Very little money seemed to have been saved for personal use, and only three individuals possessed post office savings books.

As marginal members of South African society, the Coloureds had always to make a special effort to maintain their status at Kleinzee, especially when they planned to negotiate for new perks. They deliberately avoided confrontation with the manager and they cultivated amicable relationships with bosses lower in the mine hierarchy. In some ways, as the new "working class" they had an enormous advantage over their white and black predecessors because they were better informed about company matters and individual personalities at the mine. A store of knowledge had been built up by old-timers over the years, and they got to know what went on in the homes of the senior staff through associating with the Coloured domestic servants, many of whom had been in service since 1930.

As the new workers settled in, so their leisure activities diversified. The younger men enjoyed soccer, some as players, some as spectators, but more than half of the Coloureds had no interest in sport. Many preferred reading, although the compound library had only two hundred books. Most of the reading material was in Afrikaans, the language spoken by everyone. The company subscribed to two nonpolitical periodicals, *Brandwag* and *Die Stem*, but there were no newspapers. A movie was shown once a week. There was dancing on Saturday nights, and local women (domestic servants employed by whites) were invited. There were several bands, and the company supplied a radiogram. As in the past, Sundays were days for dressing up.

Six couples now lived in the old Coloured compound, which had been transformed into comfortable flats. Their children were not permitted to attend the segregated school but were sent to the reserves for their education. A majority of workers belonged to the Dutch Reformed Mission Church; they were visited several times a year by an ordained minister. Various church groups were formed in the compound.

Although the Coloureds did the same work as the earlier Owambos and whites, as noted earlier they were not subjected to the X-ray procedure until the 1940s. IDB by Coloured workers seems not to have been a problem for the company until recently. There have always been jokes on the reserves about *blink klippies*—how old so-and-so was able to start his business from the proceeds of IDB, but there is little evidence that the Steinkopf workers were involved in serious diamond stealing from Kleinzee in the early days. Some have suggested that reserve dwellers stole from the State Alluvial Diggings at Alexander Bay (because it was state owned) and not from Kleinzee (because it was a "De Beers English operation"); that, it is said, is why the Coloured workers resented being "put under lights" when X-raying became mandatory for everyone leaving the town.

Many whites in Namaqualand over the years have coveted the lands that were set aside as reserves for the Nama and certain Coloured people. The reasons are complex, and go back to the nineteenth century when the various tracts of land were first held "in trust" by the government of the Cape Colony for the indigenous people and their descendants. In more recent times, the animosity generated by feelings of resentment and jealousy toward Coloureds over land is often expressed in unexpected ways. In January 1945, for example,

Major J. W. G. Leipoldt wrote to De Beers, Kimberley, attempting to smear the Steinkopf Coloured people. Accusing Coloureds (especially female domestic servants, but male workers, too) of IDB, he urged the company to prevent the former from working at Kleinzee. He argued, inter alia, that because some of the "quite pretentious school buildings . . . now being built at Steinkopf" were paid for by the community, the funds could only have come from IDB activity. Leipoldt suggested that "the Missionary at Steinkopf backed up by the Anglican rector at O'okiep with, possibly, a good word from the Bishops" was responsible for the liberal treatment of the Coloureds by the company.[13] Leipoldt had been questionably involved in scheelite mining with members of the Steinkopf Coloured community on their land, and his letter reflected his personal animosity against them. His accusations, all false and mischievous, were designed to destabilize future relationships with Coloured workers at Kleinzee. Long before apartheid became official policy, people with Leipoldt's prejudices were always the first to resent any liberalizing of relations with people of color.

The socioeconomic ramifications of migrant labor are complex for both workers and their families. In Steinkopf, the departure of at least one person from each household to the mines or towns has been an economic necessity for the majority of families for many years. In the 1950s, both the church and the raad encouraged migration to places like Kleinzee and Alexander Bay because they favored the compound residential system. It was argued that this arrangement facilitated worker contact with their homes and gave other members of the community an opportunity to keep an eye on kin absent from home. The raad found it convenient to demand payment of local taxes through its contact with the mine management, for which it had become the semiofficial labor bureau. Some members of the raad were paid by the mining companies to recruit labor, and the church liked the compounds because they provided a good environment for collecting dues.

The church and workers' wives and parents also considered the compound system to be desirable on moral grounds. Their rationalization argued that as workers were properly cared for (in the compounds) and well-disciplined, there was no chance of illicit sex with loose town women, and so on. But it was the economic benefits of being a migrant mineworker that were always paramount. Given the poverty at home, institutionalized migrant labor proved more rewarding than any other kind of economic activity for unskilled workers. In 1952, the majority of Coloured mineworkers earned approximately £5 14s. per month (including overtime), and by 1958, the monthly wage had risen to approximately £10. Although this was the first substantial increase in twenty years, it was indeed considerable. Cash income from farming in the dry Namaqualand region was insignificant.

Other forms of migrant labor were looked upon less favorably by the community. To take a job in towns such as Port Nolloth, Springbok, or further afield in Cape Town was believed to be fraught with hazards, over which the family had no control, and some such migrants never returned. It was also said that workers returning from those towns brought all the "undesirable" habits of town life back with them, especially when they returned with frivolous wives. The chief complaint was that they failed to send money home.

The preference for institutionalized migratory labor over individual excursions into the more "impersonal" labor market of towns and cities belonged very much to the 1950s, when many people were resisting change. But as that conservatism gave way to worker "demands" for higher wages and better living conditions, so the De Beers company was forced to change its policies. Wages increased dramatically from the 1960s onward, and special arrangements were made for workers to go home for weekends. Closer links were forged with local government on the reserves and the old compound system gave way to more comfortable living conditions. Better food and opportunities for career advancement were provided, along with houses for married workers employed in certain semiskilled and skilled jobs.

Domestic Servants

Any account of Coloured workers at Kleinzee would be incomplete without some discussion of the domestic servants. While not part of the company's labor force, domestic servants have always been of great significance to life on the mine. In addition to their affiliations with particular families, servants ("servant girls," as they were called) interacted closely with the Coloured male workers through ties of kinship and friendship. Some married while in service.

From the early days, Coloured servants got to know everything about the private lives of their "misseses" and "masters." Among the senior staff, when a dinner invitation was extended to another family, it was understood that the visiting family's maid was also invited to "help with the washing up." This was not really a chore because it entitled her to enjoy a good meal and to catch up on gossip with the host's maid. With the kitchen close to both the dining and sitting rooms, conversations could be easily overheard, and this added to a general pool of gossip and information. Maids excelled in having rich knowledge of the upper echelons of the mine's hierarchy. News spread quickly through servant networks to other white households, and thence to the Coloured workers in the compound. During my fieldwork, I was amazed at the detailed knowledge that Steinkopf women had acquired about their former employers and about what had gone on in the town generally: young domestics in the early days, they had had their ears open. What surprised me most, though, was how little they resented having been at the beck and call of their "madams";[14] poorly paid, they received only half the wage of a male Coloured worker.

The typical day for a maid in a senior staff household began before 6:00 A.M., when early morning tea was served. Breakfast had to be prepared by 6:30. Then they went on to household chores, assisting with other meals, and to be nanny to any children. Most maids were free in the afternoon, but at 5:00 P.M. returned to work. Some maids, especially those working for senior staff, received some on-the-job training in middle-class household management. They also learned to speak English and the rudiments of South African English culture, on which they prided themselves. I think it is true to say that young Coloured women from the reserves who went to work at Kleinzee in the 1930s and 1940s expected to be trained, just as their employers expected to be able to train them in their ways. One staff wife said, "I got a girl from the mission. She had some education so it was quite easy to teach her how to cook and do housework. She had never worked for anyone else before so I could teach her my way."

Close bonds of friendship and psychological dependence often developed between maids and madams in Kleinzee. In many ways, the madams needed the support and loyalty more than the maids did, and in general many of these relationships, even if not symmetrical, reflected mutual attachment. One former maid told me:

> Sometimes, when I was in my room having my time off in the afternoons my mis-sis would call me by my name from the kitchen door: "Maria, Maria, Maria," she would call, louder and louder, and I would pretend not to hear at first because it was so lovely to listen to my name being called like that—in English!

Not all domestic servants shared such sentiments, however. Most complaints came from those in the employ of white families lower on the socioeconomic scale.

Domestics in the homes of the poorer whites were often paid shockingly low wages—the equivalent of a farm laborer's pittance—and they were not allowed to eat the food they had prepared for the family. An indication of their humble status is reflected in the manner in which they were sometimes recruited. If no servant could be found through the network of Coloured maids and workers in Kleinzee, a trip might be made to a reserve to find one. In one such case, the husband traveled to the Komaggas Reserve, found a suitable *meisie* (young girl), gave her father a few shillings, and waited until she had packed her bag. She was hired for the sum of 10s. a month.

Just as there was a status hierarchy among the families who employed them, so, too, did a hierarchy emerge among the domestic servants. The wages paid varied considerably. Senior staff paid their domestics between £2 and £4 a month in the 1930s, while families lower in the scale paid between 10s. and £1. Wages increased a little in the 1940s, when the mine superintendent's family was paying £6. By the 1950s, senior staff families were paying up to £8; others paid less than half that amount.

The status of the employer was of enormous importance to domestic servants. To work in the mine manager's or the mine secretary's household gave the maid an edge over servants who worked in the motor mechanic's or painter's household. It was a question of "class": maids identified with their madams through "the master's" occupation. In the wider context, we might say that domestic service provided a means for geographical and upward social mobility for Coloured people living on the reserves and in small towns in Namaqualand. These women were often able to select their employers through the male migrant labor network or by word of mouth from domestics already employed at Kleinzee.[15] As put by one former domestic servant:

> I would never have accepted a job with Mrs. Rabie. She paid badly, gave her servants lousy food, and she herself was very common *[onbeskof]*. My mother worked for the doctor's wife at Concordia [another mining town]. So when Mrs. Parkinson [the manager's wife] at Kleinzee wanted a maid I knew that was where I should go.

The Marginal Status of Coloureds

I have pointed out that Coloured contract workers did the same work the white Namaqualanders and the Owambos had done before them, and that they were culturally similar to the white Namaqualanders, speaking the Afrikaans language and belonging to the same religious denomination. In some ways, though, their status was very different on the mine, particularly as they were not confined to the compound barracks to the degree other workers had been. However, the Coloureds were not well-liked by the majority of the white population, notably the Afrikaners, and in the 1950s the security department started to regard them as serious security risks, although grounds for the suspicion were never substantiated. Their close association with domestic servants was frowned upon, and some white men were clearly jealous that only Coloured men had access to single women. When the Rec Club committee hired an excellent Coloured band to play at the New Year's dance in 1951, some families boycotted the event, referring to it as the "Hottentot dance." Even the Owambos, in their time, looked down on the Coloureds, whom they called "Bushmen." The Coloureds, in turn, had negative feelings about living in the compound in which the Owambos had been housed. This attitude seems to have derived from their association with other black Africans with whom they were in competition for jobs on the copper mines.[16]

By 1961, Coloured workers were earning much better wages than they had in the past, partly because they had started to be rewarded for long service and partly because their qualifications and skills were being recognized. They no longer did pick-and-shovel work, this work having been taken over by newly recruited, black contract workers from the Transkei and Ciskei (see chapters 9–11). The blacks lived in segregated compound barracks (now called hostels) several miles out of town.[17] Many semiskilled, and some skilled, jobs on the mine had, in fact, now been taken over by Coloureds, as is reflected in the wages they received (see table 8.1). Although the state's apartheid policy was now firmly entrenched throughout the country, economic forces were playing their part in undermining the principles of job reservation: there were not enough whites available to fill all the skilled and semiskilled jobs and these were now filled by Coloureds, and black South African workers exclusively were meeting the demand for pick-and-shovel workers to do bedrock cleaning and other menial jobs.

Table 8.1. Coloured Workers' Wages on Kleinzee Mine, September 1961

Daily Wage	No. Workers	%
50–80 cents	158	58.74
85c.–R1.05	39	14.50
R1.10–R1.30	58	21.56
R1.50–R2.55	13	4.83

Note: One man (manager of the dairy) earned R104-47 per month.

Source: KA, file on Coloured workers, 1961.

Pension Plan for Coloureds

The company had no pension plan for Coloureds until the mid 1960s. Nor were there any procedures with regard to sick pay, accident pay, and light-duty pay. Each case was treated separately, whether it was sickness, death, or pension benefits in old age. As an example we have the case of Manie Williams,

8.1. Sunday Afternoon
Senior staff and their families on a Sunday afternoon outing, 1930.

Cricket Match. Dec 26. 1931.
KLEIN ZEE v PORT NOLLOTH.
Blaauw Pan

8.2. Christmas Cricket
Cricket on Blaaupan. Kleinzee v. Port Nolloth, Boxing Day (December 26), 1931.

8.3. Spectators under the Flag

The Blaaupan cricket pavilion. Note the Union Jacks (two of them!) flying on the "club house" (1931).

8.4. Sundown

The nineteenth hole at Geelpan golf course, 1932. A car acts as bar and tea room. Most people have their backs to the setting sun and the southwest wind.

8.5. Going Golfing
Senior staff golfers posing with their well-dressed Coloured caddies at the new course in the river bed, 1954.

8.6. Waiting for Their Men
Women on the Richtersveld reserve waiting for contract workers to return, c. 1960.

8.7. Home Again
A contract worker arrives at his village, c. 1960.

who after eighteen accident-free years of exceptional service as a *bakkie* driver, in March 1961, at age sixty-three, complained of feeling ill. When the mine doctor seemed unable to help him, Williams resigned and went home to Steinkopf. Six months later it was learned that he was in Groote Schuur Hospital, Cape Town, with cancer of the lung. Married, and with a daughter still in school, Williams died in the Springbok Hospital on October 30, 1961. Head office agreed to pay his widow R133 a year (£5 10s. a month) until the child left school. If the widow remarried the allowance would cease.[18]

Thomas Cloete, also from Steinkopf, aged sixty-seven, who had worked for the company for nineteen years as compound cook, decided he wanted to retire in 1964. Head office debated his case and authorized a pension of R142 a year (£5 18s. 6d. a month).[19]

Abram Vries, aged fifty-seven, had worked for the company for more than twenty-six years. When he told the doctor in January 1965 that he was too weak and old to continue working at the recovery plant, the doctor recommended that he retire. The manager agreed, noting that Vries had a wife and four children still dependent on him. Head office offered to allow him R240 a year (£10 a month) at the pleasure of the company.[20]

Isaac Cloete, aged sixty-two, who had worked for the company for twenty-eight years as a cobbler, wished to retire at the end of October 1965, after having had three operations at Groote Schuur Hospital for perforated ulcers. Cloete, who had put all his eight children through teacher-training programs, was put forward, as a loyal company servant, for a long-service gold watch. Head office agreed and also awarded him a pension of R468 a year (£19 10s. a month).[21]

Although the company resolved these four cases to the satisfaction of the workers and their families, there was no policy by which cases could be treated routinely, which would have removed some of the anxiety for Coloureds surrounding retirement, accidents, sickness, retrenchment, and resignation. De Beers left such matters unattended to for too long. The new black African workers who had been recruited from the Transkei and Ciskei also needed to have their benefits from De Beers clarified, but they did at least have some protection (such as it was) from regulations based on acts of Parliament. At the end of January 1958, there were approximately 430 black workers at Kleinzee. More were recruited the following year and thence annually as mining operations expanded.

In 1961, there were 354 Coloured workers, but a high proportion of them were now doing semiskilled and skilled work. It is ironical that the Coloureds, who were receiving higher wages than blacks, had to wait until the company had revised its policies regarding social benefits to a new group of workers. However, given their marginal status in South African society, this apparent anomaly is entirely consistent with their official position as defined by the Population Registration Act (see note 1).

Part II

◆

Oppenheimer's New Empire

The era of individual discovery and prospecting—a time that to some people was one of glamour—had given way to the commerce of diamond production and company-town life. Now the latter paved the way for a monstrous expansion of the industry and the building of a large new company town to accommodate a Kleinzee workforce ten or more times that of the preceding period. The details of that expansion—especially its social effects—are considered in the chapters that follow.

9

The Modernization of Kleinzee

Although having enormous corporate power, De Beers has always been required to tailor its mining and other operations to chapter and verse of state legislation. Thus, when the Precious Stones Act was amended in 1927, the parameters and direction of diamond mining in Namaqualand were radically changed. The new act prevented further prospecting and mining everywhere in the region—with the exception, of course, of Kleinzee:[1] its nineteenth-century freehold status gave it immunity from certain clauses in the new legislation. Without that immunity, the mining operations on the Kleinzee property by Cape Coast and De Beers could not have taken place, and these companies would not have extracted diamonds weighing 1,635,787 carats, worth £14,060,164, during the thirty-year period that ended in 1956. That year, those diamond deposits were exhausted.

A total shutdown of operations was cleverly averted in late 1956, following negotiations between Oppenheimer and the South African government, whereby De Beers obtained a lease to mine and prospect the adjacent property of Annex Kleinzee. It was not, however, until 1961, following the passing of the newly amended Precious Stones Act (1960), that De Beers was given the green light to expand its operations on a gigantic scale. The company spent millions of rand prospecting most of its coastal properties, it modernized its outmoded mining technology and infrastructure at great cost, and extended its mining operations to the three rich alluvial complexes now fully under De Beers control.

The Buffels Marine Complex, which included the properties known as Sandkop, Annex Kleinzee, Dreyer's Pan, Karreedoornvlei, Tweepad, and

Oubeep, extended some forty kilometers north of the Buffels River and five kilometers to the south of it. The diamonds in this area are associated with well-rounded fluvial gravels occurring in deep potholes, gullies, and crevices at the bedrock level on a series of archaic raised beaches. The Buffels Inland Complex consisted of the deposits of diamonds on the inland properties, such as Langhoogte and Nuttabooi, to the north-east of Kleinzee, adjacent to the Buffels River some forty kilometers upstream. The Koingnaas Complex was located roughly sixty-five kilometers south of Kleinzee on the properties of Somnaas, Koingnaas, Swartlintjie, Langklip, and Mitchells Bay. The high-grade gravels in this locality tend to occur in patches, in areas of depressed bedrock.[2]

It took the company several years (until the 1960s and early 1970s), using highly sophisticated equipment, to prospect and assess these new mining complexes fully. In the ensuing years there have been periods of maximum production followed by carefully managed periods of operational restraint, with minor worker lay-offs from time to time. By comparison with the old operations, the scale of mining has been enormous—and without a complete shutdown. In 1990, when I visited the new Kleinzee, the combined production of the three complexes was reported as 964,375 carats for 1989, valued at a US$150 million or more; 39,546,464 tonnes of overburden were stripped and 5,862,875 tonnes of ore were treated.

Oppenheimer died, at the age of seventy-seven, on November 25, 1957, before the official amendment of the amended Precious Stones Act had been passed. But he had ingratiated himself and De Beers so successfully with the government of the day that he knew before his death that his Namaqualand empire was about to be realized. This monstrous expansion of the industry called for the creation of two new towns to accommodate a workforce ten or more times greater than during any previous period in Kleinzee's history. One was built virtually on top of the old Kleinzee, retaining its name. The other, Koingnaas, was built near the mining complex to the south. A mining center was established at Langhoogte on the site of the Inland Complex, and workers commuted to Kleinzee. The white employees and their families now lived in the two "suburban" oases of Kleinzee and Koingnaas, and the black and Coloured workers in hostels on the peripheries of these towns, under the requirements for well-planned towns in the heyday of apartheid.

The modern town of Kleinzee flaunts a 1970s-style suburban character. Its four thousand or so residents enjoy the benefits of ample fresh water piped from the Orange River and electricity from the ESKOM grid system. There are trees, shrubs and lawns, recreational and sporting facilities, schools,

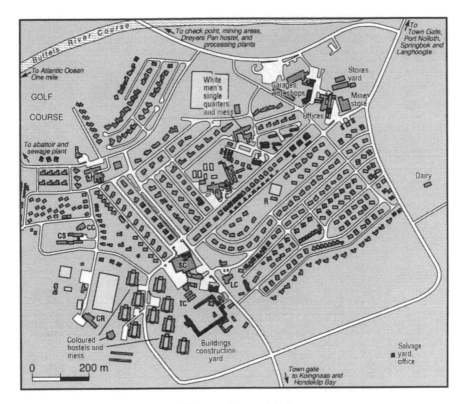

Kleinzee Town, 1992

churches, a modern hospital, library, cable television, a supermarket, a shooting range, tarred roads, an airport, and every conceivable kind of club and voluntary association, ranging from *jukskei* (similar to horseshoes, but played with yoke-pins) to gavel (competitive debating). The town, and everything in it, was built by De Beers to be the headquarters of its alluvial diamond operations in the region.

It took years to complete the modern Kleinzee, but long before the trimmings of modernity had been completed the white population (357 strong, including 165 children) was living very comfortably. By the beginning of 1967, the *Cape Coast Chronicle* reported that eighty-four houses were available for married couples and that sixty-two automobiles were owned. The newspaper also took delight in exaggerating the gluttonous habits of the townspeople, who were credited with consuming 5,310 pounds of beef, 3,092 pounds of mutton, 858 pounds of pork, 1,083 pounds of poultry and cold meat, 2,132 loaves of bread, 10,396 pints of milk, and 11,400 eggs in February alone. By 1968, better attention was being paid to the leisure needs of the Coloured and black workers. The hostels were improved and the first annual Coloured and African athletic meetings were held on one of the new playing fields constructed for people of color.

In April 1969, Jack Blamey, the last of the managers to serve both the old and the new operations, retired after nearly twenty years in office. Most of his farewell speech reviewed his years as manager and dwelt on the important changes that had taken place during that period: more people, more houses, more specialists to introduce new techniques of mining and retrieval. This expansion, he said, would continue with even greater intensity after he left.

Seventeen new houses were scheduled for completion early in 1970, with a further 10 percent per year until 1974. Thirty-two garages for private cars were to be built outside the security gate, and more were planned. Construction had begun of new, two-storey quarters for single white workers; there would be flatlets for other single white employees. Blamey outlined plans for additional classrooms and a school library for the white school. Construction of a new recreation club—the pride and joy of the white employees—had already begun, and plans were in progress for extensions to the Coloured and black hostels; there would be married quarters for selected Coloured families. Further improvement of the sports facilities for Coloureds and blacks were also under way. Plans for mining at Koingnaas had been made: houses and single quarters were being built there for whites, and a recreation club, sporting facilities, and a company store were planned. Blamey also announced that, to conform with the laws and requirements of the policy of apartheid, there was to be "a Coloured township and a Bantu hostel" at Koingnaas.

Soon after Blamey left in 1970, the status and importance of Kleinzee in the mining world was acknowledged with the appointments of a general manager and a divisional engineer. Mining operations now expanded rapidly and more workers had to be hired. Others were recruited to maintain the infrastructure of the two towns. The water supply was still further improved, the company acquired a new Baron aeroplane, and a new sports field, with a turf cricket pitch, was opened in March. By March 1971, all new white employees were given lavish welcoming receptions at the club.

Meanwhile, the company ignored the level of poverty among the Coloured population in Namaqualand—poverty intensified by drought and factory closures. Some of the old-timers at Kleinzee felt something ought to be done. The women revived the Women's Work Party and rallied its benevolent forces to collect foodstuffs for the destitute people of Port Nolloth and the large number of Steinkopf people in dire need of basic provisions. Starvation and sickness among the Coloured and Nama people, who lived a few hundred meters outside the company's main security gate, prompted the establishment, by the women, of a soup kitchen and clinic for them in 1973. Eventually, the state moved these people to Lekkersing, out of the company's way and everyone's sight.

Just before the tarring of the roads in 1971, general manager J. D. Frazer invited Chief Jeremiah D. Moshesh, minister for the interior of the Transkei government, to visit the mine, in recognition of the company's reliance, during the expansion, on the Transkei (and Ciskei) for cheap labor. The new hostels for Coloureds and blacks were built at this time. By the mid 1970s, great efforts were made to improve the recreational and other facilities for people of color. A combined nonwhite athletics meeting took place in November 1974—the first of its kind since the beginning of the mine—and in May 1975 soccer players and athletes went to Kimberley to compete in the De Beers Inter-Mine Black Athletic Championships. In 1974, a church for the Coloureds was dedicated by the Dutch Reformed Mission Church, the Calvin Protestant Church, the Anglican Church, Roman Catholic Church, and the Methodists. The following year, the Zonderberg Primary School for Coloured children was opened. For whites, a memorable event in 1974 was the arrival in March of Nicky Oppenheimer, Harry's son, with his touring Anglo American cricket team. The team turned out to be enormously talented and versatile: challenging Kleinzee at cricket, golf, and squash, they won every match. Another big event in 1974 was the declaration, on October 17, of "open town" status.[3]

If June 1976 is remembered by other communities in South Africa for the first major student uprisings in Soweto, and the massacre associated with it, for Kleinzee it was a year of opulence—parties, weddings, and VIP comings and goings. The highlight of the year was the 1926–1976 golden jubilee celebration, an elaborate and extravagant ritual occasion attended by visitors from all over South Africa. Amateur videos of the ceremonies capture scenes that would have been impossible and absurd in the late 1920s—an elaborate procession led by high-kicking drum majorettes from Springbok and the Springbok cadet band. Accompanied by horseback riders, floats, bicycles, and clowns, they paraded through the town to the main sports field, where the whole town, in all its segregated glory, was entertained. A funfair featured carousels. Rugby matches were played, the first between teams from Kleinzee and Oranjemund: the main game, as if to assert the hegemony of De Beers and Anglo American over the rest of the world, was between a combined Kleinzee-Oranjemund team and Cape Town's famous Villagers Rugby Club. In the evening, the white people enjoyed ritual eating and drinking at an *ox-braai* (barbecue) and a beer fest, followed by a dance at the rec. club.

The end of the decade witnessed several important technological changes and the introduction of new methods of drilling and prospecting. But the main improvement was the establishment, in June 1978, of an electricity sub-station fed from the ESKOM grid, which now provided unlimited power at lower cost to the company. The decade's end also brought signs that the company wished to bury certain aspects of racial segregation. In January 1979, Joseph Vries, Paulus de Klerk, and George Cloete, all Coloured men from Steinkopf, and several white Namaqualanders received, at the same ceremony, awards from D. J. van Jaarsveld, the general manager, marking twenty-five years of service. All were accompanied by their wives, and the occasion marked the first official "mixed race" function at the rec. club. A similar celebration was held in November. The color bar had not vanished, but the company was making an effort to change. The white community showed little reaction to these changes, although a fashionable minority, as if to protest against the policy of nonracialism, attempted to transform its own unexciting image by organizing fashion shows for beautiful people. Some of this ilk wanted to teach others how to use chopsticks and to introduce go-go dancing. When van Jaarsveld, who had been responsible for many of the liberal innovations, left in February 1982 to take up the general manager's position at CDM, he was entertained at the rec. club at what appears to have been a rather dull cocktail party and dinner. Van Jaarsveld's real admirers were the black workers at the Dreyer's Pan hostel, who paid tribute to him, on their turf, at an evening of tribal dancing.

On May 14, 1985, after nine weeks of intensive negotiations, a formal agreement was signed between the National Union of Mine Workers (NUM) and De Beers Namaqualand Mines Division (NMD) that provided for collective bargaining and representation of rights for contract and other lower-paid workers, regardless of race. The significance of this agreement was commented on by the general manager in a public statement. He pointed out that it constituted the first recognition of an agreement between an emergent trade union and a company in the diamond sector of the mining industry.

Meanwhile, food and drink remained an obsession among the white residents of Kleinzee and Koingnaas. The annual ox-braai was well attended, the Rendezvous Restaurant was opened, a medieval dinner was organized at Koingnaas by the chief nursing sister, and wine-tasting evenings became common, as did "pub nites" and "ladies' nites." Many of the clubs (for example, the gun, fishing, golf, and bowls clubs) had members-only bars. Arts and crafts (especially pottery) flourished among some of the white women, a debating (gavel) association was formed, a museum was planned, and the dramatic society was very active. During the 1985 recession in the diamond market, some white employees (and many blacks) were laid off.

A New Era Begins, 1986

When the market recovered in 1986, the company decided to improve its relations with the Coloured people in the Namaqualand reserves on whom it relied for labor. Steinkopf was offered a community center and a photocopier for the secondary school; Komaggas received assistance with its sanitation system. Leliefontein (the community that supplied the fewest workers) got only a typewriter for its primary school.

De Beers Consolidated Mines, Ltd., celebrated its centenary in Kimberley in March 1988. There were no celebrations at Kleinzee to mark the occasion, despite a visit from the Transkei chiefs; the latter might have added dignity to the ceremony and provided another political feather for De Beers' cap. Instead, De Beers waited until November 26, when it announced its new shareholder scheme. All employees were now given the opportunity to acquire ten De Beers shares within a year. These would be paid for by the company. Some people thought this a marvelous idea, but others felt there must be a catch and asked why the company wanted to give away its shares. De Beers shares went up in value by 30 percent the next year, and the company reported that a million carats had been produced.

The company now made it clear to all its employees that apartheid would no longer be tolerated, announcing that, among other things, the Zonderberg (Coloured) School and the Kleinzee Private School would be amalgamated. In preparation for these changes, a series of formal meetings were held with foremen and departmental heads to explain the new policy and get it in perspective. The company called this new overhaul in policy "organizational renewal" (OR). One of its several aims was to get rid of objectionable stereotypes and racist language at work, and all employees were now to call each other by their first names. Organizational renewal was received with mixed reactions, and the Coloured workers, especially, thought it hilarious that, after all these years of institutionalized subservience, they were now being told to call the "baas" by his first name. Those who refused were criticized by management and said to be suffering from the "*meneer* [mister] syndrome." A few decided that "uncle" would be more appropriate, and many white foremen had now to get used to being addressed as extended kin.

When I arrived at Kleinzee to begin fieldwork in July 1992, institutional apartheid had theoretically been abolished by the company. But social segregation was still very evident.

10

The Paterson System

Some business professor among the Scots
Scientifically fits folk into slots.
How many decisions you make per day
Determines what perks should come your way.

And so we find under wide skies
Where gold is clawed from the grey earth
That in Welkom differing houses rise.
Each type a sign of the tenants' worth.

Black gardeners sprinkle a close cut lawn,
And wattle trees wave beside the hedge:
Bougainvillea's crimson blossoms adorn
Ambition's concrete outer edge.

Here is architectured caste
Among the close suburban whites.
And black men saunter lithely past
To other graded living rights.

      —Ninian Smart, "The Paterson Scale (A Method Anglo-
      American Uses to Grade People)"

The expansion of the diamond industry in the 1960s called for new methods and techniques of mining to satisfy the market demand for gem-quality diamonds. Most of the new areas to be mined were covered with massive sandy overburden, sometimes to a depth of thirty-five meters, all of which had to be removed before large-scale productive mining could begin. Another concern was housing a much larger workforce and paying acceptable salaries and wages to disparate ranks of workers.

New Mining Technology

The operation of any form of strip mining requires costly equipment and the labor to operate and maintain the machines. In 1979, the earth-moving and loading fleet at Kleinzee included low-bowl scrapers, bulldozers, dump trucks, front-end loaders, and hydraulic excavators. Improvements and additions to the overburden fleet were made from time to time. The dragline, put into service in 1982, was able to strip 11.5 million tonnes of earth a year, in swoops taking sixty to seventy tonnes at a time. Such mechanization made it possible for more than 800,000 cubic meters of overburden to be moved in a month, an operation carried out on a three-shift basis, so that the work could go on nonstop, day and night. The company describes the process as "a progressive operation": as soon as one area has been mined out, it becomes the dumping ground for the overburden of the next section, and so on.

10.1. The Dragline
Each scoop can move seventy tons of overburden. Photo c. 1990.

10.3. Driver Number One
Cornelis Goosen, the first excavator driver at Kleinzee, in 1949. Now in retirement at Springbok, he is a former owner of Dikgat Farm.

10.2. Dragline Operator
The late Daniel Cloete, in retirement at his home on the Concordia Reserve, 1993.

10.4. Moving the Top Layer
Scrapers shifting overburden, c. 1990.

10.5. Getting the Gravel
Loading diamondiferous gravel after the overburden has been removed.

10.6. Bedrock Cleaning
Contract workers cleaning bedrock where the richest deposits of diamonds are found.

10.7. Washed and Washed Again
Photo shows the complexity of a modern washing plant.

Overburden stripping exposes the ancient beach terraces that contain the diamondiferous ore, mixed with fine sand, gravels, boulders, and other material such as hard green clay. The terraces, which average only a meter in depth, lie above present sea level and are shallow compared with the overburden. The nature of each terrace is determined by the character of the bedrock surface, where most of the richest diamond-bearing ore is trapped. Some of this material can be moved by hydraulic excavators, but most requires backbreaking hand shoveling and sweeping. In certain areas, the terrace consists of hard conglomerate, which has to be drilled and blasted before loading can take place. After the preliminaries, the ore is bulldozed into stockpiles, loaded into thirty-five-ton diesel rear-dump trucks, and taken to the treatment plants for the complex process of extracting the diamonds.[1] In 1989, forty-seven tonnes of overburden and diamondiferous ore had to be processed to produce a single carat of diamonds.

At the treatment plant, the diamondiferous gravel is dumped into a hopper that feeds a crusher. After crushing, gravels are screened and oversized material is crushed again. The graded gravels are then washed in a scrubber to get rid of clay, and another process (similar in some ways to the old rotary pan) separates heavy material from light. The idea is to drive the heavy concentrate containing the diamonds to the bottom of the pan. The considerable quantities of light gravels are taken off the top and removed to the tailings

10.8. Fortress Diamond
The heavily guarded recovery plant where diamonds are separated from the heavy concentrate.

10.9. A New Place to Live
A section of the new Kleinzee town.

10.10. Hostel
Dreyers Pan hostel (compound) for black contract workers located two miles outside the new town.

10.11. Stop Here!
The checkpoint at the east end of the town, c. 1990.

10.12. Entering the New Company Town
Welcome to the new Kleinzee.

10.13. Totsiens!
Retiring after thirty-five years' service to De Beers, Jan "Plaas" Cloete (right) bids farewell to a fellow worker, 1993.

dumps. The diamond-loaded concentrates are then transported, under heavy security, to the final recovery plant.

The final stage takes place in an enormous, windowless fortress on the north bank of the Buffels River. Only selected employees and security people are permitted to enter the inner chambers of this sacred edifice, the icon of De Beers Namaqualand Mines. Although the recovery plant is visible from every part of the town, no mythology informs those on the outside about its inner mysteries; no oral tradition betrays its secrets. However, one small pamphlet, printed by the company itself, allows some information: inside the fortress, the concentrates are bombarded with X-rays—because "when you shine an X-ray beam through a diamond, the diamond glows brightly. When it glows . . . a detector . . . quickly sends a message to an air blower. The blower sends a jet of air towards the glowing diamond and knocks it out of the line of gravel."[2] The diamonds are then sorted by trustworthy workers, cleaned with acid, weighed, and finally transported to head office.

New People: New Needs

Mining on an enormous scale called for a workforce much larger than the region could supply, and labor had to be recruited from other parts of South Africa and from as far afield as the United Kingdom. In January 1993, De Beers Namaqualand Mines employed 2,409 people—1,805 of them involved in the Buffels Marine Complex based at Kleinzee, 576 in the Koingnaas Complex, and 28 in the Buffels Inland Complex at Langhoogte. Three-quarters of the workforce—some with, some without families—were housed in Kleinzee; the remainder lived in the new town of Koingnaas. (In January 1932, Cape Coast employed fewer than 200 people.)

It took a massive building program to accommodate this multi-occupational workforce. New shopping facilities, modern medical and recreational services, and proper schooling had to be provided, together with banking and postal services. The company's "municipal" obligations meant there also had be a guaranteed supply of acceptable water, plus a sewage system, roads and sidewalks, a library, and electricity for industrial and domestic use. New security measures brought in more elaborate entanglements of barbed and razor wire, computerized surveillance gadgets, and new checkpoints to handle the increased volume of traffic It is no exaggeration to say that (leaving aside the security elements) De Beers created a modern, suburban-type town in the South African semidesert, planned to suit the assumed needs of its white employees. Even the Coloured and black workers experienced immense material improvements, and the town amazed the Namaqualand people to a degree far surpassing their wonderment at the old Kleinzee when it was built in 1929.

Discrimination against the Coloureds and blacks continued, of course. In 1993, nearly 19 percent of the 2,409 employees were classified as black, 61 percent as Coloured, and nearly 20 percent as white. Although the correlation is not perfect, the majority of the black and Coloured employees worked in unskilled or semiskilled jobs; in the main, whites occupied the rest.[3] There is now enormous diversity of occupations: as well as working in every facet of the mining industry, company employees are also engaged in construction, housing, maintenance, supply of utilities, recreation, social services, and so forth (see table appendix 2.3). The list of occupations is formidable, especially if compared with that at the mine in the 1930s. As in the past, everyone permanently resident in the town is either in the company's employ or is a spouse or child of an employee. The population has the character of the essential company town.

Formal Administration

Among the occupations missing from the list in the above-mentioned table are those of policeman, minister of religion, lawyer, and municipal administrator. The company employs its own security men and women, and the South African Police, who are based just outside the main gate, have access to the town only because they are needed to make the actual arrests of anyone accused of IDB. Priests and ministers of religion regularly visit the mine to hold church services, but to enter they must first obtain permission from the security department. Lawyers have no place in town because the company has its own "law," codified as custumals in the Policies and Procedures handbook. Labor disputes are arbitrated through union representatives, using procedures clearly set out in the handbook.

In short, the total absence of a town hall, mayor, town councillors, or municipal workers enables the company to control of all its employees, with the proviso that all criminal matters and civil torts fall under South African law. *Policies and Procedures* provides guidelines for local management by an executive committee (EXCO). The committee consists of the general manager, the assistant general manager, the mine superintendent in Koingnaas, the administrative manager, the chief engineer, the metallurgical superintendent, the senior personnel manager, the senior medical officer, the chief security superintendent, the chief geologist, and the section manager. This group wields enormous power over all employees, their dependents, and any visitors residing with them. Real power, however, is vested in the general manager, who can override his committee or act unilaterally if he wishes. Nowadays, some general managers portray themselves to their employees as self-appointed "mayors"; they try to keep in touch with the people—an approach that allows them to find out what is going on in town. General managers have used a variety of managing styles over the years, but in all cases their authority derives from the company.[4] I do not, however, wish to ignore the importance of gossip—of information "errand-running" to the general manager. Some employees seek to control and manipulate information for their own ends. I was in fact amazed at the number of self-appointed informers ready to relay to people in high office their opinions with respect to any event they considered important.[5]

The Paterson System

Following the lead of Anglo American, De Beers decided in the early 1980s to abolish racial discrimination in work, housing, and play. These enlightened policies, designed to be part of the move to build a new South African society, included the creation of what was called a progressive wage system. After 1946, in the context of the color bar, various systems of job evaluation had been used in the South African mining sector to set wage scales, notably acts of Parliament related to job reservation designed to protect the level of white wages, especially on the mines. Anglo American, in its attempt to cope with rising inflation in the early 1970s, was the first company to depart from established practice by experimenting with new ideas of job evaluation, increasing the wages of its black workers.

Mine managers, feeling that the new ideas tended to discriminate against white clerical workers, opposed this "progressive wage system," with its proposed single "unified" wage scales. Their resistance led Anglo American to look for "a standardised job evaluation system which could be used throughout the corporation [to] facilitate planning in terms of a standardised wage structure as well as allow for personnel to be transferred from one company to another within the corporation."[6] The system finally chosen was the Canadian-Scots Paterson plan,[7] which was so successful in the eyes of Anglo American and other companies in the mining industry that by 1982 the whole industry was using it.

The Paterson system is designed to grade all jobs entirely on the degree and level of decision-making capabilities involved. The system identifies six levels of decision making. Paterson calls these levels "bands," and each band is correlated with a level of organization.

Table 10.1 Paterson Bands: Income, Decision-making, and Organizational Levels

Band	Wage Range, Kleinzee Mine (rand per month, 1993)	Decision-making Level	Organizational Level
F	n.a.	Policy making	Top management
E	9,654+	Programming	Senior management
D	5,253–9,654	Interpreting	Middle management
C	2,618–5,252	Routine	Skilled workers
B	1,333–2,617	Automatic	Semiskilled workers
A	959–1,332	Defined	Unskilled workers

Source: Table based on Len Le Roux, "A Guide to Job Evaluation Systems Used in South Africa," South African Labour Bulletin 10, no. 4 (1985): 72–92.

The system is in fact much more complex: each band is further subdivided, giving a total of twenty-eight divisions. The Paterson system arranges the whole workforce into a number of what Max Weber would call status gradations based on one criterion, decision making, a term that seems to suggest also the notion of responsibility. What this achieves in practice is a convenient way of fixing wage and salary scales and the number of privileges an employee is allowed. For example, in Kleinzee, one needs to be in band C or above to get a house; one needs to be in the D to E band to get a car allowance; all in the E band get heated swimming pools; all of those in the A band and most of those in B must live in hostels segregated from the main part of town.

My analysis of wage distribution in the context of the Paterson band system on the Kleinzee mine in 1992–93 did not produce startling results, especially when the indices of "race" and ethnicity were introduced. Blacks and Coloureds occupied the lower Paterson bands and earned the lowest wages.

Blacks earned somewhat less than Coloureds, although a few higher-level jobs were held by nonwhites (see figure 12.1 and appendix table 12.2). Under the De Beers New South Africa nonracial policy, records of racial origin are not supposed to exist.

What effects do calculated schemes, such as the Paterson band system, have on the structure of single-industry company towns? Are they really designed to improve the lot of all the employees, eliminate racism, and ameliorate the problems of inequality and social differentiation in general? Or are they no more than part of the scheme of things to make the industry more efficient and productive? It is difficult to answer these questions, but the Kleinzee experience—past and present—suggests that all such schemes are the result of rational decisions of a board of directors based (explicitly or not) on political expediency and economic prudence. Others have shown similar conclusions for mining and factory towns elsewhere in the world.[8] Aubrey Michalowsky (a physician who studied Kleinzee in his research on the effects of living in an isolated mining community) concluded that "although the Paterson band system is based on decision making and was introduced [at Kleinzee] as a guideline for remuneration, one of the resultant effects is that De Beers has created a society of social classes and the inhabitants have therefore become very class conscious."[9]

The Paterson band system orders people according to their decision-making abilities as these complex qualities are evaluated by foremen, supervisors, department heads, and so on. But the initial level into which each employee is slotted is, by and large, predetermined by the occupation itself. In other words, as should be obvious, all employees have their starting wages or salaries laid down according to the Paterson system's definitions; they are then reevaluated by the same system when merit and other criteria are applied later in their careers. Top management, senior management, and middle management always have an edge over everyone else. There is thus a strong suggestion that for the majority, hard work is not necessarily rewarded. Paterson, the system's originator, argues inter alia that the scheme curbs "dog-legging" of wages among unskilled workers; that is, it prevents discrimination of the kind experienced by the Owambo workers in Kleinzee in the late 1940s. Paterson, incidentally, supports his claim with the more recent example of Namibian mineworkers.[10]

The dominion that companies and their head offices hold over their mining and other single-industry communities begins, I suggest, long before the town plans are drawn up. In the Namaqualand alluvial mines, the network of companies involved, as venture capitalists, figured there was an opportunity for them to make a killing. Predicating a future for themselves in the region, they saw that they must wrest control of how events would pan out out, so to speak. Meanwhile, with very different scenarios in mind, the prospector-discoverers and small syndicates were attempting, futilely, to negotiate their own futures. The ability of the big company to achieve its goals is largely a question of its control of capital and the supply of technology, but the certainty of success depends equally on the company being able to maintain total control over the lives of the people it employs.

Occupation provides the obvious general index of each employee's status and income. However, it is the kind of housing allocated that places employees more accurately and formally in structural positions—positions that are created by the company's industrial philosophy of maximizing profit through a pragmatic system of social differentiation, formed within the context of state policy and the ideology of white South Africans. The application of the Paterson band system is a product of that philosophy.

Houses and Flats

Graduated accommodation—a variety of comfortable houses and flats—is provided for managerial, professional, administrative, and certain predetermined skilled and semiskilled employees. In January 1993, nearly 70 percent of the 475 white employees were comfortably accommodated in houses. The other 30 percent or so of whites were allocated superior "bachelor" accommodation (vastly superior to the hostels) situated in the center of town. Fewer than 100 Coloured employees were allocated houses (generally smaller in size than the whites') or flats designed for married couples. Only two black employees were allocated houses: one was the company co-pilot; the other was a senior clerk.

The Paterson system has proved to be a great boon to the company when it comes to the allocation of accommodation. Six housing categories are matched with corresponding bands. For example, employees in upper bands, D to E, are allocated houses with main bedrooms and en suite bathrooms, plus two other bedrooms and a bedroom-study. There is also a lounge, dining room, kitchen, pantry, laundry, bathroom, shower cubicle, veranda/pergola with French doors, family room, heated swimming pool, double garage, and servants' quarters. An employee in band C has a house with three bedrooms, kitchen, laundry, bathroom, toilet and shower, single garage, and servants' quarters.

Having a spouse is, in itself, not a qualification for obtaining a house. In fact, the rule is for family accommodation to be provided only for permanent employees in the C1 Paterson band and higher, which eliminates all the married workers in the A1, A2, B1, B2, and B3 bands. All the black workers recruited from the Transkei and Ciskei (constituting roughly 20 percent of the total labor force), although married, are disqualified from acquiring houses because of their location in the Paterson system. It is not difficult to see how the nonracial Paterson system presently continues to discriminate against both black and Coloured people through their class membership in a world historically based in apartheid. The Paterson system also discriminates in favor of high-status whites. A single parent, if in the E or upper D bands and in custody of a child, is entitled to a house under the Paterson system. Some divorced couples, with both working for the company and both in the Paterson upper grades, have been granted separate houses.

No distinction made by the Paterson system creates more jealousy and rivalry between employees than those made in the allocation of housing. Some of the resentment comes from people who have families in other parts of the country but no house in Kleinzee because they are below C1, but the greatest jealousy is felt by those who have a company house but feel they should have a better one. In fact, the Paterson system, especially in the housing sphere, rather than reducing the tensions and conflicts between potential rivals, accentuates them. The company places great stress on matching employees with what it calls ideal units, and worrying about "correct" (*sic*) allocations of houses as these became vacant. When people of equal status are competing for a house, they are judged on service points relating to their respective pensionable service. And when both husband and wife are employed by the company, the spouse with the higher Paterson rating determines the house category.

One working wife blatantly refused to move into a higher house category because she was jealous that her husband ranked above her in the Paterson system. Conversely, many husbands in the lower C Paterson category have felt threatened and out of place when their wives got jobs that put them up a notch in the housing hierarchy. The company pays a settling-in allowance equal to 50 percent of the wife's salary, which draws attention to her superior status in the household.

The main jealousies, however, occur between members of different households, some of whom resent being lower in the hierarchy than they feel they ought to be. People are, in fact, labeled as much by their houses as they are by their occupations. It is not so much the obvious differences such as the addition of a swimming pool or the services of a company-paid gardener that rile people; it is more the size of a neighbor's carpets or the presence or absence of a *braaihok* (barbecue hut). Such small items highlight minor status differences that many people are reluctant to accept.

Some Coloured people who have moved far enough up the occupational scale over the years to qualify for a house say that the dwellings allotted to them are inferior to those given to whites in the same Paterson band. As one person put it: "The committee [that allocates housing] expects us to live in what amounts to servants' quarters. . . . So much for equality with whites!" This woman was referring not only to the style of house she had been allocated; her complaint had more to do with its location in the west end of the town, in an area set aside for Coloured housing in the 1970s as one of the requirements of apartheid legislation. (The state inspector of housing at that time tried to get the company to build a wall to mark the division between the two racial zones. The company decided to plant a row of trees instead.) Even today, some white townspeople still refer to that part of town as Soweto, even though some white families have been housed there since 1990.

Houses, like everything else on the mine, are built, owned, and allocated by the company. In the old Kleinzee, all furniture, too, was supplied by the company, largely for security reasons. Personal property that could not be X-rayed, such as radios and golf clubs, could not be taken out of the fenced-in area when an employee left. In the new Kleinzee, people both bring their furniture with them and take it away when they leave, all shipped at the company's expense. Termination of contract automatically terminates occupation of accommodation. If an employee dies, the widow or widower is permitted to remain in the house for three months; on retirement or resignation after satisfactory service, an employee and family may remain up to a month in the house; employees summarily dismissed may be required to leave immediately— "tomorrow or at management's discretion."

Housing and utilities are provided without cost to employees, and although occupants are expected to keep their houses clean, their gardens in good order, and the front pavement swept, the back of each dwelling is tidied by the parks and gardens department. The company assumes responsibility for the maintenance of all buildings, painting the inside of houses every five years, the outside every seven years; carpets, too, are replaced every seven years. E banders get special treatment—gardeners to maintain and improve lawns, hedges, and flower beds, attendants to look after swimming pools, and so forth. Some middle and lower D banders express jealousy at not belonging to the "special perks" elite, and a few high-ranking wives were once reported to have felt put out because a general manager's wife had changed the color of her en suite bathroom every year. Employees in basic housing were quite unaffected by her eccentricity because it did not impinge directly on their status.

Most houses have servants' quarters. These consist of a small bedroom and adjoining three-piece bathroom. Most families employ domestic servants, but some use the quarters as guest accommodation when they have visitors or need extra storage space. The company stipulates that "immediate family"—for example, parents or grandchildren—may remain in town for one year only; permission is renewable on request. Casual visitors may stay up to three months, but the company specifies in all cases how many visitors one can have, based on the size of house. No one other than immediate family is eligible for company-subsidized benefits such as schooling and hospitalization.

Single Quarters and Hostels

Allocation of housing to single men and women at all levels in the C band of the Paterson system is done by the senior personnel manager's staff. Those regarded as graduate or professional employees (for example, nurses and teachers) or in regular jobs rated as upper C are housed in single flats. Those in the lower C band are accommodated in recently renovated single quarters that were built in 1929.

But in January 1993, most employees at Kleinzee were accommodated in one of the three segregated hostels. The term hostel—more accurately, mine hostel—came into use in South Africa in the late 1960s to refer to the bachelor quarters provided for migrant contract workers in mining communities. In Kleinzee, the first use of the term coincided with the massive expansion of the diamond industry. Hostels are, in fact, no different from compounds, although they do provide better living conditions, notably food and recreational facilities. In 1993, all 457 black employees (with two notable exceptions) were housed at the Dreyer's Pan hostel, about five kilometers to the north of Kleinzee town, while the majority of the 1,477 Coloureds lived in the hostels located on the periphery of Kleinzee and Koingnaas. A significant number of Coloured employees commute each day from the Komaggas Reserve, bused in by the company. This is a perk much resented by many Steinkopf people.

While the Paterson system does not make any distinction between employees based on South African racial stereotypes, it could hardly be said to constitute an affirmative-action scheme to combat racial discrimination. A handful of Coloured employees, as noted above, live in the flats and single quarters, and a number of Coloured families have been allotted houses in the white part of town. But the real test of nonracial action is to be found in the hostel system. Company rules say that houses and flats are allocated to married employees in the C1 band and above, and that hostel rooms are allocated to single-status employees in the A and B bands. But by and large, everyone in the A and B bands are black and Coloured. Some whites tried to live in the hostels but found "the people too different." Later they managed to find accommodation elsewhere (e.g., in servants' quarters). Some were promoted into the lower C band.

Allocation of hostel rooms is done by a committee under the direction of the superintendent of community services. This team is also responsible for the general administration of the hostels and, with the chief catering manager, for providing subsidized meals to the workers. Their duties and the manner in which they carry them out resemble very closely those of former compound managers.

Guest Houses

The hierarchical nature of the housing system extends also to the six guest houses that accommodate the company's official guests and other visitors. Once again, position in the Paterson band system determines, with a few exceptions, where the guests stay. The Lodge enjoys a country club setting. Like Lorelei, at Koingnaas, it provides temporary accommodation for visiting dignitaries—the likes of Harry Oppenheimer, medical specialists, veterinarians, managing directors of major suppliers to the company, interviewees for D3 jobs and above, and transit employees in D3 positions and above.

Four other guest houses put up relief and transit employees below D3 positions. Arrangements may also be made to house visiting clergymen and their families (only one night without charge) and friends and relatives of single employees. Friends and relatives pay commercial rates for food and lodging.

Clubs

The company went out of its way, when the new town was being built, to ensure that its employees would have adequate sporting and recreational facilities—according to needs as determined by the company. The Kleinzee Recreation Club was created to provide facilities for dances, cinema shows, and other gatherings for white employees. The club also houses a badminton court, two general bars, a ladies' bar and lounge, and a restaurant. Only members are admitted—a policy that pretty well guarantees a whites-only clientele. Numerous subsidiary clubs meet the demand for a wide range of sports, from golf, cricket, and rugby to jukskei (yoke pin), darts, and target shooting. Other clubs and associations meet for arts and crafts and photography. Among other activities there is a dramatic society, a youth club, a women's work party, and a *vrouesendingsbond* (women's missionary association).

The Dreyer's Pan hostel for black workers (which closed after the layoffs in 1993) had its own recreation hall and catered for biweekly film shows, drama productions, weight lifting, and other indoor entertainment. The Dreyer's Pan hostel was designed by management at that time to be a self-contained "total institution" within the confines of the mining area. It had its own self-service company store "to cater for the Black workers who were seldom permitted to visit town." It was comprehensively stocked with clothing, footwear, electrical appliances, sewing machines, and linen. The sections for ladies' and children's wear were popular, most migrant workers taking gifts home to their families after each contract period. Workers living at Dreyer's Pan were at one time not allowed to visit the Kleinzee company store in town, with its vegetable market, grocery sections, butchery, hardware, men's and ladies' drapery, and fancy-goods sections. The black workers were told they could place written orders.

The Westend Club, a recreation club built for Coloured residents, is located on the outskirts of the town, facing the ocean. The club provides facilities for soccer, rugby, and netball. Dances are held frequently and there are several excellent bands. There are regular cinema shows, and two bars—a men-only bar and a ladies' bar and lounge. When Dreyer's Pan hostel closed in 1993, the remaining black contract workers were moved to town, where they began using the Coloured club. A few visited the bar in the Kleinzee Rec. Club, and although they were not refused service, they were asked to apply for membership before returning. The matter was taken up at a meeting of National Union of Mine Workers (NUM) and company officials, where the question of club membership was explained. While the blacks present at the meeting accepted the explanation that the Rec. Club was a private organization, the exclusive nature of the club did bring home to them the reality that race is not the only criterion for discrimination. A few blacks have, in fact, joined the Rec. Club—none of them from the lowest levels of the Paterson system.

The experience of patrons at the Westend Club was quite different. Membership requirements were not carefully monitored and, to my knowledge, no one was ever asked to produce a membership card. When my wife and I visited the club for the first time to have a drink, we were severely reprimanded by the barman for entering the "long bar," which was regarded as an exclusive male preserve. Our reception in the adjacent ladies' bar was quite different, and the same barman delighted in serving us double shots. Although everyone was very friendly, no one seemed to understand why we would want to join them for drinks. Later, we heard that some of the Westenders felt that our purpose in visiting their club had been to do them honor, and it was only after they learned of our Steinkopf and Richtersveld connections that we were treated as if we were full members of their club.

11

Church, Ritual, and Home Ties

No visitor to the modern company town of Kleinzee could fail to be impressed by the facilities that the De Beers company has erected in the semidesert for many of its employees, both in and out of the workplace. The creation of these amenities does not, however, make the company a welfare organization. De Beers is a gigantic industrial and commercial enterprise, whose purpose in Namaqualand is to mine diamonds for enormous profit. When all the viable diamondiferous gravels have been exhausted, the mine will close and the amenities will cease to exist.

Thus, while the company must be given credit for its innovations and social services, these are no more than essential parts of the general scheme of industrial efficiency. The creation of sporting and recreational facilities and the establishment of libraries, schools, and first-class medical facilities has little to do with great concern for worker welfare or happiness. For it is the company that decides what facilities are appropriate for each "class" of employee, as determined by occupation and racial and ethnic labeling. As we have seen, similar principles apply in the allocation of housing, all this differentiation now being predetermined and ossified by the Paterson system. Given the hierarchical nature of company mining towns, there should not be anything remarkable about these simple strategies for maintaining people in optimum contentment at relatively low cost and effort.

The one social arena that figures little in the organization of all company towns

155

is religion. This domain, and especially that of "church" as an institution, deserves serious consideration, because the notion of a "company church" neither accords nor harmonizes with the structural disposition of these towns. There are two rather obvious reasons. First, religion is the only institution over which a company has no claim; and second, because religion has a sectarian quality that often generates discord and negative attitudes toward the company's established order.

The topic is of particular importance because religion is often the only arena that mediates between worker attitudes toward the local community and their associations with the outside world—as workers themselves define those localities. At the present time, De Beers requires no divine assistance to maintain profits. De Beers does not ask a bishop to bless the dynamite at Langhoogte to make the blasting more effective or to make the dragline on the sandy beaches scoop, strip, and swing more quickly. Nor does the company need a dominee to hold prayer meetings to pray for more migrant laborers to work on the bedrock and do the menial jobs in town; it does not even pray for rain to fill empty reservoirs. Van Onselen has an interesting discussion of company attitudes toward specific churches, and religion in general, in colonial Southern Rhodesia. He argues that religion was perceived by both the mining industry and the state as a potentially powerful threat that called for their intervention in the religious life and activities of compound inhabitants.[1]

While De Beers stipulates formally that nothing "which offends good taste as it is understood in Christian Societies" may appear in the local newspaper, it does not promote religious activity. Unlike sport and recreation, religion (church) seems never to have been considered particularly necessary to keep people contented. In fact, in Cape Coast days, management would have preferred to bar the dominees from holding services in the white compound. (One dominee, as I have shown, not only discouraged his flock from working on Sundays, but encouraged IDB in his affirmations from the pulpit that God put diamonds in Namaqualand soil for the benefit of the Namaqualanders.) But to have refused a dominee entry to the compound would have invited worker dissatisfaction and possible depletion of the labor force.

In 1930, for the Anglicans "church" meant the occasional visit from the rector of Namaqualand; for the Roman Catholics it meant getting permission from the manager to attend mass at the Port Nolloth mission; for the white NGK members in the compound, it meant the quarterly *nagmaal* (communion) services from a visiting dominee; and for the Coloured NGK members it meant an occasional visit from a minister associated with the *sending* (mission) church.

Nowadays, the company leaves it to the people to invite clergy from the outside to minister to their needs, but feels little obligation to provide any more than space for religious activity—namely, the church buildings. Old Kleinzee had no church building, and services for the white staff were held in the mess, near the single quarters, and for the workers, in the compound. When the community expanded in the 1970s, three church buildings were constructed: one for the black migrant workers who lived out of town in the Dreyer's Pan hostel complex; another for Coloured people, on the west side of town near the Zonderberg school; and a third for whites, in the center of town. All these nondenominational buildings were built during the apartheid years. Each congregation invited priests or ministers from Port Nolloth, O'okiep, Springbok, Steinkopf, and Alexander Bay, and the visiting clergy held services in different buildings along racial lines. The Anglican priest, for example, cele-brated three communion services—one at 10:00 A.M. in the Kleinzee church, another at 3:00 P.M. in the Coloured church, and another in the Dreyer's Pan church in the evening. In the 1980s, when Coloured priests were appointed in Namaqualand, members of the white congregation at Kleinzee virtually stopped attending services; some said: "We don't like being ministered to by Hottentots."

By the early 1990s, when the company began its nonracial policies, the vis-iting Coloured Anglican priest invited everyone to attend services in the church originally built for Coloureds. A sizeable contingent of black men from Dreyer's Pan hostel showed up, as did a few black domestic servants and a couple of visiting wives from the Transkei or Ciskei. The rest of the congrega-tion were Coloured people, married and single. When I did my fieldwork in 1992–93, only one white adult attended these services—a woman and her two young children. The services were always interesting. The black group sang the hymns in Xhosa and added beautiful harmonies to the melodies sung in English by the rest. The scriptural readings were sometimes in English, sometimes in Afrikaans, sometimes in Xhosa. The priest delivered his sermons in either Eng-lish or Afrikaans, an excellent translator rendering them into fluent Xhosa. The acolytes, servers, and the thurifer were all Coloured boys and girls. Two black subdeacons assisted the priest. Each Sunday, after the singing of the final hymn and while the rest of the congregation was dispersing, the black cohort sponta-neously formed its own recessional. The women tapped rhythmically on their hymn books and bibles, the whole group chanting an animated Xhosa melody as they shuffled toward the door. While the emotions expressed in these ritu-als suggest public displays of Xhosa ethnicity, they are also strongly rooted in the village life with which they identify in the Transkei and Ciskei. These ritual exercises never excluded other members of the congregation, and anyone who showed interest was encouraged to join in.

The reluctance of whites to attend nonracial services is partly the result of the conjunction of racial and class prejudices, but it must surely be related also to the general indifference to religion and church in many parts of the Western world. Such agnostic indifference cannot, however, account for what some Kleinzee people said: "A lot of the blacks have got AIDS," and "Why would we want to associate so intimately with blacks? Their culture is quite different from ours." Some whites feared what other whites in town might think of them if they crossed the color bar; others feared cultural pollution if they identified with blacks.

In November 1992, Kleinzee had twenty-one denominations. Among them were the white Anglicans, Roman Catholics, and NGK; a Coloured NGK congregation; another for blacks; two congregations of the Apostolic Faith Mission; seven splinter Black Zionist groups; African Methodist Episcopalians; two "Ethiopian" churches; and the Christian Fellowship. Early in 1993, the seven Zionist churches, whose members had been at variance for some time over several undisclosed issues, with the help of a company official united, calling themselves the United Zionist Church.[2] Black workers take church matters very seriously, insisting on the right to express their beliefs through ritual association. Uniting the seven Zionist groups solved a problem both for the members and for the company. Had the congregations not united, the company would almost certainly have received requests from each congregation for space in which to worship.

Amakhaya Rituals

Closely associated with church affiliation are the many *amakhaya* (literally, people of one's home) associations formed by black migrant workers who live away from home. In fact, my account above of a ritual "innovation" by a group of Xhosa workers in a nonracial church presents an example of activity closely related to the culture of amakhaya association in general. Amakhaya are essentially support groups with elaborate ritual involvement that facilitate the maintenance of ties with kith and kin when away from home.[3]

In February 1993, when many black employees were being "retrenched" or retiring, co-workers (all members of one church) took advantage of the free time after church one Sunday to bid farewell to their "brothers" and "sisters." The whole congregation was invited to attend, and everyone assembled at the Westend Club, which had recently been opened to all races. At the club, all the blacks in the congregation, and a few Coloured men, sat in a

"square circle" in the main reception room, while the Coloured women prepared a delicious potluck meal for everyone present. Lamb ribs and chops
were *braaied* outside on the coals; two kinds of rice, coleslaw, *sousboontjies*
(haricot beans in a sweet-sour sauce), and lots of tea were served. The occasion was very proper, very middle-class. Beer was not served. The men wore
nicely tailored suits, wearing ties, socks, and shoes to match. They looked
more like mine officials than migrant contract workers, some being attired as
if to emulate the sartorial taste of a past manager. The women, too, were
fashionably dressed, all wearing hats. No one fitted the stereotype of a South
African migrant peasant worker, and no one looked like an urban amakhaya.

Several people who were due to leave the mine within a few weeks were
honored at the ceremony. The first—the wife of a man who had recently been
retrenched—was about to leave with her husband for the Ciskei (the man
was working overtime that day, and could not attend). Donations were called
for and the money was placed on a Bible. Various people spoke, giving the
woman advice, urging her and her husband not to forget them or the other
people at Kleinzee. Appropriate Bible passages were quoted, and hymns were
sung. Every so often, the women clapped in unison and the men tapped their
feet. When the woman who was being honored was given an opportunity to
reply, she spoke deferentially, but not submissively, in a biblical genre, being
careful to *hlonipha* (show respect for) the men as if they were all her husband's brothers.[4]

The next ceremonial round was similar, but since the person was a lay
minister with high status the performance was more complex and lasted
longer. The ceremony was divided into a number of liturgical modules, each
built around a sermon by a self-appointed speaker. Strict silence was observed
while each man spoke, until some guests felt it appropriate to start singing a
hymn; then everyone joined in. Sometimes the words of the hymn seemed to
stress a particular sentiment, and often one verse was deemed sufficient.
When the singing stopped, the speaker generally continued, but any slight hesitation on his part was taken as a signal that another speaker could take over.
Some were firmly, but not rudely, interrupted, generally by one of the women
who led the singing, at some unspecified time, providing others with the opportunity to silence the speaker for speechifying too intensely, or for going off
topic. Sometimes an aggressive speaker simply ignored the signals and continued
his sermon. One orator cleverly dominated for about an hour, deflecting many
spirited interruptions with phrases from the book of Revelation. His sermon
was, indeed, very long, but it was carefully thought out, always relevant, and
always political, urging everyone—those remaining at Kleinzee and those

returning to the Ciskei—to stick together. He spoke a good deal about matters back home, and how important it was for people to fulfil their obligations to home. A traditionalist, he used the Xhosa word *Qamata* for God, thereby avoiding the old missionary term *uThixo*.[5]

In sharp contrast to this traditional oration, two other speakers talked about the virtues of De Beers and the improvements that had occurred over the years. One of them said:

> When I first came here [more than twenty years ago] we black people had to ride in an open lorry whether we were going to work or church. And you had to listen to the baas [sic] so that he would not get kwaai [mad at you] because you were not where he wanted you to be when he wanted you. Now things are very different. Everything is softer, and you can ride in the comfort of a bus or a car. . . .
>
> De Beers can't help having to retrench people. . . . This [we hear] is happening all over the world. . . .
>
> When I first came here, we people, who lived at the Dreyer's Pan Hostel, were not allowed to shop in town, so we had to write out our shopping lists and give them to a security guard who would buy the goods for us.

A lay minister being honored that day received an assortment of gifts—a briefcase "to keep him busy," half a dozen large tumblers, "so that he would never be thirsty," a crucifix with a built-in clock, "so that he would always be on time." These gifts from the community were all displayed for everyone to see, but later he asked that they be rewrapped for him so that he could enjoy another surprise when he was welcomed by his family at home next week. He then thanked everyone in a short speech in Xhosa, switching to English near the end. He told people how apprehensive he had been when he left home (near Queenstown) twenty-six years earlier. "I worried whether I would find my church at this place, Kleinzee, to which I had been recruited." Outlining what he was going to do in his retirement, he said, "The first thing will be to buy some property near Queenstown on the reserve [which is] as you know, just like Steinkopf . . . then I am going to build a house."

I have focused on the above going-away ceremonies because they illustrate the importance to the workers of keeping home ties alive. Kleinzee, despite its remoteness and closedness, seems to be a preferred location for these Ciskeians and Transkeians to work. Kleinzee is not Johannesburg, but the disadvantages of isolation seem to be outweighed by the opportunity to save, especially now that the National Union of Mine Workers and De Beers have established an acceptable working relationship and there has been improvement in wages.

Much of the complexity of hostel life is mediated by the amakhaya groups. The men hold regular private meetings to discuss village matters, clan affairs, burial-society business, and South African political issues. Many of these issues overlap with the church domain, and together they effectively keep workers abreast of both affairs at home and everyday problems related to hostel life.

Company Goodwill Visits to Home Villages

In recent years, the company has reinforced amakhaya principles, perhaps unwittingly, through "goodwill" visits to the Ciskei and Transkei by its management.[6] In September 1982, the general manager visited Ntabethemba in the Ciskei and the Herschel district in the Transkei. The manager traveled in one of the company planes with a retinue of six employees, three of them blacks. The group was well received by the local people and entertained at Chief Mehlomkhulu's home, where sheep were slaughtered to mark the occasion.

Back at Kleinzee, later in 1982 management encouraged intermine tribal dancing. Dreyer's Pan hostel and Black Mountain hostel from O'okiep competed in sections devoted to Pondo and Pondomise. Traditional songs were sung by the visiting Sterkspruit Senior Secondary School Choir. The following year, a group of Ciskeian chiefs visited the mine as distinguished guests of the company. In 1983, the company financed the building of a teachers' quarters at the Amavundle Higher Primary School in the Thornhill area of the Ciskei and purchased eighty desks for the pupils; later, company representatives visited the area for a celebration. Around the same time, there were reports of a fantastic exhibition of tribal dancing in Kleinzee by workers from the Dreyer's Pan Hostel. Pondo, Hlubi, Xhosa, and Timitie groups all took part.

In September 1987, management presented long-service awards to black workers at their homes in the Ciskei and Transkei, while they were on leave. In his speech, the general manager thanked the recipients for long and loyal service: "The Company places much value on dedicated service because of the benefits to both the Company and the employee. . . . While honouring these employees, we must remember, however, that their wives have also played a role . . . [by] looking after their homes and children."[7]

Two years later, the Ciskeian and Transkeian chiefs were back again in Kleinzee, at the invitation of the general manager, to hold "formal discussions over three days on matters of mutual interest." They also met with hostel residents for informal talks and enjoyed performances of tribal dancing and a soccer game. In 1990, long-service awards were again celebrated in the Transkei and Ciskei, the general manager taking an impressive group of senior staff with him. The company of course has a hidden agenda in its public-relations paternalism.

If the wages the company pays its contract workers remain low, De Beers perceives the deficit as being made up in other ways. The general manager explained this aspect of the paternalistic system to me: "The meals in the hostel are subsidized to an enormous amount by the company. Each meal costs us R11.60 and the workers pay only R2.70 on the average for a meal coupon. . . . Accommodation in the hostels is provided free of charge, and workers are transported free of charge to the Transkei and Ciskei at the beginning and at the end of each contract at the company's expense. Free transportation to the Ciskei and Transkei is also provided for workers to attend funerals of near kin."

It is, in fact, a common sight to see busloads of black contract workers and their wives on their way home, waiting for clearance at the main security gate. The typical scene is a crowded bus, the front half of which is occupied by women; the men (the husbands) sit behind them. The luggage rack on the roof is loaded with boxes of goods purchased at the company store—groceries, clothing, furniture, and appliances. These excursions are regarded by the company as special concessions at the company's expense. A number of brick cottages at the west end of the town have been built for the women, who are permitted to stay for the two-week period coinciding with the end of their husbands' contracts, thereby making it possible for couples to travel together to their rural homes with their purchases from the company store.

Unlike those employees (largely white) who are housed in fine, self-contained, self-sufficient, suburban-style dwellings, black migrant hostel dwellers are given little choice but to regard their time spent on the mine as extensions of home, rather than home itself. Put another way, we might say that, over the years, all black contract mineworkers have regarded their lives at Kleinzee as temporary extensions of the boundaries of their home communities. The same applies, and for much the same reason, to Coloured workers, who have been involved in migrant labor at Kleinzee for a much longer period, and to the white Namaqualanders of the 1930s. My generalization about these issues of boundary extensions should not be interpreted as applying to housing alone: it really derives from a structural reality—that the lower employees are on the socioeconomic scale, the harder they have to work at keeping their personal lives and associations in good repair, both at home and while they are employed on the mine. The link between home, wages, and bread and butter are very real.

Home Ties of Coloured Workers

Coloured workers, like the blacks, also observe ceremonial occasions before they leave the company's employ. When a man from Komaggas decided he had had enough of company-town life and retired after thirty-nine years of service, his co-workers organized an outdoor party for him, after work at the dairy where he was employed. About twenty men were present. Cold beer was served, and pounds of sheep ribs and *boerewors* (country sausage) were grilled on the coals. His white overseer, who was specially invited to the party, made the first speech, wishing Jan Plaas well. In his nostalgic reply, Jan told everyone how he had come to Kleinzee as a laborer, training as a knock-off trammer on the haulage in the mining area.

> At that time [early 1950s] there were no fancy machines. We worked with mules, and what was called the donkey haulage [mechanical winch], in places where the continuous haulage line did not reach. When the first excavator arrived, it could barely do the work that the pick-and-shovel workers had done. Things were very different here at Kleinzee in those days. The pay was pretty bad, but in other ways life was very cordial and pleasant here. It was almost as if we were all brothers and sisters—just like one big family.
>
> One day, in 1952, when I was on leave, I received a message from the new compound manager telling me to report for duty the following Monday to start a new job at the dairy. That Sunday, a lorry from Kleinzee passed through the Komaggas reserve. I got a ride and reported for duty the next morning. That is how I got my job here in the dairy.

Jan went on to urge his friends to be loyal to each other as workers, loyal to the dairy, and loyal to the company. Everyone present then formed a line and filed past Jan individually. They shook hands, made little personal speeches, gave advice, and thanked him for his friendship over the years. Jan in turn gave advice to each person.

The occasion, although not linked to any particular church or congregation, had a strong religious character and closely resembled the ceremonies for retiring black workers. The Coloured reserves are not as far away as the Ciskei and Transkei, but it is still imperative for workers to maintain close ties with home, and while at home to maintain a network of relations with Kleinzee. As with black workers, the company has made an effort to promote public relations, making goodwill visits to the Coloured reserves. In 1985, Allan Hendrickse, a Coloured member of Parliament, and his wife were invited to attend the tenth anniversary of the Zonderberg company school for Coloureds. The next year, Coloured schoolteachers from Steinkopf, invited to visit Kleinzee for a day, were taken on a mine tour.

Home Ties of White Workers

When a white employee leaves the service of the company, there are currently no out-of-the-ordinary farewell rituals such as I have described for Coloureds and blacks. An employee who ranks high in the Paterson system may be entertained by management at select parties at the club, although these have been reduced in number in a decade of cutbacks. Most people are simply "partied" by their friends, but not much more. Thus, we cannot, strictly speaking, say these white people are honored by amakhaya principles.

There are, however, important church affiliations among Afrikaans-speaking whites, and these need to be carefully considered in this regard. The majority of the Afrikaans-speaking whites in Kleinzee are members of the NGK, the largest Dutch Reformed church in South Africa. Very active, the congregation has nevertheless distanced itself spatially from the mine community by worshipping in the Grootmis church built in the 1930s. The dominee spends a good deal of time in Kleinzee, however, visiting his parishioners for coffee and cocktails, but because he is not employed by the company he and his family live across the Buffels River, in the Grootmis hamlet. The Grootmis church is now almost entirely dependent financially on dues received from the Kleinzee members. Without those contributions, there would be insufficient funds to pay the dominee's salary, and in this sense the parishioners can be said to control the congregation, if not own the church. In the old Kleinzee, an affiliation of this sort with the Grootmis church would not have been possible because of security restrictions.

It is my belief that the Kleinzee NGK members joined the Grootmis church because it provided a spatial, as well as symbolic, home base that offset some of the isolation of company-town life. Among the whites, the Afrikaners are the only group that feels the need to cultivate its identity through a church, an identity that substitutes, as it were, for the amakhaya principles associated with blacks and, to a lesser extent, the Coloureds.

If many Afrikaans-speaking whites see the church as a substitute for maintaining ties with the outside world, what can be said of the English-speaking whites? I venture to suggest that the English employees in Kleinzee feel little need to reinforce their ties with the wider world—neither through church nor special involvement with their former communities—because of the false security they derive from their privileged socioeconomic position. The same can also be said for the Afrikaans-speaking people in general, but in the context of this De Beers mining town, where being English counts so much in determining rank, many Afrikaners feel the need to cultivate another social arena to protect their identity.[8]

12

The Racial and Social Determinants of Income

When the policy of apartheid was officially proclaimed in 1948, institutionalized racial segregation had existed in South Africa for many years, as witnessed by the various statutes of the Union. But the new policy was part of a carefully contrived strategy devised by the ruling class to give the state stronger legal backing in its control and subjugation of indigenous peoples, their descendants, and various non-European immigrant populations. Central to the policy of apartheid and all the repressive legislation, old and new, related to it was the Population Registration Act (1950), a devious piece of racialist legislation that provided neither a definition of race nor a clear definition of what was meant by the term *color*. A white person, for instance, was defined as "a person who in appearance obviously is, or who is generally accepted as a white person, but does not include a person who, although in appearance obviously a white person, is generally accepted as a Coloured person." A native (today known as a black), on the other hand, was defined as "a person who in fact is or is generally accepted as a member of any aboriginal race or tribe of Africa." A Coloured person was negatively defined as "a person who is not a white person or a native."

What is so significant about these definitions is the detail that they are based largely on indices of association and acceptance—that is to say, not necessarily on color. Thus each of the three so-called racial groups were further divided into ethnic groups. For example, natives were regarded as being either Xhosa or Zulu or Sotho, and so on, Coloureds as Cape Coloureds, Malays, Griqua. . . .

Neither Cape Coast nor De Beers developed race policies of their own. Like other industrial corporations in South Africa, appropriate social conventions and state laws were simply incorporated into company policy to maximize labor efficiency. Thus, while racial (e.g. color) discrimination of some sort has always been present in the history of Kleinzee, race has never been the sole factor in determining the socioeconomic positions of employees. The detail that race and class divisions often coincide, and that determination of status is often a function of group attitudes toward physical differences, does not demonstrate the primacy of race in determining hierarchies of this sort. Ideas about race and status are, in fact, often closely related.

Ethnicity and Occupation

I want now to reexamine the composition of the mine's population in terms of varieties of social differentiation, bearing in mind that every form of stratification is always modified by the ideas and attitudes (positive and negative) that different groups have about race and its companion, color. Crucial to the better understanding of this hierarchical system is full consideration of the importance of ethnic components.

The history of Kleinzee's workforce reveals, over and over, as I have illustrated in earlier chapters, how important ethnicity has been in shaping the social ecology of the town and the workplace. In 1930, for example, the official working class consisted entirely of white contract workers: these laborers were housed in the compound, isolated from the other members of the community. Afrikaans-speaking farmers and peasants, recruited from the surrounding region, they constituted an ethnic group with a distinctive culture. They spoke a dialect of Afrikaans, often married kin such as cousins, and shared many customs with the local Nama and Coloured populations. They received special recognition from the state, which courted their votes in a number of political elections in the 1930s. The state also brought pressure on Cape Coast to reward them with twice the wage paid to Coloured and black workers at that time. For a short period (1926 to 1927), Coloured and white pick-and-shovel workers received roughly the same daily wage, and it was the state's influence and the general prejudices of the day, not the company's, that imposed the criterion of race in the workplace, thereby influencing the socioeconomic hierarchy of the mine—an example of ethnic identity preceding institutionalized racism.

Ethnic identity and bias of another kind was also the basis of recruitment at the top of the mine hierarchy in those years. Everyone entrusted with even a modicum of responsibility was expected to have at least one British colonial attribute. The senior officials were South African English, and all but one had been commissioned officers in World War I. One had also fought for the British in the Boer War. Further down the social scale, the majority of the supervisors (foremen), too, were South African English, and they were assumed, therefore, to share political sentiments with their superiors. Even the guards (security staff), who were all ostensibly Afrikaners, upheld (or were expected to uphold) English political sentiments, a quality that was a major criterion when they were selected to guard the company's diamonds. An anecdote will serve as illustration: When Dr. D. F. Malan defeated General Smuts in the 1948 election, one of the guards, who had been recruited from the lower reaches of the Buffels River, was appalled: "Wat gaan ons nou met daardie hoerkind Malan maak"? ("What are we going to do now that that son-of-a-bitch Malan is in power?") he is reputed to have told a senior official. But, as Malan's Nationalist Party policies gained strength among the majority of white voters in South Africa, so Namaqualanders, like this security guard, shifted their political allegiance away from Smuts. Yet they retained their feelings of loyalty to the company, largely, I suspect, because they had been so effectively influenced by the senior officials over the years. Company hegemony and slanted goodwill was always apparent at election time in the 1930s and 1940s. Employees were transported to the polling booth at the police station, outside the town, having been instructed by a senior official where to make the X on their ballots. Family members of these Namaqualanders, living in Grootmis and further upstream along the Buffels River, were similarly instructed to support English interests. For Major Orpen, the chief protection officer, a vote for Smuts was a vote for the British Empire, Cape Coast, and De Beers, and he took it upon himself to make sure that as many people as possible in the local region cast their ballots in that direction.[1]

But as sole owner of the mining town and most of the surrounding farms, the company did more than simply exert influence on individuals and groups: it possessed naked power, and it used it from time to time to discipline people, especially to control the destiny of ethnic contract workers at the bottom of the socioeconomic scale. Earlier, I showed how, in 1944, rather than increase the wages of Namaqualand workers, the company replaced them with Owambos, who were paid a fraction of the Namaqualanders' wage. When the Owambos were recalled by the South-West African Administration, the company found it both easy and convenient to replace them with Namaqualand Coloureds.

The company has always used principles of ethnic exploitation in its recruitment of cheap labor to meet its needs, a common practice in the mining industry generally since excavation takes place in remote areas.[2] Although each group was regarded as a separate racial category in South African terms, recruitment by the company was based on common ethnic criteria, not on race—a practice that made it easier for companies to devise a variety of techniques to control labor more efficiently, and pay them less.

The recruitment of Xhosa-speaking contract workers from the Ciskei and the Transkei involved Kleinzee management with a group of workers who identified themselves specifically with so-called tribal affiliations, such as Pondo, Pondomise, and Fingo, and with their home districts and villages (see chapter 11). Over the years, the company exploited those ethnic and amakhaya involvements to maintain a stable workforce. The policy's success is evident: many worked for the company long enough to reach retirement. Another indicator of stability is that in 1993 all the Xhosa-speaking contract workers were married.

Once again we observe that ethnicity, not race, has been the basis of labor recruitment. Sometimes, however, a notion of ethnicity is transformed by management into an idea (usually false) about race that rationalizes a stereotypical attitude toward a group of workers. For example, it has been and still is a common assertion that only blacks are physically capable of carrying out such strenuous work as wielding pick and shovel at bedrock level; Coloured workers are said to be physically too weak to do such heavy work, notwithstanding that all the pick-and-shovel work had earlier been done by Coloured workers and, earlier still, by whites. After many Ciskeian and Transkeian workers were retrenched early in 1993, part of the heavy work was again done by Coloureds. In March 1996, the *NM Chronicle* reported that a team of Coloureds were the hot-shot bedrock cleaners in the Koingnaas mining division. And not only were they Coloured: they were *women*.

After 1960 or so, as the town's population increased in size and diversity to meet the demands of industrial expansion, so the implications of ethnic (and racial) diversity became more complicated. Among the whites, the English continued to occupy higher positions than did the Afrikaners, supporting the traditional view that "De Beers is English." And in language use, despite attempts by the company to foster trilingualism (Xhosa, Afrikaans, and English), even today English predominates in the pages of the *NM Chronicle* and in communications from the general manager. Although since 1994 more space has been given in the *NM Chronicle* to the Afrikaans language, there is no Afrikaans or Xhosa version of *Policies and Procedures*, the handbook of custumals and guidelines used to administer the mine.

While the successful exploitation of labor by mining companies is generally explained in terms of the institution of migratory labor and the compound system, the ruthless efficiency of those two complementary institutions is closely related to the manipulation of the complex of ethnic differences and groupings. Divide-and-rule strategies are common for maintaining the system, especially in the compounds.[3] The history of Kleinzee is as much a history of institutionalized interaction between ethnic strata and class divisions as it is of the production of alluvial diamonds. Racialism, in the sense of discrimination against certain nonwhite groups, cannot be denied, but even here one must insist that racial stereotypes and prejudices are fashioned by the culture of ethnicity and are not simple responses toward biological difference. Thus, while Xhosa and Owambo contract workers resemble each other physically as black Africans, they differ enormously in language and culture, social organization, and their expectations from the company, which paid them and treated them accordingly. Similarly, the white contract workers of the 1920s and 1930s constituted an ethnic group and were given wages, living quarters, recreational opportunities, and a diet as the company saw fit. Coloureds, too, working for the company in various capacities and at different times since 1927 received similar treatment, having their needs met as the company considered appropriate.

The "De Beers is English" sentiment is readily recognized by many in their comprehension of the history of De Beers. Its importance was brought home to me one day early in November 1992 while I was waiting to interview someone in a peripheral part of town. Unexpectedly, a white, Afrikaans-speaking worker appeared through a side door. We introduced ourselves by giving our surnames simultaneously, as is the custom in Namaqualand. Within a minute, he began to tell me about his early life on the lower reaches of the Buffels River and how, after the discovery of diamonds, poor farmers sold their farms for mere pittances. We discussed the fencing-off of Kleinzee and other properties by De Beers, and he recalled his father telling him that in the 1930s, as the company acquired more power in the magisterial district, all the roads leading to the fishing sites on the coast had been closed to the Namaqualand public. This white, Afrikaans-speaking man then asked me who owned the diamond industry. I was given no time to reply and he dealt angrily with the question himself.

> Yes, they were all Jews [to begin with], the whole lot of them: Barney Barnato, all the Oppenheimers and the Dunkelsbuhlers. And that Rhodes bloke, he was also a Jew, an English Jew [En daardie Rhodes Kêrel was ook 'n Jood—'n Engelse Jood] . . . all those people worked with the English [companies] using American money. . . . What is the Anglo American [company all about] if this is not true? Just look at the canning industry—fruit and jam. It used to belong to Rhodes, now it belongs to Anglo American which also owns [nearly] all the vineyards and orchards . . . [in South Africa].

The man's outburst was a composite text (not entirely accurate) directed at individuals (Rhodes and the Oppenheimers) and ethnicities (Jewish, English, and American). However, the full meaning and significance of his lecture came to me much later, after I had talked to other Afrikaans-speaking employees about the top echelons of the company's hierarchy. Many indicated how much they resented the dominion of "the English" in everyday affairs. As one man put it, "If one of us Boers wants to get to the top, he's got first to work hard at being like the English." How might this be achieved by an individual? He must associate with the English, and especially, he must get an English wife. He gave various examples, including his observation that one Afrikaner's rise to distinction in the company's hierarchy was related to a pattern of serial monogamy: over time, the man had three wives, each ethnically more English than the last.

Gender and Occupation

Ethnicity is not the only factor that determines, or influences, a person's status or class. Male gender preference has always loomed large in the occupational scheme, and management has been a male preserve since the beginning of Kleinzee. This of course is not surprising. No woman was employed in any capacity by the company until the 1940s, when a white nursing sister, a female schoolteacher, a postmistress, and a woman cook for the white single men were appointed because of a shortage of trained males. The company was reluctant to employ wives of employees, as could be seen in the 1940s: head office objected to an employee's wife helping out with typing in the mine office when the male clerk joined the armed forces.

The exception to the exclusion of women from the workforce in the early days was the employment of Coloured servants by married employees. But these were not the company's servants, although the manager had to authorize their admission to the town. Over the years, more women began to be employed, although as late as the 1950s, wives of company employees were not encouraged to take jobs, reflecting the general attitudes and practices in South Africa.

By the 1970s, after the expansion of mining operations and the building of the new town, most stenographic and many clerical positions were filled by women. Women became cooks and cashiers and dominated the nursing and teaching professions. Today, even the security staff includes women. And as more secretarial and other white-collar jobs were created, so it was in the interest of the company to exploit the cohort of married women, since they were already housed, and many were looking aggressively for gainful employment. The fact that their husbands worked for the company seemed not to matter any more, and wives ceased to be regarded as security risks. For example, the general manager's wife was allowed to become senior executive secretary in the mine office, in charge of the administration of mine policy. In a previous era, such an appointment would never have been made—first, because of her sex, and second, because she was the manager's wife.

In January 1993, there were 306 women in the company's employ. They made up nearly 13 percent of the workforce. While no woman was represented in either the D or E bands in the Paterson system, 55 women had good jobs in all the C bands; among them were senior hospital workers, teachers, administrative officers, nurses, personnel officers and assistants, and accountants. Women were also well represented in both the A and B bands. In the B1 to B4 range, 152 women held roles such as junior supervisors, clerks, diamond sorters, security guards, and sales assistants. In the A bands, 99 women were employed as laborers, cleaners, and helpers, and in other odd jobs in the town. All but three of these were Coloured women. At the lower end of the B band, Coloured women outnumbered whites two to one. Higher in the scale, the reverse occurs, the majority of the better jobs being occupied by white women. For example, there are 22 whites but only 4 Coloureds in the higher C range. Only one black woman was employed by the company in 1993.

Women domestic servants continue to be employed. The majority are still Coloured women from neighboring reserves and small towns, although a few black women have now entered domestic service. It was difficult to obtain reliable data of wages paid to domestics in the 1990s. Many families paid only R60 a month, plus food and lodging; one family paid R100 a month, plus the extras. Domestic servants from the Komaggas Reserve have been able to take advantage of the company's daily commuter bus service. Some years ago, the company gave employees an allowance for a maid of R75 a month, which seems to reflect the average wage at that time.

It is not easy for women in general to find work in a man's mining world. Even low-paying jobs in domestic service require knowledge of local networks to find suitable employers. In the company's occupational sphere, astute micropolitical maneuvering is especially necessary when wives of employees negotiate entry into the local job market. Much depends on the husband's position, on personal networks, and on the woman's relations with other employees' wives in town. Some women seem to get the job they want without difficulty; others never find work, or have to be satisfied with second or third choices. More time than was available to me would have been needed to explore in greater detail the rivalries, conflicts, and tensions relating to the women's job market, where access to employment by the company is so closely intertwined with the status of a husband's occupation. Women who never get the job they apply for because the system rules against them suffer devastating psychological effects.

Salaries and Wages: Old and New

The introduction of the Paterson band system was designed to order everyone employed by the company in a new hierarchy based on assumed decision-making capability. In practice, this meant that everyone was arranged in a rigid system of differentiation based on occupation (see chapter 10). A highly skilled operator of complex machinery in the mine area told me: "I will never get past that C2 rating unless I get a new job. This Paterson idea is the worst thing De Beers has done for its workers." His judgment was surely correct because, as he himself observed, other employees with fewer skills, less decision-making potential, and less responsibility (e.g., telecom technicians, farm foremen, and draughtsmen) were earning more than he did simply because their occupations were tied to bands labeled as requiring higher decision-making skills.

It was never the company's intention to be involved in these kinds of problems. The Paterson system was accepted as an objective system that would abolish racial (and ethnic) discrimination in work and play, create a progressive wage system, standardize the wage structure, and so on. Moreover, because the system was believed to "objectify," it was supposed also to "simplify" decisions relating to such matters as the length of an individual's vacations, the quality of housing to be allocated, who should receive car allowances, who would be entitled to welcoming and farewell parties, and so forth.

Initially, the Paterson system worked to the advantage of the unskilled and certain semiskilled workers (bands A and B); these workers received wage increases immediately after the system was introduced. It also helped the NUM to negotiate higher minimum wages levels and increase the range of wage scales.[4] But it was the senior staff (D2 bands and higher) whose salaries and perks increased enormously. This was because their decision-making qualities received higher recognition. However, as many C-band employees observed, once placed in a Paterson category, it is very difficult to move up a band without changing jobs. A latent function of the Paterson system has been to maintain job reservation, which in turn perpetuates old racial and ethnic categories under the banner of "objective" job evaluation. None of these observations should be surprising: it has been often been pointed out that, as a strategy of cost minimization, the capital immobility of the mining industry in general encourages the control and exploitation of labor by companies.[5] In fact, the history of Kleinzee mine illustrates that the general pattern of social differentiation has remained much the same over the years, despite the expansion of mining operations and the increase in the size of the workforce to maintain it. From the point of view of De Beers, the Paterson system has been ideal.

Incomes under Cape Coast

When mining operations got into full swing in the early 1930s, the company employed more than two hundred men, all of them carefully ranked according to occupation and status, and paid accordingly. That hierarchy is summarized in table appendix 2.1 in terms of occupation, income, and race (ethnicity), based on reports and pay slips for January 1932. As chance would have it, the acting manager of the day (the equivalent of a general manager) earned exactly £100 a month. This coincidence automatically expresses all other salaries and wages in terms of percentages of the top salary earned. The table also shows all monthly incomes in ratio to the general manager's. Thus, the higher the ratio, the lower the relative wage, as shown in figure 12.2. For example, the Coloured guard's ratio of 22.22 is much higher than that of a white guard's ratio of 7.14, and the latter's ratio, when compared with that of a supervisor (3.33) reflects the wage gap between them. The ratio also, of course, reveals their respective statuses in the community. The distribution of incomes speaks for itself quantitatively, but as we have seen in earlier chapters the meaning of these inequalities must also be appreciated.

Incomes under De Beers

All 2,409 employees on the De Beers payroll in 1993 experienced very different lives from those who lived and worked at Kleinzee in the 1930s, making the best of life with brackish water, inferior housing, sandy roads, low wages, absence of proper recreational facilities, barbed-wire fences, and four locked gates. The fences remain, but the four locked gates have been replaced by computerized checkpoints (see chapter 13). By 1993, the general manager and his senior staff were impressively housed, and the next level of employees—modern-day equivalents of the old supervisor, compound manager, medical orderly, and so on—enjoyed vastly improved housing. In 1932, there were fewer than a dozen family units; in 1993, there were about 350. All the new houses were bigger, better built, and more comfortable, and any employee in C band or higher was now entitled to a house or flat.

This shift in the boundaries of income and privilege for many employees preceded the introduction of the Paterson system by many years as De Beers responded to trends in the early 1970s. The company by then knew that professionals and others (including many semiskilled workers) would not accept jobs at Kleinzee unless they were given appropriate housing, better recreational facilities, and more attractive incomes and benefits. Married white employees lower in the mine hierarchy were also provided with good housing. Given the shortage of skilled and semiskilled white labor, qualified Coloured employees filled the vacancies, and some married Coloured employees now received acceptable housing in the west end of the town.

Black contract workers continued to be housed in overcrowded, all-male barracks, now called hostels. Unlike the old compounds, the hostel complexes had shops, pubs, church buildings, and better recreation facilities. But they continued to be segregated from the rest of the town. De Beers did, however, make significant improvements in wage and salary structures over the years, and the introduction of the Paterson system, despite its rigidity, has helped remove some of the extreme discrepancies between workers' earnings based on race and ethnicity. For example, in 1932, the earning ratio of the average Coloured Namaqualand laborer was 20; in 1993, the corresponding ratio for Coloured laborers was between 9.37 and 13.1. That may be contrasted with the almost total lack of change in average earning ratios for white Namaqualand workers: in 1932, the ratio for contract men was 11.11; the comparable 1993 earning ratio for the seventy-five white workers in the lowest Paterson bands had changed hardly at all (11.24). Generally speaking, then, the overall pattern of the wage structure has remained much the same, as can be seen in figures 12.2 and 12.3.

Quantitative Trends and Correlations

The quantitative data presented in tables appendix 2.1, 2.2, and 2.3, and figures 12.1, 12.2, and 12.3 with respect to income, occupation, gender, race (ethnic group), and position in the Paterson system speak for themselves. But some interpretation and qualifications are necessary. I carried out my research during a period of major retrenchments and retirements, which tended to distort the "normal" composition of the workforce as it had been constituted over the preceding five years. The majority of the eighty-five retrenchments between January 1 and March 16, 1993, were black contract workers from the Transkei and Ciskei, which added to the general decline in the number of A and B Paterson band members. As a consequence, the Dreyer's Pan hostel was closed and all the remaining black workers were moved into town, to be housed in the vacant rooms of the hostel previously set aside exclusively for Coloured workers.

In analyzing the general distribution of income at Kleinzee in 1993, I did not have access to personal files, as I did for 1930 (see table appendix 2.1). I therefore decided to base all my estimates on the lower end of the income range paid to employees in each band. For example, I assumed that all C3 band employees earned R1,868 a month, although the salary range allotted to them was R1,868–R2,014. I thereby underestimated the incomes of employees who had reached the top of their scales. Moreover, my estimate of a general manager's salary is based on the lower, rather than higher, incomes in the E band, and includes the manager's car allowance of R2,500. None of my calculations of income at any level take into consideration overtime or bonuses.

Table appendix 2.2 provides the basic data of all monthly incomes in January 1993, expressed in terms of an employee's position in the Paterson system, in combination with gender and race, using terms adopted by the company that, by and large, correspond to conventional South African usage. Nothing remarkable emerges from this tabulation, given the regional location of the mine and its historical background in South African society. The Coloured employees, the majority of whom come from the Namaqualand reserves, constitute the largest ethnic category (61.31 percent of the total labor force). Though roughly equal in number in January 1993, whites (19.71 percent) and blacks (18.97 percent) generally carried out very different kinds of work, as table appendix 2.3 shows. During the peak of apartheid, it would have been illegal for the two lone blacks to have filled the skilled positions reflected in bands D and C. Similar restrictions would have been placed on those Coloured employees now occupying 30 percent of all the positions in the C and D bands. The reason for blacks not being the largest category, given their numerical superiority in Southern Africa, requires historical and regional explanation: such background has been given indirectly in earlier chapters.

A comparison of the occupational profile of the mine in 1993 (table appendix 2.3) and the corresponding profile in the 1930s (table appendix 2.1) shows a marked trend away from institutionalized racial and ethnic discrimination, but this does not mean that there has been a decline in the pattern of stratification. On the contrary, while the Paterson system got rid of formal racial and ethnic discrimination, it created a new logic for rigid differentiation based on occupation— a logic that will have the effect of slowing down the process of job equalization in the future.

Figure 12.1

Wage profiles of black, coloured, and white employees according to their relative positions in the Paterson band system, Kleinzee mine, January 1993. (See also table appendix 2.2.)

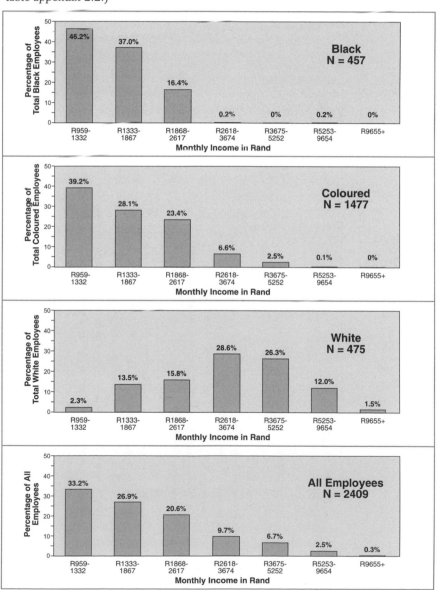

Figure 12.2

Income ratios Kleinzee, 1932

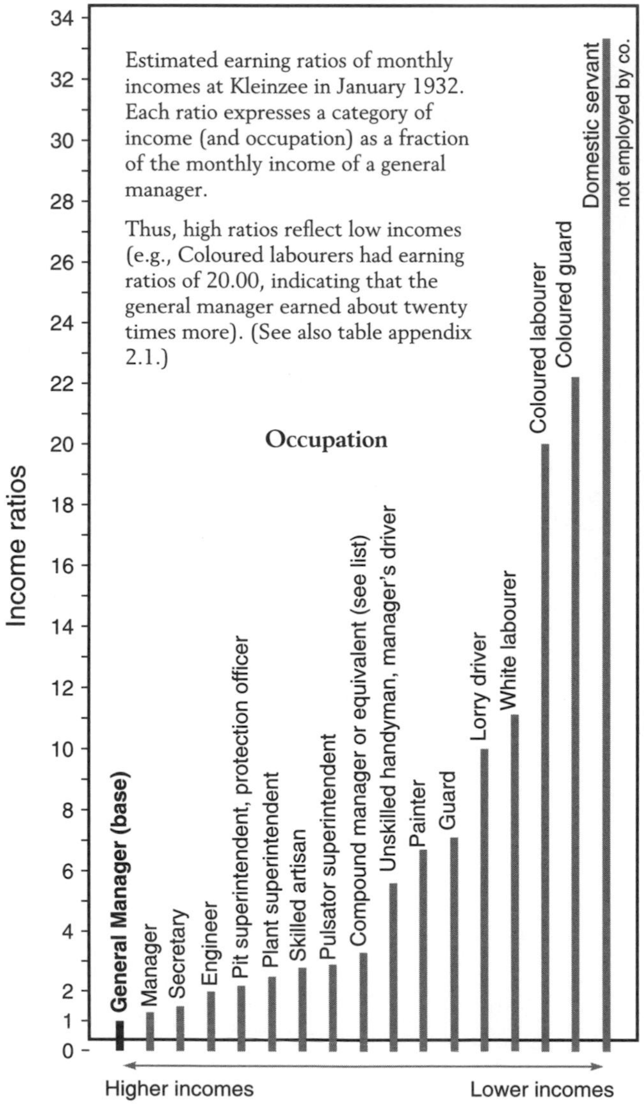

Estimated earning ratios of monthly incomes at Kleinzee in January 1932. Each ratio expresses a category of income (and occupation) as a fraction of the monthly income of a general manager.

Thus, high ratios reflect low incomes (e.g., Coloured labourers had earning ratios of 20.00, indicating that the general manager earned about twenty times more). (See also table appendix 2.1.)

Occupation

Income ratios

34
32
30
28
26
24
22
20
18
16
14
12
10
8
6
4
2
1
0

General Manager (base)
Manager
Secretary
Engineer
Pit superintendent, protection officer
Plant superintendent
Skilled artisan
Pulsator superintendent
Compound manager or equivalent (see list)
Unskilled handyman, manager's driver
Painter
Guard
Lorry driver
White labourer
Coloured labourer
Coloured guard
Domestic servant
not employed by co.

Higher incomes   Lower incomes

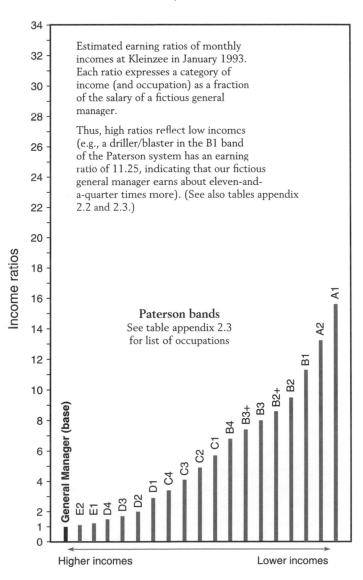

Figure 12.3

Income ratios Kleinzee, 1993

Estimated earning ratios of monthly incomes at Kleinzee in January 1993. Each ratio expresses a category of income (and occupation) as a fraction of the salary of a fictious general manager.

Thus, high ratios reflect low incomes (e.g., a driller/blaster in the B1 band of the Paterson system has an earning ratio of 11.25, indicating that our fictious general manager earns about eleven-and-a-quarter times more). (See also tables appendix 2.2 and 2.3.)

Paterson bands
See table appendix 2.3
for list of occupations

Income ratios

34
32
30
28
26
24
22
20
18
16
14
12
10
8
6
4
2
1
0

General Manager (base)
E2
E1
D4
D3
D2
D1
C4
C3
C2
C1
B4
B3+
B3
B2+
B2
B1
A2
A1

Higher incomes   Lower incomes

13

Obligation and Loyalty in a "Closed" World

I n the preceding chapter I examined some of the dimensions of socio-economic differentiation and stratification within the Kleinzee mining community. I turn now to a discussion of a number of themes relating to employees' encapsulated lives. These include an analysis of some of the rituals relating to crossing company boundaries, the obligation many employees feel toward the company, and the part that company hegemony plays in cultivating the syndrome of paternalistic attitudes.

Closedness

There are many examples of "closed" communities and institutions existing in partial isolation from the rest of the world, not so much because of their geographical remoteness but because of their structural character. These include asylums, boarding schools, military bases, company towns, monasteries, convents and nunneries, detention camps—even native reserves. However, to claim that such communities are totally closed and self-sufficient no longer rings true in today's world of rapid travel and lightning-fast telecommunication. On the other hand, the social and psychological consequences of living in this type of community, as Goffman showed, need to be carefully considered.

Residents of Kleinzee report that when the place gets on their nerves, producing what they call Kleinzee-itis, the simple cure is to leave town for a weekend, or even for a few hours. In the early days of the mine, before the town was declared "open," spontaneous getaways were never possible, and people had to tolerate their claustrophobic attacks until they went on their annual leave. Nowadays, since the construction of a new highway (a super-highway, by Namaqualand standards) from Port Nolloth to Cape Town, it is possible to make the 780-kilometer journey for a weekend. But most people looking for a quick fix for their Kleinzee-itis go to Port Nolloth, a seaport with very little to commend it. Others, not wishing to risk the effect of the cold, foggy Port Nolloth winds on their joints, drive to a rocky campsite sur-rounded by thorn trees at the foot of the Kamiesberg Mountains. Still others weekend with kin at Steinkopf, Komaggas, Springbok, and neighboring com-munities. Workers from the Ciskei and Transkei take every opportunity to have a few days off work at company expense to attend funerals at home.

These little escapes from the barbed-wire encampment and the hum-drum, controlled existence of the town are seen by people as safety valves—quick relief from the cabin fever of the fenced-in, single-industry town in the semidesert. "When you feel you can't stand it any more, when you are about to go over the edge, you just think about going out [of the gate] for a while. Sometimes, all you have to do is to go to Port Jolly [Port Nolloth] for the day and you feel better. Sometimes you just drive out on the Springbok road for a few hours and you feel okay."

The apparent freedom to come and go from town is, of course, colored by the fact that nobody leaves or returns without being processed by security officials at the main checkpoint. The rigid term *closed*, as applied to human association, suggests a more useful abstraction, *closedness*,[1] the condition of being relatively shut in, or off, from something else. The notion of closedness also implies a closed-open continuum, with single-industry company towns at one end, "real" cities at the other. Company towns and comparable forma-tions can all be said to possess qualities of closedness that separate them from the wider society. Perceptions of those qualities reside not only in the minds of insiders but also in the minds of people looking in from the outside. More-over, the condition of being encapsulated, separate, or closed does not imply simple, orderly structural relations within the given social formation. The op-posite is, in fact, the case, because everyday, common human conflict is exac-erbated by the structural ambiguities inherent in the fiction of institutional completeness.

Rites of Entrance and Departure

Boundaries and Thresholds

Entering and leaving Kleinzee nowadays is never automatic for anyone, whether the person be the general manager or a bedrock sweeper. The town might be more open than it was in the 1930s, now that mass X-raying and luggage searching have been discontinued (with the exception of in the mining areas). Yet the formalities related to coming and going remain as involved as crossing a border into a foreign country. In order to enter the town, all residents have to present personal bar-coded cards issued by the security department.

When my wife and I first arrived in July 1993, no housing was available for us, so for months we had to drive the 140-kilometer round trip every day from Port Nolloth, where we rented a house. We reported at the main gate every morning, presented our coded cards to the security staff, and waited for the computer clearance that permitted us to proceed to town in our car. We always felt uneasy when we arrived at the checkpoint, and even bewildered, for reasons explained below, when we left. After several weeks of exasperating coming and going, we asked a mine official to clarify our status in the community, to be told, "When you are in, you are in: you can go anywhere [where you are allowed to go]." It was then that we realized that each time we participated in the company's portal rituals of entering, we were being transformed into "Kleinzee people." When we departed later, we were "reprocessed"; we became outsiders again. The rites of entering confirmed that, having passed through the portal, one was no longer a free and independent person but a ward of the company, a status that applied to everyone. In our case, though, we were sometimes required to relinquish our cards at the checkpoint for "safekeeping" until the next day. There was no guarantee that we would be readmitted the next morning. On several occasions we had to reapply to enter because we had no card to present to the gate person.

Our status in the town bewildered the residents: we did not work for the company, nor were we the official guests of any employee. From that perspective, we remained outsiders even when we were insiders, an ambiguity the checkpoint staff reinforced every time they processed us at the gate. No one could ever understand our status as semipermanent, long-time visitors, except as a freak category. For to be a *resident* of Kleinzee one must be employed by the company, be the spouse or dependent child of an employee, or be the visitor of an employee. Being a resident bestows many guaranteed privileges, but only for as long as one remains in good standing. In return, each resident is expected to obey the rules laid down by management and remain appropriately loyal to the company. Otherwise, the company can "put you out the gate."

The constant coming and going through the security checkpoint at Kleinzee, and the knowledge that the "roving eye" of De Beers Namaqualand Mines always knew where we were, alerted us to the significance of Van Gennep's interest in the rituals relating to the crossing of boundaries and thresholds, frontiers and portals. Van Gennep argued, as did Victor Turner more recently,[2] that all forms of transition involve ritual behavior, and that boundaries do not have to be physical boundaries like the Kleinzee checkpoint. Thus what we learned from our ordeals at the Kleinzee gate was not so much how important it was for the company to monitor movement to control diamond theft, but how people were processed for a life of closedness and submission and obedience to the company.

The Gate with a Light

Employees who work in the actual mining area pass through another gate every morning. This gate to the world of diamonds combines top security with ritualized automation. Workers travel to the mine checkpoint by bus or car, to a parking lot. They then proceed on foot to the computerized entry unit, where, one by one, they insert their bar-coded identity cards into the required slot. A door opens and the worker enters a security chamber, unaccompanied. A green light signals that he or she must proceed quickly (no loitering allowed) through another door, which opens onto the mining side of the barrier. There, hard hats and equipment are picked up, and all employees—managers and bedrock cleaners alike—are driven to the work sites in vehicles allocated to the mining area only.

At the end of the shift, an employee returns to the checkpoint, inserts his or her identity card to return through the control unit, and waits for the door to open. Once inside the chamber, the employee places items such as wallet or lunch pail on a conveyer belt and awaits the next signal. A green light over the left door indicates that one is free to continue to the outside and proceed to the parking lot. A red light signals that one has been randomly selected to undergo a body search and an X ray in another room, where more security procedures are carried out.

All vehicles and machinery, once inside the mining area, remain there permanently, isolated. At the end of their working life, they are buried under thousands of tonnes of overburden in mined-out areas.

Formal Induction

All new employees are required to attend a day-long induction at which the management informs newcomers about the general organization of the mine and tells them how they are expected to fit in. The day of instruction also involves the initiation of "novices" to life in a company town.

At the induction I attended in 1993, newcomers were told that Kleinzee was not just another small town, but a "closed community," and "you should be aware of this so that you can start learning the culture of the place." Instruction about "the culture" of Kleinzee turned out to be telling people to "anticipate stress in order to reduce the anxiety and uncertainty [they] will experience, and develop positive attitudes and realistic expectations about the place." The new employees were also told that their induction had been designed to reduce labor turnover and lost time and to increase everyone's productivity for the company's benefit.

The organization of the mine was then outlined. The various departments were enumerated: administration, mining, metallurgy, engineering, farms and estates, personnel, loss control, survey, and geology. Details of the conditions of employment were carefully explained, and by the end of the day everyone in the group probably knew more about the company than they had ever thought to know, including that Oppenheimer had established the Central Selling Organisation in 1930. At that point, diamonds were mentioned for the first time, being proudly referred to as "our diamonds." A final video was shown, portraying Kleinzee's self-contained environment, with comments on the extra perks De Beers provides for its employees. The narrator of the video concludes with the statement that the company wants to promote "honesty, integrity, and fairness" for everybody.

Reinforcement Rituals

Many institutions all over the world reward their employees for long service. The gold watch, once reserved for a select few, seems now to be presented to any employee who can survive a large number of years of unbroken service with a particular institution. I call these occasions reinforcement rituals, because they are designed to reward people who are already established in the system. They are also transitional rites, marking the change from one level to another in the life course of employment.

The first long-service award to workers at Kleinzee is offered after ten years of service, at which time every qualifying male employee, regardless of position in the Paterson system, is ceremonially presented with a blue tie, embroidered with the De Beers logo. Women get a pen. Ten-year veterans also receive a letter from the general manager. After fifteen years, the employee receives a gold watch or money (your choice), plus another letter from the general manager. After twenty-five years, the award is another (presumably better) gold watch, and yet another letter from the general manager—at which time, spouses, too, are rewarded: they receive cash for their devoted service, whether they worked for the company or not. After forty years of service, the employee, spared yet another watch, receives a "monetary award;" the spouse receives a cash bonus; and together they receive a glowing letter from the general manager.

An important component of these occasions is the group photograph, for which the recipients of awards pose formally with the general manager. A recent gimmick to recognize shorter periods of unbroken service is that after three years, everyone is entitled to purchase the maroon De Beers tie, with embroidered logo. I was not able to discover how many of these ties were actually purchased, but I did observe them worn to church on Sundays by a few black workers in the A and B Paterson bands.

Obligated Loyalty

During my research in 1992–93, I asked both current employees and a few former employees from the 1930s and 1940s about any feelings of loyalty toward the company (Cape Coast or De Beers). At first, there was little reaction to my questions, but as discussion moved to topics such as "expectation" and "obligation," everyone agreed that there was always the expectation that the company would do things *for* them because that is "what De Beers is all about"—meaning that that is the character of De Beers. There was also a sense of obligation—general agreement that Kleinzee people owed a lot to De Beers, not for the contents of their pay envelopes but because the company provided "extras" such as medical facilities, shops, a liquor store, a safe environment, good schools for their children, and free housing.[3] Thus, no matter how much individuals might quarrel with each other, object to their bosses, and hate the hot east wind, the boring weekends, the security fences, and the general feelings of isolation and closedness, most people fly a symbolic De Beers-is-the-best flag as part of their local worldview; this loyalty is their return gift to the company for the perks they receive.

A very important factor contributing to worker loyalty in companies like De Beers is the provision of social services exclusively for company workers— services not available outside the firm's domain. Firings, layoffs, and retrenchments (for example, at a time like mine closure) spell not only loss of income but also the loss of such benefits.[4] Self-interest, disguised as generosity, is clearly embodied in all the company's gifts; why, then, should employees feel obliged to return them? The answer lies, I think, in the mechanisms whereby hierarchies are maintained by both giving and receiving. If Marcel Mauss is right, then the motive to return a gift is rooted in the necessity to maintain one's position in the hierarchical system.[5] Not to return something would be to demean one's dependent position even further, especially now that worth is "objectively" defined by the Paterson system. Even the bedrock sweeper at the bottom of the scale has a position to maintain, lest the labor expected of him does not measure up to that scale. As Mauss would say, to give is to show one's superiority. To accept without returning is to face total subordination.

In some cases, loyalty to "the company" is expressed as loyalty to senior-ranking individuals. The many varieties of institutional and individual allegiance reflect structural positions in the mine's hierarchy and cultural differences associated with ethnicity. As seen in chapter 7, the Owambo contract workers in the 1940s, earning only 8d. a day, had little interest in flying the De Beers-is-best flag. In their case, wages, rations, and handouts were taken for granted, and all hell broke loose if they did not receive them at the agreed time. It was woe to any boss who stepped out of line. But the Owambos showed great loyalty toward bosses whom they felt were on their side. Similarly, while Coloured workers in the 1930s, 1940s, and 1950s displayed some loyalty to the company, they always personalized their sentiments, directing them to those senior staff whom they selected to be their "patrons."

It would be misleading to leave the impression that only the lowest-status workers ever harbored ill-feeling toward De Beers. For example, a retired engineer now living in Johannesburg said he thought that De Beers was a "social disgrace" and did not look after its employees in remote areas. In another case, when the company laid workers off in December 1992, a fairly senior employee lapsed into depression because he felt the company had shortchanged some workers; he picked up when his wife pointed out that De Beers was "not a welfare organization." The only person who to my knowledge said he felt no loyalty whatsoever to the company was one of the physicians. But he had already made plans to emigrate.

Loyalty, Obligation, and Company Hegemony

Loyalty implies the existence of a faithful and trusting relationship toward a person or entity of higher status than one's self. Obligation, on the other hand, involves a morally, or sometimes legally, binding agreement or understanding between two parties in which the less privileged or less powerful party displays bounden duty to the superior. Often this is a burdensome task. There is sometimes a suggestion that obligation involves symmetrical relationships, but this is seldom the case. It seems more appropriate, therefore, to speak of *obligated loyalty* as the attitude employees display toward De Beers. To speak only of loyalty in the sense I used the word above would be to lose sight of the extent to which the company wields naked power over all its employees, from general manager to bedrock cleaner.[6]

Claire Williams's study of labor and family relationships among working-class people in two open-cut coal mines in Australia disclosed the high proportion of people who express high degrees of loyalty toward their company. Williams (who writes from a pro-union, Marxist perspective) argues that the lack of revolutionary working-class consciousness she discovered is caused by a number of factors, with company hegemony seeming to be paramount because it prevents the formation of a political orientation toward the company. At least one-half the people in the preponderantly working-class town she studied voted for the conservative National Party.[7]

At Kleinzee, the company establishes a hegemonic grip over the workforce by sending out to employees (via management) various signals and messages. The thrust of these messages—often printed in the *NM Chronicle* and signposted in prominent places—is that De Beers is the most moral, most respectable, most generous, most accident-free, and cleanest of companies. Thus the hegemonic process complicates class, status, and ethnic differentiation; it gives rise to a complex cognitive system in which employees express obligation to the employer, communicating a vague sense of loyalty that they seem seriously to believe they owe to the company. It struck me as being an elusive system of false consciousness. The influence of normative bourgeois ideology on all segments of contemporary societies is well known.[8] At Kleinzee and other mining communities, it can be observed even among the workers in the lowest levels of the Paterson system.[9]

14

Total Institutions or Incomplete Communities?

significant part of this book constitutes a study of community in a company town in South Africa. I have, however, analyzed along with that material some of the socioeconomic processes involved in the birth and development of alluvial diamond mining on the northwest coast of South Africa during the 1920s and its expansion over a period of more than sixty years. At the center of that development was, of course, the De Beers company, whose financial and political power and influence overwhelmed all rival companies and syndicates. In the 1960s, De Beers negotiated with the state to have the Precious Stones Act amended to enable the company to begin its massive development of the industry in Namaqualand.

The success of De Beers in the Precious Stones Act negotiations reflects the range of the company's political influence in South Africa. This of course is in addition to the power it continues to wield over the diamond industry in general, including contract migratory labor. So pervasive have the socioeconomic influences of the company in the Namaqualand region been that it is not unreasonable to say that the De Beers expansion in the region has been akin to the establishment of a "little colony" (part of a larger process of "internal colonialism") within the confines of the South African state. In support of such a view, we may note that all the net profits accruing from this valuable regional enterprise are exported to metropolitan centers in South Africa and abroad.

We may also speak of a "company state," (which again relates to the "internal colonialism" idea).[1] In archetypical company towns like Kleinzee, corporate operations and regional influence are extensive, even overwhelming. When the company extended its mining operations as far afield as Koingnaas and Langhoogte, it renamed the whole of its industrial complex De Beers Namaqualand Mines Ltd., as if to proclaim full dominion over the region. De Beers also controls the destiny of many of the residents of the Steinkopf and Komaggas reserves, who, with others, over the years have become more and more dependent on the company for their livelihood.[2]

Many years of strip mining by the company has had an immeasurable and disastrous impact on the stretch of coastal land between Port Nolloth in the north and Hondeklip Bay in the south. Mile upon mile of veld has been bulldozed and removed to expose the diamondiferous gravel deposits at bedrock level. While the scale of mining in the early days (1928 to the late 1950s) was relatively small, what comprised the whole of the mining area at that time was systematically denuded of every shovelful of sand, calkrete, and gravel. During the occasional flooding of the Buffels River, the puddle from the tailings dam was swept to the ocean, together with part of the tailings, and by the 1940s, the "kleyne zee" (lagoon) was completely silted up with toxic waste and mud, destroying the fish population and leaving no chance of natural regeneration. Later, bigger plants built to the north and south of the Buffels River created larger volumes of toxic sludge, which found its way to the ocean with detrimental effects on fish populations and the marine ecology in general. Later, with the discovery of diamonds in the sea, marine mining by De Beers and other companies stirred up the ocean bed, affecting that ecology still further. The ratio of earth-moving to diamonds is immense: in 1989, roughly forty-seven tonnes of overburden and gravels were removed to produce the equivalent of a one-carat diamond, an achievement about which, to impress employees, visitors, and shareholders, the company boasts.

Wherever the aggressive forces of the mining industry have been unleashed, there is always great cost to both nature and people. And to make such an observation is far from new. Writing of the New West in the United States in 1869, Charles Brace declared: "Mining, at the best, is a sort of devil's or ghoul's work on a landscape. . . . [T]he gay wild flowers of California are dug up as if with fresh-made graves; the rounded outline of the hills is broken by heaps of dirt, . . . the whole landscape is a picture of roughness, waste, and desolation."[3]

If the physical environment suffers from the aggressive and destructive forces of mining, how do people involved in the industry fare? Although much has been written on the physical dangers and the health hazards of mining operations in general, Kleinzee, as an alluvial diamond mine using strip-mining methods of retrieval, has a relatively low injury rate; few physical health hazards are reported. But what effects does the "culture" of company-town life have on individual workers and their families? To answer that question, I turn to a brief consideration of some other human configurations, whose sociocultural systems offer insights into the character of company towns, and vice versa.

Total Institutions

While company towns may appear to share structural characteristics with contemporary towns and cities,[4] they are, in fact, very different. Archetypes of the former might be likened, at best, to factories, isolated from their urban locations and operated by a specially recruited workforce, housed in lifeless suburban replica or in single-sex bunkhouses, hostels, and compounds, or both. Company towns also lack not only the cultural heterogeneity of the city, but the freedom, too.[5]

Erving Goffman saw the sociocultural world in general as a composite of differing styles of interaction, each having "encompassing tendencies" that, in varying degrees and by different methods, capture the time and interests of its members. Some of these institutions encompass so powerfully that their natures are delineated by barriers to social intercourse with the outside so much that they are incorporated into the physical plan, using locked doors, high walls, barbed wire, water, and forests or moors. (These "encompassing tendencies" resemble the effects of what I have called "closedness.") He calls these "total institutions." Goffman's total institutions are very closed, some more than others. All were created by the dominant society and range from mental hospitals and boarding schools to army barracks and monasteries.[6]

Goffman's interest in the nature of total institutions involved him in a discussion of the contrived practice of forcibly breaking down the boundaries separating work, play, and sleep in the "outside" world—and then bringing these three basic needs together again in a "single rational plan purportedly designed [by policy-makers] to fulfil the official aims of the institution." And he noted that successful implementation of the plan by the administration depended, to a large extent, on maintaining formal social distance between a large "managed group" and a smaller supervisory staff, and keeping everyone under constant surveillance.

The parallels between the formal organization of Goffman's total institutions and those described and analyzed for Kleinzee and other company towns are not very different. Of special note, too, is the existence of a near-total institution within the already "closed" community of Kleinzee; namely, the compound, where the "inmates" (workers), especially in the 1930s, were doubly fenced in, separated from the rest of the town by the compound fence and from their homes and families by the other barbed-wire fence that surrounded the whole town and mining area. In drawing these parallels, however, it must be acknowledged that the inmates in Goffman's total institutions lacked the basic work-payment structure of civil society.[7]

Goffman's "total institution" research throws light on the cultural claustrophobia brought on by company town closedness on employees. For example, the neurosis of "hospitalitis" that he observes and analyzes must surely have its parallels in "Kleinzee-itis" and in the "cabin fever" of many Canadian mines, whose cures are effected by reducing the tension between the inside and outside worlds. And, while I do not wish to imply that workers in mining towns lose their identity completely (as Goffman's inmates are said to do), the various rites of passage through which they pass as they cross specified thresholds parallel the symbolic "stripping of possessions" as people are prepared to fill slots in the inside world. We saw earlier how in the 1930s each contract worker, on his way to work from the Kleinzee compound, was required to strip naked at one end of the change house every morning, and march down a corridor to another room where he put on work clothes supplied by the company. While the change-house routine fulfilled practical requirements associated with security, it did, in addition, define the low social position of workers in the system. The obligations of both mineworkers and asylum inmates to be stripped of their usual apparel (and appearance) resemble the requirement of novices voluntarily entering a monastery or convent as a sign of the new life into which they are entering,[8] or convicts involuntarily entering a penitentiary.

The end result of the many processes of mortification in total institutions is what Goffman calls "disculturation"—the "untraining" of people over time, leaving them "incapable of managing certain features of daily life on the outside."[9] Those who remain too long in company towns suffer a similar fate.[10]

Incomplete Communities

Despite some insights into the nature of company-town culture furnished by the above short digression into the notion of a "total institution," the implication of that label requires qualification because life in company towns is never totally complete. Life might be self-contained, from Goffman's point of view, but in a broader perspective it is always incomplete in the sense that residents are never able to determine the direction of their future in the confines of town.[11] There is always something missing: a psychosocial vacuum is never filled.

There are other examples of incomplete communities. Anyone who has visited an army base, air force base, or naval dockyard will recognize some of the similarities shared by these social formations and company towns—size, the relative isolation, degrees of closedness and dependence on a single body that wields powerful control over people's lives, rigid hierarchical structures, problems related to worker-tenant housing, and so on. Charlotte Wolf's *Garrison Community*,[12] a study of an overseas U.S. military colony in Ankara, highlights the overwhelming and rigorous domination and involvement of the military over all other community institutions:

> Economically, the military occupation is the *one* occupation and represents for most community members the primary source of monetary income and of life opportunities. All of the facilities—places to buy goods, places to meet and be entertained, places for religious services, and so on—are operated and directed by the military establishment. There is not a plurality of authorities and enforcement agencies in the military community of Ankara. There is only one: the military. School administrators, working in schools financed, directed, and operated by the military, often (not surprisingly) defer to and even utilize military authority. Voluntary associations are bound up with the military establishment: permission to exist, type of organization, time and place of meetings are dependent on military requirements. Religious services take place in military installations and are officiated by military chaplains. Family life provides no special sanctuary from this incursion. Individual and family identities and autonomy are caught under the cloak of rank and duty. Rank becomes the chief classifier of persons; and much of the family's life in Ankara is circumscribed by the father's niche in the hierarchy . . . [Moreover], for dependants, women and children, and for military personnel during off-duty time, "appropriate attire" is also prescribed.[13]

Erik Cohen's essay and review of the literature on expatriate communities also suggests some significant parallels, especially the effects of living in what he calls an "environmental bubble."[14] Cohen also observes that individuals resident in expatriate communities suffer from a high incidence of adjustment problems, despite the protection and cushioning provided by their environmental bubbles.

Elsewhere I have discussed another class of incomplete communities that shares significant structural and organizational patterns with company towns, but which are very different in other respects: these are the so-called "reserves" or "reservations" set aside for native peoples in various parts of the world.[15] In Canada, for example, as was the case in South Africa prior to 1994, these incomplete communities are under the near-total control and administration of the federal government. The state, moreover, provides, *as if it were a company*, all medical and dental services, all welfare and social services, all the revenue for social-assistance programs, and provides or subsidizes housing, and finances all education. As communities, all native reserves are very incomplete.

The inclusion of asylums, convents, military camps, expatriate communities, and native reserves within the same typological designation as company towns may seem forced and theoretically useless because the ends that they serve are not necessarily directed toward industrial capitalism. But if we focus on other similarities, notably their powerful hierarchical structures, degrees of closedness, dependency, and the important detail that each social formation is created for specific purposes, the parallels are not so far-fetched. Of possible significance, too, is the hypothesis (to which I have already alluded fragmentarily) that people subjected to a life (voluntarily or not) in incomplete communities are placed at high risk of falling victim to a number of "pathological" conditions that include high alcohol-consumption rates, depression, a variety of neuroses and psychosomatic illnesses and anxiety states, adjustment problems, cabin fever (e.g. Kleinzee-itis), domestic violence, and especially suicide. One very comprehensive study of the psychological effects of living at Kleinzee shows that 28 percent of the white residents are heavy drinkers, consuming twice as much alcohol as the general white population; that 30 percent are depressed (more than double the rate of the general population); and that about 20 percent of the white people are clinically disturbed. Regrettably, there was no discussion of suicide, death, or the death rate. However, my general (nonstatistical) conclusion, based on my fieldwork in 1992–93 and informants' recollections, is that the suicide rate was significantly high.

Lipschitz makes some important observations about the high incidence of suicide on military bases, in colleges, prisons, and urban ghettos;[16] and the *Guardian Weekly* reports on the high rate of alcohol consumption, violence, and suicide in fraternities.[17] Louise Elliott, writing recently on wife battering and domestic violence in the Canadian military, reports that the wives are regarded as "nothing" by the chaplains assigned by the military's judicial system to deal with domestic problems.[18] Living "inside a fishbowl on a military base" thousands of kilometres from home is for the wives very isolating: "There is no stability in relationships and that part of the military culture feeds isolation." The remark is reminiscent of the quality of life in company towns.

An Epilogue
Tumbler Ridge, 1994

After I had completed the Kleinzee research, I spent a few weeks in the remote coal-mining community of Tumbler Ridge, which is situated on a small plateau in full view of Quintette Mountain and Mount Bergeron, northeastern British Columbia.[1] I was attracted to Tumbler Ridge, not so much by its isolation and wilderness location or the enormity of its open-pit strip-mining procedures (which seemed to parallel some features of the Kleinzee undertaking), but because the town of Tumbler Ridge had been built by neither of the two operating companies, Quintette and Bullmoose, but by the provincial government.[2] It also seemed to provide a case study that would be parallel, if not identical, to one of a company town like Bisbee, Arizona, where the company does not own or control the housing. Tumbler Ridge had, moreover, been carefully planned as a community showpiece for municipal and architectural circles in Canada and abroad—a little utopian community for miners and their families. The scheme also made provision for the establishment of private commerce, including light industry, small business, and tourism. As a municipality, Tumbler Ridge boasted a town hall, a mayor, and aldermen, providing all the services normally offered by affluent municipalities with a population of four to five thousand.[3]

The existence of vast coal resources in the Peace River coalfield in British Columbia had been known for decades, but it was not until the early 1970s that extensive exploration gave rise to the Northeast Coal Project, "a $3 billion project involving the export of 100 million tonnes of metallurgical coal to Japan over the next 15 years," with reserves for another two hundred years. This massive plan called for the removal of two mountaintops, making the operation one of the largest open-pit mines in the world.

194

Epilogue 1. City Hall, Tumbler Ridge
The municipality in British Columbia has some of the attributes of a company town.

In 1975, a comprehensive planning program to discuss the housing of the workforce was initiated under the guidance of the provincial government of British Columbia. The following year, developer consortiums led by Denison Mines and Teck Corporation, together with the province, concluded that a daily commuting workforce from the neighboring towns of Dawson Creek and Chetwynd was out of the question. They also ruled against the setting up of work camps at the mine sites, following the general trend throughout Canada since the mid 1960s for new resource towns to be built separately from the companies' operations. However, despite the creation of organizationally distinct self-governing municipalities, companies were still responsible for housing their employees.[4] Tumbler Ridge was to be different.

The authority of the province was paramount in all these "nonmining" decisions, and its "main objective [was] the implementation of its economic and development policies including full employment, increased real income through resource allocation, price stability and regional balance." The experiment was designed to produce a socially cohesive, financially viable, self-governing community that would be conducive to the creation of a stable workforce.[5]

Tumbler Ridge was built in record time in response to this charter. In spring of 1982, there were only a few cleared patches of forest and a number of camp trailers on the muddy terrain. By 1983, the town had a permanent population of 2,359. In 1990, the population was 4,800, and in June 1994, about 4,500—all housed in comfortable dwellings with every conceivable modern amenity. In 1986, when most of the construction had been completed, there were 1,479 housing units consisting of 748 family houses, 318 comfortable mobile homes, and 413 apartments. About 80 percent of the permanent workforce at that time worked for one or the other of the two coal-mining companies, while the remainder were employed by the municipality, business and personal services, construction, education, tourism, small business, and natural-gas development. Tumbler Ridge was to provide a model on which other resource communities could be constructed—a utopian experiment in total planning—and the architects were enthusiastic in their belief that the town would create a high quality of life for its citizens and

> contribute to the attraction and retention of a stable work force. [This would be achieved by encouraging as settlers] people who enjoy the challenge of frontier living and are willing to work together to design the town's social and recreational services . . . and by providing the structure for a family oriented community, with high quality residential neighbourhoods, a downtown focus, and parks and pathways for the town's citizens, all integrated sensitively with a wilderness environment.[6]

The District of Tumbler Ridge was incorporated on April 9, 1981, and the first municipal elections, for a mayor and aldermen, were held in 1984. Today, town-government personnel include a clerk-administrator, deputy clerk, treasurer, superintendent of public works, building inspector, director of community services, an economic development officer, and a fire chief. Its public buildings include a distinctively designed town hall, public works buildings, fire hall, and police (RCMP) barracks. Municipal taxes are based on the assessed value of property and improvements, and municipal services are comprehensive by any urban standard.

Tumbler Ridge boasts a health center where related services are housed under one roof: doctor, dentist, optometrist, ambulance, public-health nurse, X-ray technician, physiotherapist, counseling, and emergency care. There are two elementary schools, a senior secondary school, a branch of Northern Lights College for advanced education and "quality life style" courses. Equinox Alternate School provides special education, and Municipal Daycare operates an innovative preschool program.

The Community Centre is the centerpiece of indoor recreation in Tumbler Ridge. This $13 million multiuse building serves the recreational and cultural needs of the residents. In many ways the center is the equivalent of the

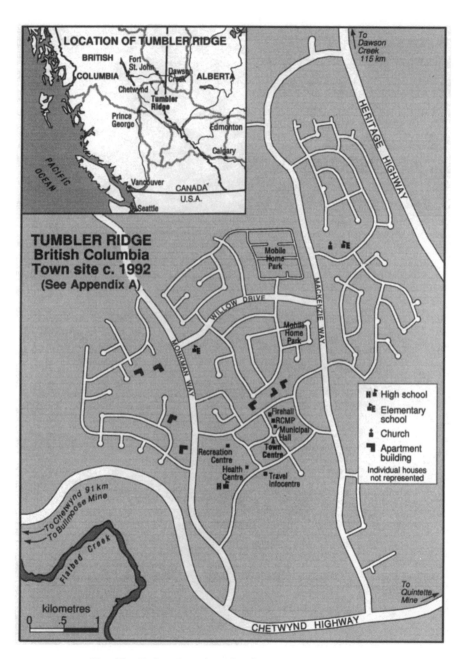

Tumbler Ridge, British Columbia, Town Site, c. 1992

Kleinzee Rec. Club, but the center, in keeping with its utopian context in a planned community, houses much more: a club for teenagers, an art gallery, a library, a cafeteria, banquet facilities, the Tumbler Ridge daycare, an elaborate aquatic center that boasts among other things a twenty-five-meter indoor pool, squash and racquetball courts, and patio sundecks.

The municipality also promotes parks and outdoor recreation—hiking, fishing, snowmobiling, cross-country skiing, canoeing, boating, four-wheeling, horseback riding, and a magnificent nine-hole golf course. It also provides baseball diamonds, soccer fields, tennis and volleyball courts, and skating rinks.

There are twelve churches and more than fifty businesses and services, including a bank, a department store, a liquor store, three hair salons, a hardware store, a garage and service station, a drug store, seven restaurants, and several clothing stores. The industrial and commercial site accommodates a branch of B.C. Hydro, machine and welding shops, a glass and collision shop, a brake-and-wheel service station, a veterinary clinic, a dry cleaner's, a propane distributor, and more.

The main transportation services to and from Tumbler Ridge are largely by the paved highway via Chetwynd, with daily bus connections and regular freight and courier services. B.C. Rail constructed a costly, freight-only electric line to link Tumbler Ridge with Port Rupert, and the mines use two trains a day to transport coal to the coast. Various private helicopter flights operate at regular times during the day; and an airport with a paved runway, four thousand feet long, and a terminal building has been built a few miles out of town.

Is Tumbler Ridge a Company Town?

James Allen would argue that Tumbler Ridge is not a company town in his terms because the operating companies, like the company in Bisbee, Arizona, in 1966, do not own or control the town's infrastructure, notably the housing (see my introductory chapter). Moreover, the administration of the town and all the social services and programs are the total concern of the provincial government. In that sense, Tumbler Ridge is a provincial incorporated town. If it is referred to as a company town, this is only because more than 80 percent of its residents are employed by Bullmoose or Quintette mining companies. On the other hand, it might be argued that the planners of this utopian community unwittingly created a community with most of the attributes of a company town. And that, by and large, the only attraction of working for a company at Tumbler Ridge is not the beautiful wilderness setting or the utopian planning of the town, but the job—the wages and salaries earned. One source gives the average individual income in 1987 as $36,000 (Canadian),[7] and the 1991 Canada Census reports that the average household income for Tumbler Ridge is about $82,375. The projected average household income for 1995 was $123,000.

In July 1994, it was apparent that the original housing plan had taken a new course. Rather than buy their own houses in Tumbler Ridge on the Central Mortgage and Housing Corporation (CMHC) plan, many miners had discovered alternative ways of housing themselves and their families. They soon concluded that they would be better off financially if they bought property in Grande Prairie, Dawson Creek, and Chetwynd and commuted to Tumbler Ridge on a semiweekly basis. For example, a man or woman with spouse and children living in the family home in Dawson Creek might travel to work at Tumbler Ridge, share an apartment with several fellow workers for four days, and spend the remainder of the week back home with the family. Property values in Tumbler Ridge dropped enormously as a consequence of this practice (coupled with the general downward trend of the housing market in North America). For example, a $75,000 home purchased in 1987 had a value of only $50,000 or less in 1994. The low prices in turn gave the two mining companies an opportunity to purchase the large number of vacant houses and apartments in Tumbler Ridge for rental purposes, thereby depressing the market still further and making the companies party to the migrancy. Many people claimed that by renting from the company at low prices, they were saving enough to buy homes elsewhere as an investment for the future.

The failure of the housing scheme was not the only feature of the utopian community to be criticized by the residents. They complained about the doctors and dentists, for example, and about lack of proper health facilities; they complained that the three-shift system imposed by the companies prevented them from getting to know their neighbors properly unless they happened to be on the same shift; and some observed that the careful, innovative physical planning of Tumbler Ridge produced, presumably unwittingly, a highly segmented physical "community" in which the three residential areas are separated not only from each other but also from everything else in the town. This latter aspect soon became evident to my wife and me when we stayed in town.

A similar "separation" philosophy seems also to have been applied in the spatial planning of each residential cluster, as is evident from the complex configurations of avenues, ways, places, streets, crescents, and loops (see town-site plan of Tumbler Ridge, map 5). Though the plan was aesthetically pleasing to some planners, made Tumbler Ridge safe for children, and ensured privacy for nearly every house and dwelling unit, it seems to have contributed to a further degree of isolation for many individuals and families. The planners, in their attempt to design a wilderness utopia for the employees of two operating companies, had, in fact, created a company town from a municipal base. In this case, the Province of British Columbia was to be the company.

What is the future for the Tumbler Ridge experiment? Alison Gill argues that formal separation of the "community system" (town) from the "corporate system" (companies) produced ambiguities and subsequent confusion in people's minds regarding their informal associations in everyday life. She blames this on the planners. Great efforts were made in Tumbler Ridge to distance the community organizationally from the resource companies—an attempt to create a sense of commitment to the community and thus a resilience to the economic uncertainty of the mining industry. But, Gill argues, regardless of how much the community might like to free itself from dependence on the mining companies, this is an unrealistic expectation.[8] Recent developments have dictated the immediate future for Tumbler Ridge itself (as distinct from the concept).

Declining prices and sales volume for metallurgical coal since 1998 led Teck Corporation to close the Quintette Coal Mine on August 31, 2000, and lay off all 500 miners. Bullmoose Mine, which employs 250, is scheduled to close in March 2003. Houses now sell for $25,900, condos for $9,900.

In chapter 13, I discussed the procedures and rituals for entering and leaving Kleinzee. While there are no high fences, locked gates, or visible security guards marking off the town of Tumbler Ridge, there are some parallels and similarities. Perhaps without meaning to, the planners of Tumbler Ridge created a town which presents a very unwelcoming image to outsiders. The absence of encouraging signals inviting them to "come inside" makes visitors feel that they are on the threshold of a private world full of "closedness." Even the WELCOME TO TUMBLER RIDGE billboard stands out starkly by itself (off the main highway) against the background of the topography after which the town is named. Outsiders are free to visit the shops, hotel, bars, restaurants, liquor store, and golf course. But few venture into the town's maze of streets and dead ends.

When my wife and I first arrived on the outskirts of Tumbler Ridge, we looked for an appropriate signal that would legitimize, so to speak, our presence in town. It was as if we needed to be given permission to enter this aloof town. As things turned out, it was the staff of the British Columbia Travel Information Centre who initiated us, providing our first contact with Tumbler Ridgers. This introduction could well have occurred at the town hall, or even at the service station, the local bar, or the check-in desk at the hotel, but none of these would have inaugurated us as capably as the two people at the travel bureau, both of whom were connected with the mining companies through their spouses. The relevant detail, however, is that some form of communication, some rite of passage, seemed necessary to facilitate our crossing of the blurred line between the outside world and the town. In truth, though, we did not count ourselves adequately incorporated into this alien territory (irrespective of the Kleinzee experience) until we had made the required journey to the actual site of the Quintette mine, twenty-five kilometers beyond town limits. Here the company's security team, in conjunction with its housing department, legitimized our presence and allotted us our prearranged accommodation in a fully furnished, company-owned apartment.

The argument presented here reiterates the simple principle that some rite of passage (and the patterns of communication associated with it) seems to be central to the processes of entry to new and unusual places; and that the complexity and intensity of those processes vary according to degrees of community closedness and the authority and power of the host institution. But why did the thoughts, emotions, and experiences that triggered the feeling of ritual readiness to be "processed" in a portal rite at Tumbler Ridge not surface the preceding night as we settled in at our motel in Chetwynd, the neighboring former frontier town? The answer is surely that the Chetwynd portal is a wide one— full of "openness," if you will—where the town was ready and waiting for us and other transients to spend a night, patronize the restaurants, buy souvenirs. As a frontier town, Chetwynd was also open for shopping sprees from loggers and coal miners, as evidenced by the rugged, easy-to-clean tables and chairs in the restaurants and the sturdy liquid-soap dispensers in the motel showers (no baths, no bars of soap, and only dark-brown towels). Unlike end-of-the-road towns such as Tumbler Ridge and Kleinzee, moreover, Chetwynd has interchangeable front and back doors, providing some of the welcoming anonymity of a drive-thru restaurant. It was Chetwynd's public and commercial orientation that gave it its openness and that distinguished it from company and company-like towns with their built-in structures of material and symbolic closedness.

Our arrival in Tumbler Ridge coincided with the start of a long weekend: both mines had shut down for the holiday, many people had left town, and most of the restaurants and some shops were closed. These long weekends, with temporary shutdowns, give people an opportunity to leave town and "get away from it all." We soon learned that people found these escapes necessary to ward off or cure the oppressive closed-in feelings they experience from time to time—what they call "cabin fever." These temporary escapes to neighboring towns like Chetwynd, Dawson Creek, and even Edmonton are so common that, as one person put it, "just when you think you are away from your neighbors, friends, and bosses [when you are out of town], who do you run into but the bank manager, a schoolteacher, and your next door neighbour—all doing the same thing." It did not take much comparative reflection to realize that the institution of long weekend shutdowns was a close parallel of Kleinzee's "De Beers weekends," when the mine closed at noon on certain Saturdays to give people an opportunity to leave town for a couple of days—"to get away from it all" as a cure for, or to offset, Kleinzee-itis.[9]

Appendix 1

Dr. Hans Merensky and Alexander Bay

Parallel diamond discoveries occurred at Alexander Bay, north of both Kleinzee and Port Nolloth, shortly after the Oubeep discovery on August 15, 1925, south of Port Nolloth. In this appendix I clarify Dr. Hans Merensky's role in the establishment of the Namaqualand diamond industry and indicate how his short-lived operation in the region lost out to the state, and how Oppenheimer (and his business consortium) acquired most of "Merensky's" fabulous diamonds.

Merensky (1871—1952), a geologist, was the son of a German missionary who arrived in South Africa in 1904 to carry out some geological surveys. He was detained for five years by the South Africa government during World War I in a camp near Pietermaritzburg. On his release in 1924, virtually penniless, he was put on the track of a platinum deposit by prospectors, which led to his discovery of the fabulous 48 kilometer platinum reef in the Lydenburg district—a discovery that left him comfortably off, if not enormously rich.[1]

While Merensky was visiting his family in Germany in 1926, after a twenty-year absence, he went to London for a few days on matters related to his platinum enterprise. There he heard a rumor in the wings of the London Stock Exchange that diamonds had been discovered in Namaqualand. He immediately cabled his secretary in Johannesburg to verify the rumor. Eight days later, as he walked into the foyer of the Adlon Hotel in Berlin, the receptionist handed him the reply:

PROSPECTOR NAMED CARSTENS HAS FOUND DIAMONDS IN NAMAQUALAND.[2]

The diamonds had in fact been discovered more than eighteen months

Appendix 1. Jack Carstens and Merensky
Jack Carstens (left) with Dr. Hans Merensky in 1930.

before, in August 1925. Merensky immediately cut short his overseas visit and arrived back in South Africa on December 15, 1926.[3] He went directly to Johannesburg to organize an expedition of experts to go to Namaqualand to investigate the diamond scene and, if possible, take options on properties. While Merensky attended to urgent business in connection with his platinum venture, the high-powered prospecting party went ahead. The group included two geologists, Dr. I. Celliers and Dr. E. Reuning, a prospector named Mare, and General Manie Maritz. Maritz was known to every Boer farmer in Namaqualand, and his job was "to introduce the two geologists to the owners of likely-looking properties."[4] When Merensky arrived in Namaqualand toward the end of December, most members of the geological team had left. Only Reuning remained.

Merensky and Reuning seem to have disliked each other: when Merensky was selecting geologists to work with, Reuning was in fact his second choice. However, Reuning had had experience of the coastal diamonds in South-West Africa and was surely the best person for the job.[5] He was prepared to be prospector, rather than theoretical geologist. In Lehmann's account,

> the two men had totally different theories about the derivation of the diamond deposits along the South-West coast. Reuning supported the river theory. He was convinced that the source of the stones was inland, and that diamonds had been

carried down to the coast by rivers, and had then been thrown back by the sea, and embedded in the terrace deposits.

Merensky, on the other hand, firmly upheld his theory that the diamonds originated from an undersea pipe, and had no connection with the stones found in the interior.[6]

Without pursuing the finer points, Merensky's theory was based on four propositions: (1) that the South-West coast diamonds originated from an undersea pipe; (2) that the presence of these diamonds is correlated with beds of fossilized oyster shells; (3) that a change in ocean currents had brought colder water, which had killed off a vast, ancient oyster population; (4) that the same current was strong enough to redistribute diamonds along the coast among these oyster populations.

Merensky's speculations do not seem to have stood the tests of time, but, ironically, his obsession with the oyster-shell hypothesis led him and his team to uncover vast riches in an incredibly short period of time. Roughly a month of prospecting yielded 6,890 diamonds, all gemstones, with a total weight of 12,549 carats and valued at about £153,000—more than £12 a carat. Reuning did most of the work, spending "days lying on the ground and crawling around in circles, looking for favourable indicators that would give him a lead for plotting new trenches across the Oyster Line."[7] Diamonds had been discovered in the area earlier, but it was Trench 3 that produced the first "oyster line" gems. Trench 4a yielded a total of 168 diamonds in one day. Ten of them weighed more than 10 carats: the largest weighed more than 71 carats—a perfect blue-white stone. Merensky was exceedingly lucky, and while his Oyster Line theory did (for the wrong reasons) lead his team in the right direction, the success of the enterprise was built on the work of the prospectors who were there before him.

As fate would have it, Merensky and Reuning were introduced to a solicitor from Springbok named Israel Gordon. Gordon, his brother, and two others had already found diamonds in the Alexander Bay area, and together they constituted an informal syndicate. They had heard of Merensky, and believing him to be rich and a potential buyer of their property they invited him and Reuning to visit their claims on December 28, 1926. Reuning and Merensky examined the claims, and Merensky decided to make an attempt to purchase them, leaving the negotiations to Reuning. That evening, Reuning reached a verbal agreement with the syndicate, which allowed a six-month option (£500 payable immediately) over the claims from February 1, 1927; and for 50 percent of the value of stones won during the option period to go to the syndicate.[8]

Within a few days, Merensky made a formal offer to buy the Gordon syndicate's property, which the latter accepted without question and signed on January 4, 1927: "£17,500 in cash, of which £1000 was payable immediately, and the remaining £16,500 on 31 January, 1927."[9]

Merensky, who contrary to the Gordon syndicate's belief lacked the capital to pay the balance of the purchase price, left Reuning in charge of the prospecting program and set off for Cape Town on January 8, 1927, to find £16,500. Reuning had already agreed to contribute £2,000, if necessary; and Merensky had funds of his own for a similar amount. But no one in Cape Town was interested, and in Johannesburg he received more rejections. His backer of previous mining ventures, Ignatius Dessau in London, refused to participate beyond £1,000. In desperation, Merensky thought of contacting the financier G. A. E. Becker, but they were not on speaking terms at the time (for reasons that were never made clear). With only a week left before the option to purchase expired, he telephoned Becker's partner H. Ohlthaver, a mining financier, who had been associated with a successful diamond enterprise in South-West Africa, to arrange a meeting. "Merensky told him about Alexander Bay and of the money it required. . . . [Merensky] asked for £12,500 at the same time promising Ohlthaver no less than 60% in the Syndicate to be formed. Ohlthaver decided to come in on these terms and gave Merensky the sum of £12,500. . . . Ohlthaver, was [incidentally] bound under the terms of [his] partnership agreement [with Becker] to offer Becker 50% of any business he might undertake."[10]

Within a few hours, the "Hans Merensky Association" (the H.M. Association) was formed: Merensky, Reuning, and Dessau together contributed £5,000, giving them a 40 percent interest. This gave Ohltaver and Becker a 60 percent interest, which they shared equally. Merensky's luck held. His friendship with Becker was renewed and they sat down together in the Rand Club to think of ways of obtaining further capital. They selected, without Ohltaver's knowledge, Sir Julius Jeppe, who was chairman of S.A. Townships, Mining and Finance Corporation Ltd., and Sir Abe Bailey, who held the controlling interest in Jeppe's company.

> The outcome was that Sir Julius, some of his own friends and certain associated companies of Sir Abe Bailey's Group also subscribed £12,500, thus making a paid up capital of £30,000. As regards the allocation of shares, Merensky received 20,000 shares as vendor's consideration, giving him therefore a 50% interest, while Becker and Ohlthaver had 25% and Jeppe 25%. There was no formal contract between the original members of the H.M. Association nor were share certificates issued.[11]

For Merensky, finding the money had proved very difficult, because he could provide no concrete evidence to support his speculations. Had he not been so remiss about keeping in touch with Reuning, who had now found more rich deposits of diamonds, the outcome could have been very different. The telegram to Merensky reporting Reuning's success was never received because Merensky was not in his office and could not be located. It read: SIX DAYS [OPERATIONS] COULD COVER THE TOTAL SUM. Reuning had carefully worded the telegram so that only Merensky would understand that a significant and valuable find of diamonds had been made.

Merensky did not return to Alexander Bay until February 2, 1927. Only then did he hear the incredible news that, in his absence, the total number of diamonds recovered was 2,762, weighing 4,309 carats, an average of more than 1.5 carats per stone and valued at about £26,500. When Reuning learned of the large participation given to Jeppe, which he regarded as quite unnecessary, and of Merensky's dismissal of his own request for one-third participation in the association, he was incensed.[12] And so he should have been: he had done most of the work and made most of the decisions regarding the siting of trenches and pits.

Merensky now applied to the minister of mines for permission to start mining, asking that, after the discoverer's claims had been allotted, the rest of the Alexander Bay area should not be thrown open as a public digging, as was customary in the case of alluvial discoveries, but should be leased to a competent concern. The H.M. Association offered to negotiate with the government for a lease of the area on terms of either one-third of the profit or one-quarter of the gross value of diamonds accruing to the government.[13]

The proposal was turned down and everything was held in abeyance until the new bill designed to amend the Precious Stones Act of 1925 was passed. After the government's refusal, Merensky drove to Cape Town to alert the prime minister to the dangers of throwing the area open to diggers, who already were descending on Port Nolloth. One, it would flood the market with gemstones, and two, many fortune seekers might perish in the semidesert. While Merensky's mission to the prime minister was surely inspired by a genuine sense of altruism, he must also have wanted to protect his and his associates' financial interests.

On February 22, 1927, the government issued the first of several proclamations prohibiting prospecting for diamonds until further notice. The ban applied to all Crown land and farms (except, as we have already seen, Kleinzee because of its freehold status). Prohibition came into force on February 25, but a grace period of eight days was allowed to wash gravel already excavated.

The issue of discoverer's rights had complex ramifications. After looking

into the matter, the state eventually recognized five different deposits of diamonds, based on the existence of terraces above the existing sea level. In
other words, it was accepted that the Alexander Bay diamonds had been deposited on these terraces at widely different periods, thereby "proving" the
existence of multiple deposits, and making the issue of multiple discoverer's
certificates consistent with the law. Discoverers' certificates were eventually
issued to Reuning, Caplan, Papert, Gelb, and Sonny Kennedy, all of whom
had discovered diamonds at different times and on different terraces. The
discoveries of Caplan, Papert, Gelb, and Kennedy all preceded Reuning's discoveries. Merensky was not a discoverer in this sense.[14]

In the meanwhile, the state was planning to establish the state diggings at
Alexander Bay.[15] To simplify the procedure, the minister of mines suggested
that the H.M. Association acquire all the certificates associated with all the
diggings. Negotiations began immediately and were eminently successful: the
H.M. Association now owned all five of the discoverer's rights. Further discoverer's certificates were later issued to Solomon Rabinowitz for his important
Buchuberg discovery, and to a prospector named Dunkels for a questionable
discovery.

Oppenheimer

When Oppenheimer saw the quality of H.M. Association's parcel of diamonds on the tables of the Diamond Board for South-West Africa in Cape
Town at the end of February 1927, he was greatly perturbed: a prospecting
parcel of 6,890 gemstones weighing 12,549 carats, valued at roughly
£153,000, had been unearthed in just over a month. A huge deluge of gemstones from Alexander Bay could prove fatal to the diamond industry, which
Oppenheimer was determined to control. So, on behalf of the Diamond Syndicate, he made an offer to the minister of mines to buy the total output of the
Alexander Bay fields, provided no more diggings were proclaimed after the
present ones were worked out. He also resolved to acquire a significant interest in the H.M. Association. By July 1929 he had bought £500,000 worth of
shares, and within another four months he dominated the group.[16] At the
same time, Oppenheimer was scheming to acquire Kleinzee and all the farm
options acquired by G. S. Ronaldson, a Kimberley businessman (see chapters
1, 2, and 3). His plan was to establish Cape Coast Exploration Ltd. by the end
of 1927 (see chapters 2, 3, and 4).

But first Oppenheimer had had to get to the H.M. Association and acquire a controlling interest. As a first step, he approached his friend, G. A. E. Becker (Olthaver's senior partner) and negotiated an agreement with him. The main points of the agreement, dated April 2, 1927, were as follows:

1. Oppenheimer would purchase a 4/25th share in the H.M. Association capital of 62,500 shares of £1 each; i.e., 10,000 shares, at £15 each.
2. Oppenheimer would be granted the sole right until April 30, 1927, to buy a further 68/125th interest; i.e., 34,000 shares at the price at which the Diamond Syndicate was prepared to sell, and could sell to any other person.
3. Becker was to use his best endeavors to secure for Oppenheimer the sole and exclusive right to purchase all the diamonds produced from the association's areas, properties, and claims.[17]

This agreement was possible because Becker had bought out Olthaver's share in the H.M. Association in March 1927. By way of an incentive to play the Oppenheimer game, Oppenheimer told Becker that he would seek to get him appointed as a director of the Consolidated Diamond Mines of South-West Africa Ltd.

Having got his own way in his negotiations with Becker, Oppenheimer, acting for the Anglo American Corporation and Solly Joel (the Barnato Brothers), who had agreed to come in on a 50–50 basis with Oppenheimer, purchased Becker's and Merensky's entire interests, thereby achieving a 74 percent interest in the H.M. Association.[18] The details of this maneuver may be summarized as follows:

(1) Becker received a total of £500,000 between April 5, 1927, and July 12, 1929, from Oppenheimer's purchase of 25,475 shares @ £19.60 (approx.) per share.
(2) Merensky received £1,103,750 from the sale of his 20,750 shares @ £53.2 per share. These include Dessau's 1,000 shares bought for £1,000, for which Merensky paid £25,000.
(3) Jeppe retained his 16,275 shares, constituting 26 percent of the total holding in April 1927.

It was not until July 1929 that all these transactions had been completed, thereby changing the character of the H.M. Association to a more formal joint venture controlled now by trusts and companies as follows:[19]

Kimberley Investment Trust, 16.95%;   Oppenheimer's domain
(Sir Ernest Oppenheimer)

Anglo American Corporation 20.435%   "
(Oppenheimer Chairman)

Barnato Brothers;   36.575%   "
(Solly Joel, et al.)

Sir Abe Bailey's Group,   26.04%
(includes Sir Julius Jeppe)   ———
                                100.00

The new Precious Stones Act, having been amended and modified many times since it was first tabled, was finally passed in November 1927. It was the state's intention, under the new act, to control both the production and disposal of diamonds to prevent a flooding of the market that would ruin the industry. Serious altercations between the H.M. Association and the state ensued. Eventually, the state proclaimed the five blocks of discoverers' claims at Alexander Bay to be an "alluvial digging," as from March 17, 1928, which enabled the H.M. Association to work its claims, rather than prospect. The same proclamation decreed that the whole of the Alexander Bay area, exclusive of the discoverers' claims, be a State Alluvial Diggings in terms of (sections 75–77) of the new act.

The H.M. Association began mining in earnest immediately on March 17, 1928, and by January 1929 it employed 240 white workers, mainly Namaqualanders, in accordance with the state's regional political and economic policy. By the end of August 1929, all claims had been worked out and all conglomerates crushed and washed, producing a total of 461,394 carats during that 17 ½ month period.[20]

The politics of the negotiations between the H.M. Association and the state became a major preoccupation after the passage of the new act because it involved not only how much mining was permitted, but also guidelines for the release and sale of diamonds. In these matters, Oppenheimer was always active, forging financial and micropolitical alliances between the parties. He was also a master evaluator and, after inspecting the parcel of "Merensky Diamonds," he realized that their superior quality and size put them in a class of their own—one that no other mine at the time could compete with. When the H.M. Association applied for the release of its diamonds, the "bort and the rubbish" were excluded from the parcel to increase its value still further.

The State Alluvial Diggings, established in March 1928, was now producing its own diamonds. Thus, when the H.M. Association applied to the state for the release of 100,000 carats for sale in August 1928, the minister regarded the request as premature. Talks between Oppenheimer and the minister followed, and by October the government had changed its mind. However, while it agreed to release of 100,000 carats of Merensky diamonds, the release was conditional on the Diamond Syndicate's purchasing 100,000 carats of state diamonds at the same time. Clearly, the delay on the part of the government was to enable the State Alluvial Diggings to produce sufficient number of quality stones in order to obtain the best deal from Oppenheimer's Diamond Syndicate. The state continued to control the H.M. Association until it went into voluntary liquidation on October 31, 1929.

The story of the H.M. Association and Oppenheimer's connection with it does not end with its voluntary liquidation because the diamonds had still to be sold. In 1929, there were a series of negotiations for the renewal of sales agreements due to producers' dissatisfaction with the method of selling their diamonds through the Diamond Syndicate. With regard to the Merensky diamonds, Oppenheimer, representing the syndicate, ceded the agreement with the H.M. Association to the Diamond Corporation as from January 1, 1930. Eventually, according to Rudd and Watson, "the Diamond Corporation not only took over the H.M. Association's stock of diamonds for £3,199,369, but also the Syndicate's stock of [the cartel] Conference Producers' diamonds for £4,932,000 and the syndicate's stock of nonconference (excluding the H.M. Association) diamonds for £4,901,186."[21]

By 1929, Oppenheimer was in full control of the diamond industry. He became chairman of De Beers in 1929, not because the company wanted him but because De Beers needed his power and influence. Oppenheimer continued his efforts to secure control over production of all important sources of diamonds in South Africa and South-West Africa except the State Alluvial Diggings.

Appendix 2

Income Comparisons

Table 2.1. Monthly Income of 208 Employees (with Occupations) on the Kleinzee Mine under Cape Coast, January 1932.

Category	Occupation	Monthly Income	Ratio of Income to a General Manager's
Senior Staff N=5	General manager (equivalent)	£100	–
	Manager	£75	1.33
	Mine secretary	£65	1.54
	Mine engineer	£50	2.00
	Mine pit superintendent	£45	2.22
	Protection officer	£45	2.22
Staff N=19	Plant superintendent	£40	2.50
	Skilled artisan (not regarded as staff by senior staff)	£36	2.77
	Pulsator superintendent	£35	2.86
	Compound manager	£30	3.33
	Medical orderly	£30	3.33
	Assistant protection officer	£30	3.33
	Storekeeper and manager's clerk	£30	3.33
	Assistant plant superintendent	£30	3.33
	Supervisors (11)	£30 (or less)	3.33
Handymen, drivers, painter, guards N=17	Unskilled "artisan" handymen (4)	£18	5.55
	Driver (manager's car)	£18	5.55
	Painter	£15	6.66
	Guards (9)	£14±	7.14
	Lorry drivers (2)	£10	10.00
Laborers N=167	Laborers (white) (138)	£9±	11.11
	Laborers (Coloured) (28)	£4-11-0	20.00
	Guard (Coloured)	£4-10-0	22.22
Domestic servants N=8	Domestic servants (Coloured) (8)	£3 or less	33.33

Note: All employees are white unless otherwise indicated. The eight domestic servants listed were not employed by the company.

Table 2.2. Average Monthly Income, January 1993, of All 2,409 Male and Female Employees on the Kleinzee Mine

Monthly incomes (in Rand) as determined by Paterson Band*	Black Employees			Coloured Employees			White Employees			All Employees		
	M	F	T	M	F	T	M	F	T	M	F	T
A1–A2 R959–1,332	211 (8.75)	–	211 (8.75)	483 (20.04)	96 (3.98)	579 (24.03)	8 (0.33)	3 (0.12)	11 (0.46)	702 (29.14)	99 (4.11)	801 (33.25)
B1–B2+ R1,333–1,867	169 (7.0)	–	169 (7.0)	365 (15.15)	50 (2.07)	415 (17.22)	40 (1.66)	24 (1.00)	64 (2.66)	574 (23.83)	74 (3.07)	648 (26.90)
B3–B4 R1,868–2,617	74 (3.1)	1 (0.04)	75 (3.14)	317 (13.16)	29 (1.20)	346 (14.40)	27 (1.12)	48 (2.00)	75 (3.12)	418 (17.35)	78 (3.24)	496 (20.60)
C1–C2 R2,618–3,674	1 (0.04)	–	1 (0.04)	88 (3.65)	10 (0.4)	98 (4.06)	117 (4.90)	19 (0.80)	136 (5.64)	206 (8.55)	29 (1.20)	235 (9.75)
C3–C4 R3,675–5,252	1 (0.04)	–	1 (0.04)	33 (1.37)	4 (0.16)	37 (1.53)	103 (4.27)	22 (0.91)	125 (5.20)	136 (5.64)	26 (1.08)	162 (6.72)
D1–D4 R5,253–9,654	–	–	–	2 (0.08)	–	2 (0.08)	57 (2.36)	–	57 (2.36)	60 (2.50)	–	60 (2.50)
E1–E3 R9,655++	–	–	–	–	–	–	7 (0.29)	–	7 (0.29)	7 (0.29)	–	7 (0.29)
All Bands	456 (18.93)	1 (0.04)	457 (18.97)	1,288 (53.50)	189 (7.85)	1,477 (61.31)	359 (14.90)	116 (4.82)	475 (19.71)	2,103 (87.30)	306 (12.70)	2,409 (100)

*M = Male; F = Female; T = Total

Note: This table shows relative positions in the Paterson band system and illustrates social differentiation by "race." Some bands have been collapsed. The numbers in parenthesis show percent of total workforce. See also figure 12.1.

Table 2.3. Paterson Band Listings for Various Occupations, Showing Income and Racial (Ethnic) Distribution

Number of Employees	Summary of Occupations	Paterson Band Range	Average Monthly Income (approx.)	Ratio of Income to General Manager's
7 All white	General manager	E+	R15,000 includes car allowance	–
	Other senior managers and professional staff (e.g., physicians)	E	R12,500 includes car allowance	1.2
41 40 = White 1 = Black	Other managers; divisional, section, and mining engineers; plant and security superintendents; loss-control coordinator; industrial relations and community services superintendent; assistant plant superintendents; etc.	D2–D4	R9,385 includes car allowance	1.60
19 White = 17 Coloured = 2	Senior mine foremen, retail-store manager, project accountants, mine secretary, dragline overseer, chief technician, etc.	D1	R5,684	2.64
162 White = 125 Coloured = 37	Social therapist; senior industrial relations officers; senior training officers; senior telecom technician; senior lab. technologist; senior industrial rel. officer; senior draughtsman; matron; maintenance planners; information center coordinators; various engineering foremen; department heads and assistant accountants; training officers; schoolteachers; senior security officers and surveyors; plant, mine, and farms foremen; senior sister; design draughtsmen; chief sorter; head chefs; chargehands; buyer; etc.	C3–C4	R4,463	3.36
235 White = 136 Coloured = 98 Black = 1	Welder, transport officer, telecom technicians, stores supervisors, riggers, nurses, preprimary teachers, plumbers, patrol mechanics, personnel trainee, panel beater, junior engineer, fitters, electricians, diesel mechanics and fitters, carpenters, butchery supervisor, boilermakers, auto electricians, liaison officers, security officers, PRO, painters, masons, jr. draughtsmen, buyer, etc.	C1–C2	R3,146	4.77

(Table 2.3, continued)

Number of Employees	Summary of Occupations	Paterson Band Range	Average Monthly Income (approx.)	Ratio of Income to General Manager's
496 White = 75 Coloured = 346 Black = 75	Warehouse controller; carpenter (unqualified); training assistants; teacher grade 1; staff nurse; secretaries grade 4; shift, road, haulage, records, farm, bedrock, liquor store, plant, prospecting, and rec. club supervisors; drilling, blasting, and stripping supervisors; meat cutters; dairyteam leader; assistant security officers; probe and augerdrill operators; vacation students; crane operators; security guards; senior clerks; secretaries; assistant masons grade 3; maintenance planning clerks; large front-end loader, dozer, hydraulic crane, and haul-truck operators; various electricians, diesel fitters, and boiler makers; airfield controller; etc.	B3–B4	R2,242	6.69
648 White = 64 Black = 169 Coloured = 415	Various bus, truck, and shovel operators; front-end loaders; typists and word-processor operators; surveyor's assistants; spray gun operators; various clerks; security guards grade 2; printing machine operators; painter hands; printing machine operators; powerstation operators; nursing assistants; librarian; meat cutters; hospital receptionist; drillers and blasters; field servicemen; crane truck and DMS operators; cooks grades 1 and 2; carpenter's assistants; bedrock teamleaders; various unqualified diesel fillers; boilermakers, electricians etc.; waitresses; tractor operators; swimming pool supervisors; shepherds; sewage plant operators; sales assistants; security guards grade 1; plant operators grade 1; drill hole operators; diamond sorters; drivers; dairy operators; barmen; various apprentices; etc.	B1–B2+	R1,600	9.37
801 White = 11 Black = 211 Coloured = 579	Swimming-pool attendants, stores helpers, stable attendant, senior cleaners, wine steward, sandblasters, roads helpers, retail assistants, probe drill assistants, pavementbreaker operators, nursery-school helper, meat packer, maintenance and lawnmower attendants, laundry and kitchen assistants, jackhammermen, hospital helpers, farm-hands, brickmaking and auger drill helpers, artisan helpers, cleaners, laborers, bedrock cleaners, etc.	A1–A2	R1,145	13.10

Note: Table shows estimated numbers for all 2,409 employees on the Kleinzee mine, January 1993. Unlike in table 2.2, incomes are given as mean averages of various bands, not the lowest in each range; thus, many workers in band A1 earn only R959, not R1,145.

List of Abbreviations

AACA	Anglo American Corporation Archive, Johannesburg
CA	Cape Archives, Cape Town
CAD	State Archives, Central Archives Depot, Pretoria
CAP	William and Jack Carstens, private papers
CAST	Consolidated African Selection Trust
CDM	Consolidated Diamond Mines of South-West Africa Limited
ct.	Carat—unit of weight for precious stones, equal to 200 milligrams
DBA	De Beers Consolidated Mines Archive, Kimberley
DOA	Deeds Office Archive, Cape Town
IDB	Illicit Diamond Buying and Trading
KA	Kleinzee Museum Archive
LSEA	London School of Economics and Political Science Archive
R	Rand—South African currency adopted in 1961
RTZA(L)	Rio Tinto-Zinc Corporation Archive, London, U.K.
RTZA(N)	Rio Tinto-Zinc Mining and Exploration Ltd. Archive, Newbury, U.K.

Notes

Preface

1. The results of this research can be found in Peter Carstens, *The Social Structure of a Cape Coloured Reserve: A Study of Racial Integration and Segregation in South Africa* (Cape Town: Oxford University Press. 1966).

2. Elsewhere, I have described the process of dealing with the past and the present in one intellectual system as the diasynchronic method; i.e., the process involves coming to terms with sociocultural relationships both in time (diachronic) and in space (synchronic). Readers used to Radcliffe-Brown's artificial distinction between diachronic and synchronic might find the neologism "diasynchronic" confusing. My only intention here is to caution against making the false distinction between historical and sociological analysis, a legacy inherited from Comte's awkward distinction between social dynamics and social statics. See Peter Carstens, *The Queen's People: A Study of Hegemony, Coercion, and Accommodation* (Toronto: University of Toronto Press, 1991), p. xvi.

3. See Jack Carstens, *A Fortune through My Fingers* (Cape Town: Howard Timmins, 1962), pp. 65 ff.

Company Towns: An Introduction

1. See, for example, Charles A. Beher Jr. and Nathaniel Arbiter, "Distinctive Features of the Mineral Industries," in Edward H. Robie, ed., *Economics of the Mineral Industries: A Series of Articles by Specialists* (New York: American Inst. of Mining, Metallurgical Engineers, 1976); James Allen, *The Company Town in the American West* (Norman: University of Oklahoma Press, 1966); and J. Douglas Porteous, "The Imposed Total Environment: Pattern and Response," in *Man-Environment Systems* vol. 2 (1972) pp. 63–64. For detailed discussions on the antiquity of mining in Europe, see, for example, Oliver Davies, *Roman Mines in Europe* (Oxford: Clarendon, 1935), and Georg Agricola, *De Re Metallica*, trans. from Latin by H. C. and L. C. Hoover (New York: Dover, 1950 [1556]).

2. Lewis Mumford, *The Culture of Cities* (London: Secker & Warburg, 1946 [1938]), pp. 143–222.

3. John S. Garner, *The Company Town: Architecture and Society in the Early*

219

Industrial Age (New York: Oxford University Press, 1992), pp. 3–4; see also Richard V. Francaviglia, *Hard Places: Reading the Landscapes of America's Historic Mining Districts* (Iowa City: University of Iowa Press, 1991).

4. Agricola, *De Re Metallica*, pp. 25–26, 77–78, 97–99. See also Allen, *Company Town in the American West*, pp. 4–8, 33–34.

5. *Encyclopedia of the Social Sciences* (1963), vols. 3 and 4, s.v., "Company Towns"; Allen, *Company Town in the American West;* Francaviglia, *Hard Places*, Garner, *Company Town: Architecture and Society*, and idem, *The Model Company Town: Urban Design through Private Enterprise in Nineteenth Century New England* (Amherst: University of Massachusetts Press, 1984); and "Leclaire, Illinois: A Model Company Town (1890–1934)," *Journal of the Society of Architectural Historians* 30 (October 1971): 219–27; John Gaventa, *Power and Powerlessness: Quiescence and Rebellion in an Appalachian Valley* (Oxford: Clarendon, 1980); Rolf Knight, *Work Camps and Company Towns in Canada and the U.S.* (Vancouver: New Star, 1975); Rex Lucas, *Minetown, Milltown, Railroad: Life in Canadian Communities of Single Industry* (Toronto: University of Toronto Press, 1971); "Life in a Company Town," *New Republic* 82 (September 1937): 171; Keith Petersen, *Company Town: Potlatch, Idaho, and the Potlatch Lumber Company* (Moscow, Idaho: Latah County Historical Society, 1988); J. Douglas Porteous, "The Nature of the Company Town," *Transactions of the Institute of British Geographers* 51 (1970): 127–42; Porteous, "Imposed Total Environment," 2:63–64; Porteous, "Gold River—an Instant Town," *Geography* 55 (1970): 317–22; and Porteous, "Social Class in Atacama Company Towns," *Annals of the Association of American Geographers* 64 (1974): 409–17; D. H. Mould, "The Company Town that Outlived the Company: Haydenville, Ohio." *Journal of Cultural Geography* 5 (1985): 71–86; M. M. Mulrooney, "A Legacy of Coal: The Coal Company Towns of Southwestern Pennsylvania," *Perspectives in Vernacular Architecture* 4 (1991): 130–45; Bob Russell, *More with Less: Work Reorganization in the Canadian Mining Industry* (Toronto: University of Toronto Press, 1999); Crandall Shifflett, *Coal Towns: Life, Work, and Culture in Company Towns of the Southern Appalachia, 1880–1960* (Knoxville: University Press of Tennessee, 1991); John S. Spratt, *Thurber Texas: Life and Death of a Company Coal Town* (Austin: University of Texas Press, 1986). For an example of the political economy of "development" in an Indonesian mining town, see Kathryn M. Robinson, *Step Children of Progress* (Albany: State University of New York Press, 1986).

6. Allen, *Company Town in the American West*, pp. 4–5.

7. On Appalachia, see, for example, Mould, "Company Town that Outlived the Company," and Shifflett, *Coal Towns*.

8. M. I. A. Bulmer, "Sociological Models of the Mining Community," *Sociological Revue* 23 (1975): 85.

9. Allen, *Company Town in the American West*, pp. vii–xi, 4–9.

10. Larry Roland Stucki, "The Entropy Theory of Human Behavior: Indian Miners in Search of the Ultrastable State during a Prolonged Copper Strike" (Ph.D. thesis, University of Colorado, 1970).

11. The idea that some contemporary planned mining towns resemble suburbs is not new. In Canada, for example, the planned aluminum mining town of Kitimat in northern British Columbia and the nickel city of Thompson in northern Manitoba have both been referred to as southern suburbs without a downtown core. See Leonard B.

Siemens, *Single-Enterprise Communities in Northern Canada*, Occasional Paper No. 7, series 5 (Winnipeg: Center for Settlement Studies, University of Manitoba, 1973).

12. See *Hoover Handbook of World Business* (Austin, Texas: Reference Press, 1993). See also Colin Newbury, *The Diamond Ring: Business, Politics, and Precious Stones in South Africa, 1867–1947* (Oxford: Clarendon, 1989), and Anthony Hocking, *Oppenheimer and Son* (New York: McGraw Hill, 1973).

13. John Smalberger, *Aspects of the History of Copper Mining in Namaqualand, 1846–1931* (Cape Town: Struik, 1975). See also Owen Letcher, *Namaqualand: Cradle of Mineral Development in Southern Africa* (Johannesburg: n.p., 1932; repr. from *Mining and Industrial Magazine*); and Jan Marais, *O'okiep Copper Ltd., 1937–1987* (Springbok: O'okiep Copper Co., 1987).

14. See A. J. H. Goodwin, "Metal Working among the Early Hottentots." *South African Archaeological Bulletin* 11 (1956): 46–51.

15. See also Robert Ramsey, *Men and Mines of Newmont* (New York: Octagon, 1973).

16. See Mouat's comments on the culture of hard-rock mining in general. Jeremy Mouat, *Roaring Days* (Vancouver: University of British Columbia Press, 1995), pp. 68–72; see also Cedric E. Gregory, *A Concise History of Mining* (New York: Pergamon, 1980). It did occur to me that there might be some merit in invoking Eliade's metaphors to highlight the differences between hard-rock copper mining and alluvial diamond strip mining. But, however intriguing Eliade's fanciful analogy between obstetrics and hard-rock mining might be, the paradigm seems to misrepresent workers' sentiments toward their work. See Mircea Eliade, *The Forge and the Crucible* (London: Rider, 1962), pp. 41–44. Smalberger, *Aspects*, pp. 104 ff., includes three early photographs of copper miners (c. 1890). One shows a group of miners (men) preparing to go underground at O'okiep. Another shows miners transporting the mined ore for breaking and sorting by hand. In the third photograph, a dozen or so Nama and other black women can be seen sorting copper ore for bagging.

17. Half-ton tip trucks on rails. The word *cocopan* is probably derived from the Xhosa/Zulu word *nqukumbana*, a scotch cart that was used to transport diamondiferous gravel and "blue ground," among other things, on the very early South African diamond fields in other parts of the country. See *A Dictionary of South African English*, 4th ed., s.v., "Cocopan," and "Scotch Cart," Jean Branford, with William Branford.

18. Newbury, *Diamond Ring*.

Chapter 1

1. For some early accounts of the power and influence of De Beers, see Gardner F. Williams, *The Diamond Mines of South Africa: Some Account of their Rise and Development* (New York: Macmillan, 1902); Alpheus F. Williams, *The Genesis of the Diamond*, 2 vols. (London: Ernest Benn, 1932); Hedley A. Chilvers, *The Story of De Beers* (London: Cassell, 1939); T. E. Gregory, *Ernest Oppenheimer and the Economic Development of Southern Africa* (Cape Town: Oxford University Press, 1962). More recent works include Brian Roberts, *Kimberley: Turbulent City* (Cape Town: David Philip, 1976); Edward Jessup, *Ernest Oppenheimer: A Study in Power* (London: Collings, 1979); Patrick Harries, *Work, Culture, and Identity: Migrant Laborers in Mozambique and South Africa, c. 1860—1910* (Portsmouth, N.H.: Heinemann, 1994), esp. chap. 3.

2. The hunch that alluvial diamonds might be found in the Namaqualand region goes back to the nineteenth century, but it was only after the discovery of rich diamond deposits near Luderitzbucht in 1908 that serious attention was paid to the possibility that equally rich deposits might exist on the coastal strip south of the Orange River. See P. A. Wagner, *The Diamond Fields of Southern Africa* (Johannesburg: Transvaal Leader, 1914). There is a claim, poorly documented, that Ernst Martin, a hotel keeper at Aus, found seven small diamonds in 1909, near Alexander Bay. However, of all the early diamond prospectors in Namaqualand before the first discovery in 1925, special recognition must be given to three pioneers, William Carstens, Fred Cornell, and Solomon Rabinowitz. See Fred C. Cornell, *The Glamour of Prospecting*, facsimile ed. (Cape Town: David Philip, [1920] 1986); Carstens, *Fortune through my Fingers*; B. J. Rudd and V. U. T. Watson, *History of the Namaqualand Diamond Discoveries* (Johannesburg: E. Oppenheimer & Son, 1956). See also letter, Graaff's Trust to W. Carstens, 26 Aug. 1919; letter, F. Cornell to W. Carstens, 6 Nov. 1919 and 26 Feb. 1920, CAP; and Eric Bruton, *Diamonds* (London: N.A.G. Press, 1970), p. 59. The Union of South Africa geological survey, 1940 (pp. 79–101) also contains useful details on the occurrence of Namaqualand diamonds.

3. Rudd and Watson, *History of the Diamond Discoveries*, p. 30.

4. Dr. John Thoburn Williamson was born in Montfort, Quebec, 10 February 1907; he died in Mwadui, Tanganyika, 7 January 1958. Educated at McGill University (Ph.D. in geology, 1933), he joined Anglo American as a geologist in 1934. After a year he went to Tanganyika in the employ of the Tanganyika Diamond and Gold Development Company. In 1940, he discovered diamonds while prospecting under great hardship. In 1942, he became director of Williamson Diamonds Ltd. Williamson later entered into an arrangement with De Beers that gained him a personal fortune as well as adding to the De Beers wealth. See Heinz Heidgen, *The Diamond Seeker: The Story of John Williamson* (London: Blackie, 1959).

5. Solomon Rabinowitz set up a trading store on the Steinkopf Reserve in 1906 and, like William Carstens of Port Nolloth, prospected for minerals in Namaqualand. Shortly after Jack Carstens's discovery in 1925, Rabonowitz and several others formed a syndicate that made funds available for further diamond prospecting.

6. Dr. W. A. Humphrey's negative conclusions seem to have been influenced by his employer since a few months later, after his contract with Relly expired, Humphrey reported on Jack Carstens's discovery in some detail to the South African chapter of the Royal Society. See "Note on an Occurrence of Diamonds near Port Nolloth," *Transactions of the Royal Society of South Africa* 14, part 3 (1926): 217–18. See also P. A. Wagner and Hans Merensky, "Diamond Deposits on the Coast of Namaqualand," *Transactions of the Geological Society of South Africa* 31: 1–42. An interesting but coincidental aside to Relly's visit is that, many years later, his grandnephew, the late Gavin Relly, became chairman of Anglo American.

7. I want to point out that it was the "crater" and surrounding area that Dr. Reuning wanted Merensky to see before he went prospecting at Alexander Bay. But by the time Merensky arrived in Namaqualand (in late December 1926), Carstens and Ronaldson had already taken an option on Annex Kleinzee. Olga Lehmann, *Look beyond the Wind: The Life of Dr. Hans Merensky* (Cape Town: Howard Timmins. 1955), p. 61.

8. For a more detailed account of the Kleinzee discovery, see Carstens, *Fortune through My Fingers*.

9. See A. C. Clarke's 1928 report on Cape Coast's properties. Clarke notes the strong concentration of heavy minerals at this site—garnets, staurolite, ilmenite, and so on. A. C. Clarke, report on the Namaqualand Diamond Properties, 1928 RTZA(N).

10. See Gregory, *Ernest Oppenheimer*, pp. 170–71.

11. Robert Ripp (or Repp), an English sailor, later traveled with Sir James Alexander as cattle keeper, hunter, fisherman, and interpreter during the latter's expeditions to Namaqualand and Damaraland in 1836–37. A letter from John Montagu, the colonial secretary, dated 22 June 1850, details the nature of the initial grant. See James E. Alexander, *Expedition of Discovery into the Interior of Africa*, 2-vol. facsimile (Cape Town: Struik, [1838] 1967), pp. 5, 150–53, passim; see also Deeds Office, Cape Town, file 724/1851; Clanwilliam vol. 8, 1.9. 1852.

Chapter 2

1. Ronaldson formed other secret "partnerships" from time to time. In 1927, for example, he was in "partnership" with Solomon Rabinowitz, north of Port Nolloth (presumably in the Buchuberg area); later, the latter filed an unsuccessful lawsuit against him. Ronaldson, with Van Praagh, was also involved with a German prospector in another mineral enterprise (probably iron) in South-West Africa.

2. Consolidated African Selection Trust Ltd. (CAST) was active in Namaqualand from 1927 to about 1943. See C. A. Kidd, "CAST in Namaqualand," RTZA(N), 1983. See also Selection Trust and CAST archives now housed with RTZ Corporation in St. James's Square, London, and RTZ Mining and Exploration Ltd., Broadway, Newbury, Berks., U.K. There is also a very useful collection housed in LSEA.

See also Peter Greenhalgh, *West African Diamonds, 1919–1983: An Economic History* (Manchester: Manchester University Press, 1985), esp. pp. 46–47.

3. Kidd, "CAST in Namaqualand," p. 5; and A. J. Wilson, *The Life and Times of Sir Alfred Chester Beatty* (London: Cadogan, 1985), pp. 154–57.

4. LSEA letter, Wilmarth to Secretary of CAST, 7 Mar. 1927. See also CAST letters to Van Praagh, 21 Jan. and 14 Feb. 1927.

5. Kidd, "CAST in Namaqualand," pp. 7–8.

6. It is also important to realize that the 10 percent purchase from CAST, in late February 1927, was made before Oppenheimer had acquired any interest in the H.M. Association at Alexander Bay (see appendix).

7. See Gregory, *Ernest Oppenheimer*, pp. 170–71.

8. Clarke did not submit his final report until February 1928. Although not complete, it was very thorough, with excellent photographs of the mining areas. It also dealt with aspects of the twenty-seven farms and proved an invaluable document for Cape Coast and, later, for De Beers. Oppenheimer received his own copy; two copies went to Anglo American and two to H. T. Dickinson, the consulting engineer.

9. Ronaldson had a serious nervous breakdown when he received the news; he went to England for electroshock treatment. Another view is that his illness had been brought on by his futile attempt to outmaneuver Oppenheimer in the Namaqualand diamond venture.

10. Rudd and Watson, *History of the Diamond Discoveries*, p. 58.

11. DBA, Cape Coast Exploration Ltd. minutes, February 21 to April 1930. I was unable to locate any document relating to the partnership between Ronaldson, Van

Praagh, and Rabinowitz; it must, however, have been common knowledge at the time, judging from its prominence in contemporary oral tradition.

12. Ibid., minutes, 15 Aug. 1930.

13. Ibid., 21 Sept. 1928. See also KA letters, Rich to Ronaldson, 29 Oct. 1928, and Anglo American to Major Monro, 19 Jan. 1929.

14. Ibid., 21 Jan. 1936. That the full amount of £3,000 was not paid can be explained only by the fact that Ronaldson's £750 "bonus" to Carstens in December 1927, for his work, was deducted from the principal sum. This small settlement was of course quite separate from Ronaldson's other debts to his "partner," which would include Carstens's share of all sales of all the properties, not to mention the profits from diamonds. See also earlier correspondence on this matter. KA, letter, Parkinson to Dickinson, 19 Mar. 1930; and KA, letter, Dickinson to Parkinson, 31 Mar. 1930.

15. Oppenheimer's appointment to the chairmanship of De Beers coincides with his acquisition of Merensky's residual interest at Alexander Bay for more than £1 million.

16. DBA, letter, Clara Saunders to Ernest Oppenheimer, 6 Dec. 1934.

17. DBA. See Saunders report, 11 Feb. 1926.

18. DBA, ibid.

19. DBA, microfilm roll 23A, m. 31–36. Unless otherwise stated, the documents used in this discussion were located on microfilm, as indicated above. The period covered is from late January to 26 May 1927.

20. DBA, telegram, Oppenheimer to Hirschhorn, 15 Mar. 1927.

21. Ibid., letters, Hertog to De Beers, 18 Mar. 1927, De Beers to Saunders, 18 Mar. 1927.

22. Ibid., letter, Haarhoff, Hertog, & Lange to Duncan & Rothman, 29 Mar. 1927; and letter to Oppenheimer, 28 Mar. 1927.

23. Ibid., letter, 25 Apr. 1927.

24. Ibid., memo, 4 May 1927.

25. Ibid., letter, 25 May 1927.

26. See George Beet, *The Grand Old Days of the Diamond Fields* (Cape Town: Maskew Miller, [1931?]). Beet was born in 1853, a birth year he shared with Cecil Rhodes, Alfred Beit, and Starr Jameson—all of whom he knew well. If not, himself, part of the Kimberley establishment, as a reporter (and, later, editor) for the *Diamond News* for many years, he was well informed on the diamond industry. Of the latter's demise George Beet records:"Before his death, the late Mr. Harry Saunders, of Kimberley, sent for me and gave me all the information he could concerning the [Namaqualand discoveries]. He requested me at the same time to make it known that it was mainly owing to his own pioneering efforts that these valuable deposits in Namaqualand came to be opened up."

Jack Carstens does not mention Saunders's suicide in *A Fortune through My Fingers* but he often spoke about it in conversation. However, he does write about Ronaldson's breakdown and journey to England in 1928 for electroshock therapy.

Chapter 3

1. The actual memorandum of association of the company was signed on 29 December 1927 by seven subscribers, each of whom agreed to take out a share in the company valued at £1. The objectives for which the company was established were

quite excessive, covering every conceivable branch of mining and commerce, illustrating very clearly the Anglo American connection. Moreover, four of the subscribers were Anglo American directors; three were company employees.

2. All details and quotations in this chapter are taken from the minutes of the Cape Coast Board, unless otherwise stated.

3. AACA, board minutes, 17 Feb. 1928. See also Gregory, *Ernest Oppenheimer*, p. 342 n. 22 for his interpretation of the minutes.

4. As noted earlier, in February 1927 CAST purchased a 50 percent interest in the rights over the farms that the Ronaldson Syndicate had acquired for £30,000, and, almost immediately, Oppenheimer's Anglo American purchased 10 percent of CAST's holdings. In July 1927, Oppenheimer purchased the remaining 50 percent interest in Ronaldson's venture to give him a 60 percent interest (30% went to Anglo American and 30% to Barnato Brothers).

5. DBA, notes, 18 Feb. 1928. The records show that every farm on which options had been taken out in 1926 were registered in Ronaldson's name only. Moreover, although in partnership with Van Praagh and Jolis, no transfer of property by Ronaldson to them was officially registered until 30 Aug. 1929. It is also interesting to note that A. C. Clarke, CAST's senior man at Kleinzee, had been put in charge of the Kleinzee operation the preceding year. Clarke, moreover, was instructed to "keep closely in touch with Sir Ernest Oppenheimer . . . and discuss all aspects of the business with him at all times." LSEA, letter, secretary to Clarke, 20 Oct. 1927.

6. KA, Register of Diamonds, 1927–28.

7. KA, Digging Operations, 1927.

8. See Newbury, *Diamond Ring*, p. 355, passim, and Newbury, "South Africa and the International Diamond Trade, 1946–1970," paper delivered at the University of Toronto, October 1994 (author's photocopy).

9. Kidd, "CAST in Namaqualand," p. 30.

10. Greenhalgh, *West African Diamonds*, p. 47. See also the discussion by Gregory, *Ernest Oppenheimer*, chap. 7.

Chapter 4

1. Kidd, "CAST in Namaqualand," p. 26; and KA, Diamond Register.

2. KA, Behrmann to Cape Coast, letter, 1 May 1929.

3. See chapter 6 for a discussion of white contract workers in the late 1920s and 1930s; and see chapter 8 for comments on their status vis-á-vis Coloureds.

4. In 1930, the staff listed were: manager, L. J. Parkinson; mine secretary, V. L. M. Wilson; resident engineer, C. G. Trevett; mine pit superintendent, J. E. Carstens; chief of protection and supervisor, E. S. Witt; plant superintendent and supervisor, E. J. H. Crocker; pulsator superintendent, S. Fletcher; compound manager, O. N. Pringle; medical orderly, J. K. Mackintosh; storeman, E. F. Jackson; [office] clerk, H. Du Plooy; supervisors, W. von Gruenewaldt, W. Stevens, F. C. Wecke, A. P. Engelbrecht, W. Mostert, and U. M. von Chelius. The 6 artisans consisted of 3 fitters, 1 electrician, 1 power station attendant (J. Agenbag), and 1 carpenter. There were 10 guards, 165 white contract workers (laborers), and 35 Coloured laborers. Not employed by the company were a trader-shopkeeper (W. W. Dick and, later, D. Boynton-Lee), and 8 domestic servants. See KA, manager's report, June 1930.

5. Cf. Vera Shlakman, *The Economic History of a Factory Town: A Study of*

Chicopee, Massachusetts, Studies in History 20 (Northampton, Mass: Smith College, 1935), p. 14.

6. KA, manager to Boynton-Lee, letter, 1 Nov. 1944; manager's memo, Dec. 1944.

7. KA, Humphreys to DEBENIC [code name], telegram, 26 Oct. 1931.

8. KA, medical officer's report, 24 Jan. 1947.

9. See also chapter 8.

10. Kidd, "CAST in Namaqualand," p. 28.

11. KA, annual report, 31 Feb. 1936.

12. See KA, correspondence, June 1932.

13. KA, Humphrey report to Cape Coast, 21 July 1932.

14. Ibid., engineer Trevett's report to Humphreys, 21 July 1932.

15. Ibid., correspondence, Feb.–July 1932.

16. Ibid., manager's memo, 1 May 1932.

17. Ibid., Trevett to manager, letter, 20 May 1932.

18. Ibid., Goosen to Humphreys, letter, July 1932, translated from Afrikaans.

19. Ibid., Eliot to Humphreys, letter, 27 June 1932. See also correspondence Feb.–July 1932.

20. See chapter 8 for a translation of their joint letter to management on July 21, 1932. See also KA, correspondence June 1932, and report by Humphrey, July 1932.

21. Ibid., general manager of De Beers to manager at Kleinzee, letter, 4 Mar. 1932.

22. Ibid., memo on X-ray, May 1932.

23. KA, memos and notes, June–Oct. 1932.

24. KA, Humphreys to Beck, letter, 22 July 1932.

25. Ibid., report by Humphreys, May 1932.

26. Ibid., note on Beck's visit, 3 Aug. 1932; and Beck to Humphreys, letter, 22 Aug. 1932.

27. KA, manager's end-of-year report, 1937.

28. KA, consultants to Pifer, letter, 27 June 1938.

29. KA, Pifer to consultants, letter, 30 Sept. 1938; and Pifer to Auret, letter, 23 May 1938.

30. I located Pifer's papers in the archives of the University of Washington. These reveal his concern for detail and interest in his discipline. For another perspective, see Drury L. Pifer, *Innocents in Africa* (New York: Harcourt Brace, 1994)—an account by Pifer's son, who spent his childhood years in South Africa. The book is based on weekly letters that the young Pifer's mother wrote to her mother during the thirteen years the Pifer family was in South Africa. Interesting sections on life at Kleinzee and Oranjemund include Pifer's recollections of his life as a manager's son on a De Beers diamond mine.

31. KA, Pifer to consultants, letter, 11 Oct. 1937.

32. KA, Pifer to head office, letter, Dec. 1938.

33. KA, misc. notes, 1938.

34. KA, telegram to head office, 17 Aug. 1939.

35. KA, letter from head office, 14 June 1939; letter from director of air services, 26 July 1940.

36. KA, notes, 13 Aug. 1940.

37. KA, Wilson to head office, letter, 6 Oct. 1940.

38. KA, Beck to Wilson, letter, 22 Dec. 1941.

39. KA, Wilson to general manager of De Beers, letter, 29 Aug. 1942.

40. KA, "Reminiscences of Kleinzee," by J. D. Crafford (1976). Crafford was for many years an office clerk at Kleinzee.

41. KA, misc. notes, Apr.–Dec. 1943. Soon after World War II, police from the Diamond Detective Department arrested a Kleinzee resident, linking him to a massive IDB ring involved in diamond smuggling to Germany in support of the Axis.

42. KA, notes, 6 Jan.–10 May 1944.

43. KA, notes, 24 Apr. 1945.

44. KA, Turner to head office, letter, 28 June 1943.

45. KA, Van Rooyen's report, 1952. See also Gyngell to general manager of De Beers, confidential letter, 25 Aug. 1952; Blamey to head office, letter, 15 Dec. 1922; and report by P. E. Rich, assistant protection officer, 2 Feb. 1953.

46. See, for example, M. I. A. Bulmer, "Sociological Models of the Mining Community," *Sociological Review* 23 (1975): 61–92; and Ricardo Godoy, "Mining: Anthropological Perspectives," *Annual Review of Anthropology*, vol. 14 (1985), pp. 199–217.

47. KA, notes, Dec. 1952.

Chapter 5

1. Cf. the portrayal in *Coal Is Our Life* of the status of British coal miners in the 1950s. The authors write, "The rôle of the worker is not to direct production, it is to put himself at the disposal of the employer for a certain period of time. As a consequence of his labour power being bought by the employer the product of his labour is alienated from the immediate producer, the labourer, and is appropriated by the employer"—N. Dennis, F. Henriques, and C. Slaughter, *Coal Is Our Life* (London: Tavistock, 1956), pp. 27–28.

2. This section is drawn from KA, misc. notes and correspondence, 1928–32.

3. In July 1932, a parcel of diamonds weighing 10,000 carats was stolen from the Bitterfontein post office while in transit from Kleinzee to Kimberley. Information regarding the shipping of these gemstones had filtered through the network of IDB traders.

4. KA, Sister Madeleine to Humphreys, letter, 24 Feb. 1932.

5. KA, telegrams, 31 Dec. 1931.

6. KA, letter, 11 Nov. 1931.

7. Ibid., 4 May 1931.

8. Ibid., Humphreys to Dickinson, letter, 23 Mar. 1931.

9. Ibid.

10. Ibid., Parkinson to Dickinson, letter, n.d. (Aug. 1930?); Parkinson to Colonel Bower, letter, 30 Aug. 1930; correspondence, 19–20 Aug. 1930.

11. Ibid., notes, July 1932.

12. *Cape Times*, 9 Oct. 1940.

13. This section and the one following are drawn from KA, misc. notes.

14. Carstens, *Fortune through My Fingers*, pp. 104–5.

15. KA, mine records.

Chapter 6

1. A sizable literature deals with various aspects of compounds (hostels) and the role of the compound system in the exploitation of labor in Southern Africa. Most of these works deal, very appropriately, with compounds in the context of migratory

contract labor. See esp. Charles Van Onselen, *Chibaro: African Mine Labour in South-ern Rhodesia, 1900-1933* (London: Pluto, 1976), and two more recent works, Harries, *Work, Culture, Identity,* and T. Dunbar Moodie, with Vivienne Ndatshe, *Going for Gold: Men, Mines, and Migration* (Berkeley: University of California Press, 1994). Other important works include Jonathan Crush, Alan Jeeves, and David Yudelman, *South Africa's Labor Empire: A History of Black Migrancy to the Gold Mines* (Boulder: Westview Press, 1991); Alan Jeeves, *Migrant Labour in South Africa's Mining Econ-omy: The Struggle for the Gold Mines' Labour Supply, 1890-1920* (Kingston, Ontario: McGill-Queen's University Press, 1985); Frederick Johnstone, *Class, Race, and Gold: A Study of Class Relations and Racial Discrimination* (London: Routledge & Kegan Paul, 1976); Norman Levy, *The Foundations of the South African Cheap Labour System* (London: Routledge & Kegan Paul, 1982); Victor L. Allen, *The History of Black Mine-workers in South Africa: Techniques of Resistance, 1871-1948* (Keighley, U.K.: Moor Press 1992); Ian Phimister, *Wangi Kolia: Coal Capital and Labour in Colonial Zimba-bwe, 1894-1954* (Johannesburg: Witwatersrand University Press, 1994); Ian Phimister and Charles Van Onselen, *Studies in the History of African Mine Labour in Colonial Zimbabwe* (Salisbury: Mambo Press, 1978); John Rex, "The Compound, the Reserve, and the Location: The Essential Institutions of Southern African Labour Exploitation," *South African Labour Bulletin* 1, no. 4 (1974): 4-17; Robert Turrell, *Capital and Labour on the Kimberley Diamond Fields, 1871-1890* (Cambridge: Cambridge Univer-sity Press, 1987); Charles Van Onselen, *Studies in the Social and Economic History of the Witwatersrand, 1886-1914,* 2 vols. (Johannesburg: Ravan Press, 1982), and idem, *The Small Matter of a Horse: The Life of "Nongolozo" Mathebula* (Johannesburg: Ravan Press, 1984); Gardner F. Williams, *The Diamond Mines of South Africa: Some Account of their Rise and Development* (New York: MacMillan, 1902); and William Worger, *South Africa's City of Diamonds: Mine Workers and Monopoly Capitalism in Kimber-ley, 1867-1895* (New Haven: Yale University Press, 1987).

2. For a note on *compound,* see Jean Branford, with William Branford, in *A Dic-tionary of South African English,* 4th ed., s.v. "Compound."

3. KA, notes, 1930. For an excellent account of the blueprint of a typical South African compound, see T. Dunbar Moodie, "The Formal and Informal Social Struc-ture of a South African Gold Mine," *Human Relations* 33, no. 8 (1980): 555-74. See also Turrell, *Capital and Labour*; and Van Onselen, *Chibaro,* p. 130.

4. See Edmund Bradwin, *The Bunkhouse Man: A Study of Work and Pay in the Camps of Canada, 1903-1914* (Toronto: University of Toronto Press [1928] 1972), esp. chaps. 3 and 9; and Lucas, *Minetown, Milltown, Railtown,* pp. 38-39, 50-51. There are many parallels, despite enormous differences in the structure of the build-ings, between the lifestyle of the Kleinzee compound dwellers and that of the bunk-house men of the Canadian mining frontiers in the same period.

5. Commenting on control over labor by De Beers in Kimberley at roughly the same time, Van Onselen writes: "The control over black workers, which at De Beers had been primarily a by-product of an attempt to restrict the illicit diamond trade, became a feature of compound systems, that had nothing to do with diamonds, but everything to do with employers seeking to maximise control over labour"—*Chibaro,* pp. 130-31.

6. DBA, minutes, Cape Coast board, 9 May 1930.

7. KA, monthly reports.

8. KA, manager's reports, 1930-32.

9. Ibid.

10 KA, Parkinson to Dickinson, letter, 17 Nov. 1930.

11. KA, protection officer's report, 2 Feb. 1931.

12. Ibid., 17 Nov. 1930.

13. KA, reports, 1930-40.

14. DBA, Cape Coast board minutes, 9 May 1930.

15. Ibid.

16. KA, memo, 7 Jan. 1932.

17. KA, letter, 22 July 1930.

18. KA, Parkinson to head office, letter, 31 July 1930.

19. Ibid., 21 Dec. 1930.

20. KA, note, 16 July 1932.

21. KA, memo (probably from Pifer), 1939.

22. KA, Humphreys to head office, 28 Dec. 1931.

23. KA, manager's report, June 1930.

24. KA, Parkinson to Dickinson, letter, 29 Nov. 1930.

25. KA, Parkinson to SWFIN [code for South West Financial Corp.], letter, 10 Dec. 1930.

26. KA, Steenkamp to manager, letter, 19 Sept. 1930.

27. Ibid., 2 Nov. 1931.

28. KA, Parkinson to Dickinson, letter, 22 Sept. 1930.

29. KA, misc. notes and reports, 1930-37.

30. For two excellent discussions of the politics of migrant labor and the influence of the state on the system, see Crush, Jeeves, and Yudelman, *South Africa's Labor Empire*; and Jeeves, *Migrant Labour in South Africa's Mining Economy*. See also Colin Newbury, *Diamond Ring*, 1989.

31. For a useful discussion of wages in South Africa, see Robert Davies, *Capital State and White Labour in South Africa, 1900-1960: An Historical Materialist Analysis of Class Formation and Class Relations* (Brighton, U.K.: Harvester, 1979).

32. KA, Turner to general manager of De Beers, letter, 13 Aug. 1943.

Chapter 7

1. DBA, general manager's memo on the reopening of Kleinzee, 6 Apr. 1943. In all the company's documents, these workers are referred to as "Ovambos." I have retained that spelling when quoting from the documents. Otherwise, I follow the contemporary spelling, *Owambo*.

2. KA, secretary of De Beers to Office of Administrator for SWA, letter, 23 Sept. 1943. Consolidated Diamond Mines, Oranjemund, a sister mining community, was part of the De Beers/Anglo American diamond empire.

3. KA, administrator to secretary of De Beers, telegram, 1 Oct. 1943. For an excellent account of wage labor and labor migrancy among Owambo and other workers in Namibia, see Gillian and Suzanne Cronje, *The Workers of Namibia* (London: International Defence and Aid Fund, 1979). See also Alison Corbett, *Diamond Beaches: A History of Oranjemund, 1928-1989* (Claremont, Cape Town: Published by author, 1989) for some discussion of Owambo workers at Consolidated Diamond Mines, and Robert J. Gordon, *Mines, Masters, and Migrants: Life in a Namibian Mine Compound* (Johannesburg: Ravan Press, 1977) for the experience of Owambo workers at the hard-rock mines further north, in Namibia.

4. KA, De Beers to secretary of the interior, letter, 2 Oct. 1943.

5. KA, general manager to Holland, letter, 5 Feb. 1946.

6. KA, Ovambo Transport No. 2, n.d.

7. KA, Ovambo file, 1947.

8. A variety of confirmed rumors in Namibia and Namaqualand currently relate the financing of the South-West African Peoples Organisation (SWAPO) during its struggle for Namibian independence to proceeds of IDB from Oranjemund.

9. KA, Turner to general manager, letter, 9 Oct. 1944.

10. Ibid.

11. KA, Brinton to manager, letter, 5 Feb. 1944.

12. KA, correspondence, 22 Feb. 1944 and 13 Mar. 1944.

13. KA, correspondence, 28 Apr. 1944, 2 June 1944, 6 June 1944.

14. KA, director of native labour to manager, letter, 14 Apr. 1944.

15. KA, notes on the native compound, 13 June 1947. See also KA, manager's weekly report, 22 May 1945.

16. KA, manager's weekly report, 22 May 1945.

17. Material in the following two subsections is drawn from KA, Ovambo file.

18. KA, Klopper to manager, letter, 22 Aug. 1944.

19. DBA, Harris to manager Louwrens, letter, 8 Nov. 1944.

20. Ibid., De la Rey to manager, letter, 8 Nov. 1944.

21. Ibid.

22. DBA, Cape Coast to Adamant, telegram, 9 Nov. 1944.

23. DBA, telegram, 13 Nov. 1944.

24. DBA, Gow to manager, 8 Nov. 1944.

25. DBA, Donald McHardy's report, February 1945.

26. KA, Turner to head office, letter, 13 Nov. 1944.

27. KA, Jonker to manager, letter, 21 Nov. 1944.

28. KA, Louwrens to Jonker, letter, 6 Dec. 1944.

29. Carstens, *Fortune through My Fingers*, p. 146.

30. KA, Louwrens to inspector of mines, letter, 12 Feb. 1945.

31. KA, report, 20 Nov. 1944.

32. KA, manager's report, 24 Apr. 1944.

33. KA, Dr. A. McLean's notes, 16 May 1946.

34. KA, general report, 8 Jan. 1947, and CDM, report, 14 Sept. 1945.

35. KA, manager's weekly letter, 24 Sept. 1945.

36. KA, magistrate to manager, letter, 13 Jan. 1944.

37. KA, Toby Holland's letter, 27 Mar. 1946.

38. See, for example, Cronje, *Workers of Namibia;* and Gordon, *Mines, Masters, and Migrants.*

Chapter 8

1. *The Population Registration Act No. 30 (1950),* as amended, defined a Coloured person as a person who is "not a white person or a native [black person]." See discussion of the act in the appendix to Carstens, *Social Structure,* "Race Classification in South Africa."

2. KA, correspondence, Dickinson to Parkinson, 15 Oct. 1930; Oppenheimer to Cape Coast board, 27 Mar. 1930; Humphreys to Dickinson, 13 Apr. 1931. See also monthly returns to Department of Mines and Industries, 3 June 1930.

3. Ibid., monthly returns, 5 Aug. 1930.

4. KA, correspondence, 13 Apr. 1931.

5. KA, Coloured workers to manager, letter, 21 July 1932.

6. DBA, list of shareholders in Cape Coast, 9 Feb. 1935.

7. KA, Caplan to manager, letter, 10 Dec. 1929.

8. KA, mine secretary to Caplan, 28 Feb. 1930.

9. KA, Humphreys to Dickinson, letter, 13 Feb. 1932.

10. KA, correspondence, 13 Mar. 1930.

11. KA, Beets to Parkinson, letter, 25 Mar. 1930.

12. For more on the period covered in this section, see Carstens, *Social Structure*. For a recent autobiographical account of life in the compound at the State Alluvial Diggings (Alexander Bay) in the early 1950s, written by a former Coloured worker, see F. Pokoy, *Riemvasmaak* (Voortrekkerhoogte: Makro Boeke, 1995).

DBA, Leipoldt to secretary of De Beers, letter, 20 Jan. 1945.

e also Jacklyn Cock, *Maids and Madams: A Study in the Politics of Exploi-* nesburg: Ravan Press, 1980).

sory examination of the list of maids who had worked for the senior staff hey all came from "good" homes. The manager's maid (the one whose ked for the doctor) came from a "good" Steinkopf family, and the nt's maid and nanny came from a high-status Port Nolloth family. 's maid had been educated in a convent; later, she married into the hily in Steinkopf.

in Carstens, *Social Structure*, pp. 185-89.

oured workers, 1961.

manager, letter, 23 Nov. 1961.

l manager to secretary, letter, 22 Oct. 1964.

DM, letter, 10 Mar. 1965.

inzee office, letter, 18 Oct. 1965.

ils derived partly from back issues of the *Nama-* ewspaper. I benefited especially from Jennifer past. For the rest I have relied on oral tradition, own experiences and recollections of change. ining and mining geology, see Cedric E. Gre- ork: Pergamon, 1980). Gregory also deals miners in different parts of the world and ms. For an excellent, well-informed ac- ry, see Bruton, *Diamonds*.

with short-lived excitement. Some town in their cars to display their hey were out they were out and

an
an
trol
and
2).
on in

earch,

ure and
2); E. S.
Wilkins,
Company
Shlakman,

munities on
of Medicine,

n of the place of
1880–1960, see
a (London: Oxford

when they in they were in, as determined by the processes conducted at the East Gate checkpoint (see chapter 13).

Chapter 10

The epigraph is from *Smart Verses* (Santa Barbara: Fithian Press, 1994), p. 47.

1. See also M. Raubenheimer and P. Le Roux, *Life and Work at Kleinzee*, photographs by J. Maître (Kleinzee: De Beers Consolidated Mines, 1976). For a detailed account of the technology needed for alluvial diamond strip mining at Consolidated Diamond Mines, see Alison Corbett, *Diamond Beaches*, 1989.

2. De Beers pamphlet, n.d. For an excellent scholarly treatment of diamond mining and recovery methods, see Bruton, *Diamonds*. Bruton gives clear accounts of hand-operated water-gravitating, rotary pans and grease tables, as well as details regarding modern treatment plants and sorting with the aid of X-ray separation procedures.

3. See appendix 2, table 2.3, and figure 12.1.

4. It is important, therefore, to distinguish between individual variations in managing styles and those reflecting company strategy and policy. For an insightful study of management strategies used by five transnational firms in Canada, see Bob Russell, *More with Less: Work Reorganization in the Canadian Mining Industry* (Toronto University of Toronto Press, 1999).

5. General managers are, of course, always answerable to the company, and c be dismissed, recalled, transferred, or reprimanded by head office at any time. For elaboration of the occurrence and patterns of gossip as a mechanism of social con in single-industry towns, see Lucas, *Minetown, Milltown, Railtown*, pp. 347–51; Albert Blumenthal, *Small Town Stuff* (Chicago: University of Chicago Press, 19

6. Jacques Perold, "The Historical and Contemporary Use of Job Evaluat South Africa," *South Africa Labour Bulletin* 10 (4) 1985: 74.

7. T. T. Paterson, *Pay: For Making Decisions* (Vancouver: Tantalus Re 1981).

8. See, for example, John S. Garner, ed., *The Company Town: Architec Society in the Early Industrial Age* (New York: Oxford University Press. 19 Hunt et. al., *What the Coal Commission Found* (Baltimore: Williams & 1925); Porteous, "Nature of the Company Town," 127–42; Porteous, "The State: A Chilean Case-Study." *Canadian Geographer* 17 (1973): 113–26 *The Economic History of a Factory Town*.

9. Aubrey M. Michalowsky, "The Effects of Living in Isolated Con the South African Diamond Mining Industry" (doctoral thesis, Faculty University of Stellenbosch, 1987), p. 30.

10. Paterson, *Pay*, pp. 121–46.

Chapter 11

1. Van Onselen, *Chibaro*, pp. 184 ff. For a scholarly considerat churches in the company (coal) towns of Southern Appalachia Shifflett, *Coal Towns*, pp. 190–98, passim.

2. See Bengt Sundkler's classic *Bantu Prophets in South Afri*

University Press, 1962) for a discussion of the origin of these separatist churches and the distinction between the Zionists and the Ethiopians.

3. See Philip Mayer, *Townsmen or Tribesmen* (Cape Town: Oxford University Press, 1961); Monica Wilson, *Langa* (Cape Town: Oxford University Press, 1963); and esp. P. A. McAllister, "Work, Homesteads, and the Shades: The Ritual Interpretation of Labour Migration among the Gcaleka," in Philip Mayer, ed., *Black Villagers in an Industrial Society* (Cape Town: Oxford University Press, 1980).

4. *Hlonipha* (to show respect) carries the implication of ritual avoidance of certain people and situations.

5. *uQamata*, the traditional word for the Creator in the Xhosa language, is now favored by many Xhosa people over *uThixo* (God), which, they say, is the white man's term for God. In fact, *uThixo* derives from the Khoi word for God, *Tsui //Goab*, which, after being introduced by early missionaries, later "transformed" into Xhosa.

6. These examples of goodwill visits to workers' homes are based almost entirely on material derived from the local newspaper.

7. *NM Chronicle* 21 (September 1987).

8. See Aubrey Michalowsky, "The Effects of Living in Isolated Communities on the South African Diamond Industry" (doctoral thesis, University of Stellenbosch, 1987), pp. iv, 199, passim.

Chapter 12

1. For another account of the operation of British hegemony in De Beers, see Brian Roberts, *Kimberley: Turbulent City* (Cape Town: David Philip, 1976), pp. 62–69, passim.

2. See also Godoy, "Mining": 199–217.

In the back country of Quebec, company towns such as Shawinigan, Arvida, and Temiscaming were built to reproduce the socioeconomic hierarchy of the late nineteenth century: "The managers' houses were on the hill where they could visually dominate the workers' quarters below." Management was, of course, English, not French. See Ray Conlogue, "Urban Planning," *Globe and Mail*, May 7, 1996.

3. See, for example, Crush, Jeeves, and Yudelman, *South Africa's Labor Empire*; and Van Onselen, *Chibaro*. For more liberal interpretations and discussions, see Harries, *Work, Culture, Identity*, and Moodie, *Going for Gold*.

4. See Laurie Flynn, *Studded with Diamonds and Paved with Gold: Miners, Mining Companies, and Human Rights in Southern Africa* (London: Bloomsbury, 1992) for a detailed discussion of the National Union of Mine Workers in South Africa.

5. Godoy, "Mining": 207.

Chapter 13

1. The quality of "closedness" is inevitably associated with interstitial areas, both physical and symbolic, between communities; both Barth and Cohen refer to these as boundaries. However, given the regular interaction (no matter how small) that takes place between different communities and other social formations, the term *boundary* needs to be qualified if it is to convey the full meaning of these sometimes delicate

cultural margins and interstitial areas. A boundary indicates the limit of specific action as well as the limit itself, suggesting cessation of interaction and communication. *Threshold* seems to be a more versatile and accurate term because of its association with coming and going—with doorways and entrances and exits. Boundaries are fixed; they move only when formally altered. Thresholds refer to the processual maneuvers that individuals and groups make as they negotiate the terms of their relationships, whether or not they cross over to the other side. The dynamics of every society always involves coming and going from one place or situation to another, which in turn entails entering and leaving groups, associations, communities, and even classes and status strata. These processes take place in different ways, but it is at the *thresholds*, actual and symbolic, that people encounter situations that require them to be involved in rites of passage. These often elaborate rituals prepare them for new roles and transform them to be able to adjust to new positions. See Fredrik Barth, ed., *Ethnic Groups and Boundaries* (Boston: Little, Brown, 1969), and Anthony H. Cohen, *The Symbolic Construction of Community* (London: Tavistock, 1985).

2. Arnold Van Gennep, *The Rites of Passage* (Chicago: University of Chicago Press, [1908] 1960). Victor Turner, *The Forest of Symbols: Aspects of Ndembu Ritual* (Ithaca, N.Y.: Cornell University Press, 1967), and idem, *The Ritual Process* (Chicago: Chicago University Press, 1969).

3. This paternalistic image of the company is reflected in a number of unexpected ways. For example, when people were informed in the early 1990s that in future they would have to buy their own lightbulbs and green garbage bags, people were upset: they felt that the company was letting them down. A year or two earlier, they experienced similar "trauma" when home deliveries of bread and milk were abruptly discontinued. In both these trivial occurrences, it was not the cost of these items and services that upset people, but the rebuff they felt they had received from their patron and nurturer.

4. For some other examples, see Porteous, "Company State," 113–26; Charles T. Goodsell, *American Corporations and Peruvian Politics* (Cambridge: Harvard University Press, 1974).

5. Mauss argued that while gifts in human societies in general may appear to be "voluntary, disinterested and spontaneous, [they] are in fact obligatory and interested." Gifts may appear to be generously offered, "but the accompanying behaviour is formal pretence and social deception, while the transaction itself is based on obligation and economic self-interest." There can never be such a thing as a "free gift." Mauss was especially interested in what he called the "institutions of total prestations"; in such transactions, he said, there is an *obligation* to repay the gift. Mauss saw people as being involved in a social and psychological pattern that bound them: Marcel Mauss, *The Gift: Forms and Functions of Exchange in Archaic Societies*, trans. Ian Cunnison (London: Routledge & Kegan Paul, [1925] 1966), pp. 10–11, passim. See also a new translation by W. D. Halls, with foreword by Mary Douglas, Marcel Mauss, *The Gift: Form and Reason for Exchange in Archaic Societies* (New York: Norton 1990).

6. For a theoretical discussion of loyalty and the workplace, see Mark Granovetter and Charles Tilly, "Inequality and the Labor Processes," in *Handbook of Sociology*, ed. Neil J. Smelser (Newbury Park: Sage, 1988), pp. 175–221.

7. Claire Williams, *Open Cut: The Working Class in an Australian Mining Town* (Sidney: Allen & Unwin, 1981), pp. 91–129.

8. See, for example, Antonio Gramsci, *Selections from the Prison Notebooks* (New York: International, 1971); Frank Parkin, "Working Class Conservatives: A Theory of Po-

litical Deviance," *British Journal of Sociology* 18 (1967): 278–90; and esp. Donald Kurtz, "Hegemony and Anthropology," in *Critique of Anthropology* 16, no. 2 (1996): 103–35.

9. In 1996, the Royal Bank of Canada, in an insightful diamond-industry analysis, said: "The loyalty that De Beers commands in the diamond industry is very much a two-edged sword. On the one hand, those making a living inside the diamond trade will not risk offending De Beers by either deed or word. Dissenting voices are rare within the industry, and those voices that are raised tend to be anonymous. . . . On the other hand, there is almost universal agreement that De Beers is good for the industry as a whole. Thus, De Beers is in the position of being able to command loyalty [and also to enforce it]." I am indebted to Robert Halupka, a metal specialist employed at the Royal Bank of Canada, for this quotation.

Chapter 14

1. The "internal colonialism" idea has also been applied to other socioeconomic situations. See, for example, two articles by Robert K. Thomas, "Colonialism: Classic and Internal" and, idem, "Powerless Politics," *New University Thought* 4, no. 4 (1966–67): 37–44, 44–53. With regard to *state* and *estate*, Porteous uses both terms in separate publications: see Porteous, "Company State," pp. 113–26, and "Nature of the Company Town," pp. 127–42. See also Charles T. Goodsell, *American Corporations and Peruvian Politics* (Cambridge: Harvard University Press, 1974), and D. Barrios de Chungara, *Let Me Speak!* trans. Victoria Ortiz (New York: Monthly Review Press, 1978); also C. H. Grant, "Company Towns in the Caribbean: A Preliminary Analysis of Christianburg-Wismar-MacKenzie," *Caribbean Studies* 11 (April 1971): 46–72. See also two intriguing reports by Richard Patch from the late 1950s that throw further light on the power and influence of U.S. and Canadian companies in Peru. Richard W. Patch, "An Oil Company Builds a Town," *American Universities Field Staff Reports: West Coast of South America* 5, no. 2 (1958), and "The Role of the Hacienda in the Hispanization of Andean Indians," ibid., 6, no. 2 (1959). For Canada, see esp. L. D. McCann, "The Changing Internal Structure of Canadian Resource Towns," *Plan Canada* 18 (1978): 46–59.

2. In 1992, De Beers engaged the Environment Evaluation Unit of the University of Cape Town to carry out an impact assessment of the closure of its Namaqualand mines in 2005. I have not dealt with that research, partly for reasons of space and partly because it would have slanted my analysis too far in the direction of an uncertain future—that is, away from interpretation of the past and present. See University of Cape Town, *NM 2005 Impact Assessment* (Rondebosch: Environment Evaluation Unit, University of Cape Town, 1992); and idem, *Closure of De Beers Diamond Mines in Namaqualand*, compiled S. F. Brownlie (Rondebosch: Environment Evaluation Unit, University of Cape Town, 1992).

3. Charles L. Brace, *The New West* (New York: Press of Wyncoop & Hollenback, 1869). For an excellent study of mining landscapes in the United States, see Francaviglia, *Hard Places*.

4. In his discussion of a similar issue, Bowles asks: "In what sense are resource communities 'rural,' in that they are generally isolated in non-metropolitan areas?" See Roy T. Bowles, "Single-Industry Resource Communities in Canada's North," in *Rural Sociology in Canada*, ed. David A. Hay and Gurcharn S. Basran (Toronto: Oxford University Press, 1992), pp. 63–83.

The city, as Mumford characterized it, "is both a physical utility for collective living, and a symbol of those collective purposes and unanimities that arise under favouring circumstances." This does not mean that city life is always idyllic. On the contrary, Mumford points out, cities arise out of people's social needs and multiply both their modes and methods of expression. Since remote forces intermingle with the local, conflict is as common as harmony. Thus, while cities are noted for their freedom, architecture, and technological comfort (as well as for artists, philosophers, scholars, and poets), they are also notorious for ravaged landscapes, industrial factory districts, patches of blight and disease, slums, and exodus into lifeless dormitory suburbs and factory spores. In its social aspect, then, the city may be described as a special framework directed toward the creation of a common life and a significant social drama. Mumford, *Culture of Cities*, pp. 3-8, 479-93.

5. By *freedom* I here mean the opportunity to transform the many stranded cultural complexities of cities and the ability to create new paradigms and styles of living.

6. Erving Goffman, *Asylums* (Chicago: Aldine, 1962), pp. 4-5.

7. Ibid., pp. 10-11. See also Moodie, *Going for Gold*, pp. 15-29, 88, for a discussion of Goffman's work in relation to South African gold mines; see also Harries, *Work, Culture, and Identity*, p. 56.

8. See Suzanne Campbell-Jones, *In Habit* (London: Faber & Faber, 1979).

9. Goffman, *Asylums*, p. 13.

10. Michalowsky, "Effects of Living."

11. The terms *total institution* and *self-contained community* should not be confused with Raymond Breton's idea of "institutional completeness," which he applies to institutionally integrated ethnic communities. See Breton, "Institutional Completeness of Ethnic Communities and the Personal Relations of Immigrants," *American Journal of Sociology* 70, no. 2 (1964): 193-205.

12. Charlotte Wolf, *Garrison Community* (Westport, Conn: Greenwood, 1969).

13. Ibid., pp. 66-67, 92.

14. See Erik Cohen, "Expatriate Communities." *Current Sociology* 24, no. 3 (1977): 5-129.

15. Peter Carstens, "An Essay on Suicide and Disease in Canadian Indian Reserves: Bringing Durkheim Back In," *Canadian Journal of Native Studies* 20, no. 2 (forthcoming).

16. A. Lipschitz, "Suicide Prevention in Young Adults (Age 18-30)," *Suicide and Life-Threatening Behavior* 25, no. 1 (1995): 155-70.

17. *Guardian Weekly*, 23 May 1999, p. 20.

18. Louise Elliott, "Courage under Fire," *Globe and Mail*, 4 Sept. 1999. See also Deborah Harrison and Lucie Laliberté, *No Life Like It: Military Wives in Canada* (Toronto: Lorimer, 1994).

An Epilogue

1. Published materials on Tumbler Ridge include the following: John H. Bradbury, "Instant Resource Town Policy in British Columbia: 1965-1972," *Plan Canada* 20 (1980): 19-38; Canada, *Canada's Single Industry Communities: A Proud Determination to Survive* (Ottawa: Minister of Supply and Services, 1987); Alison M. Gill, "New Resource Communities: The Challenge of Meeting the Needs of Canada's Modern Frontierspersons," *Environments* 18 (1987): 21-34; idem, "Friendship Formation in a

New Coal-Mining Town: Planning Implications," *Sociology and Social Research* 74 (1990): 103–9; Alison Gill and Geoffrey Smith, "Residents' Evaluative Structures of Northern Manitoba Mining Communities," *Canadian Geographer* 29 (1985): 17–29; Adrienne Peacock, "Tumbler Ridge: A New Style Resource Town," *Priorities* 13, no. 1 (1985): 6–11; Ira M. Robinson, *New Industrial Towns on Canada's Resource Frontier*, Department of Geography Research Paper 73 (Chicago: University of Chicago, 1962); Wes Shera and Alison Gill, *An Evaluation of the Planning and Development of Tumbler Ridge* (Victoria, B.C.: University of Victoria, School of Social Work, 1987). See also *Tumbler Ridge Tattler*, June 1981–June 1984, and *Tumbler Times*, Jan.–Sept. 1983.

2. In 1994, Bullmoose was owned by Teck Corporation (60.9%), Rio Algom L (29.1%), Nisho Iwai Canada (10%). Quintette was owned by Quintette Coal Ltd. (Denison Mines 50% equity interest), Tokyo Boeki (10.49%), Mitsui Mining Company (12.5%), Charbonnages de France (12.01%), Sumitomo Corp (5%), Japanese steel companies (10%). In 1998, Teck Corporation owned both mines.

3. This is not to say that the Tumbler Ridge experiment in single-industry-resource town planning is unique. Tumbler Ridge parallels to some extent Mackenzie, the planned, single-industry forestry town to the east of the plateau. See Patricia M. Marchak, *Green Gold: The Forest Industry in British Columbia* (Vancouver: University of British Columbia Press, 1983). There is also an important discussion of industry versus government planning of resource towns in Robinson, *New Industrial Towns*. An earlier publication by the Institute of Local Government, Queen's University, also throws light on this question and provides a useful comparison of 145 resource towns in Canada. See *Queen's University Institute of Local Government, Single-Enterprise Communities: A Report to Central Mortgage and Housing Corporation* (Kingston, Ont.: Queen's University, 1953). See also Bowles, "Single-Industry Resource Communities," pp. 63–83.

4. Bradbury, "Instant Resource Town Policy": 19–38; Marchak, *Green Gold*, esp. chap. 11.

5. See Shera and Gill, "An Evaluation."

6. "Tumbler Ridge," report published by the District of Tumbler Ridge, July 6, 1981.

7. Canada, "Canada's Single Industry Communities," p. 57.

8. See Gill, "Friendship Formation": 103–9. Peacock's article on Tumbler Ridge, published in 1985, offered a parallel interpretation from a feminist, socialist perspective—see Peacock, "Tumbler Ridge": 6–11. A much earlier publication comes to very similar conclusions based on an overview of some studies and observations of single-enterprise communities in northern Canada. See Leonard B. Siemens, *Single-Enterprise Communities in Northern Canada*, University of Manitoba Occasional Paper no. 7, series 5 (Winnipeg: Center for Settlement Studies, 1973).

9. See my discussion in chapter 13.

Appendix 1

1. For more details of Merensky's life and career as a geologist with interests in both diamonds and platinum, see Lehmann's *Look beyond the Wind*; and *Hans Merensky: Ein deutscher Pionier in Südafrika* (Göttingen: Schutz, 1965); see also *Standard Encyclopedia of Southern Africa*, "Hans Merensky"; for more on the relationship between Merensky and Oppenheimer, see Gregory, *Ernest Oppenheimer*, pp. 163–218.

The relationship between Oppenheimer and Merensky is important and deserves future research. Both the Oppenheimer and Merensky families were German. The Oppenheimers seem to have been Jewish. Merensky's father was a missionary. Oppenheimer, through his connections with De Beers and through his own company, Anglo American, became closely associated with British interests. He was knighted in Britain and honored by British and South African universities. Later, according to Karla Poewe, "He became famous for his discoveries of platinum, chrome, diamonds and phosphates, for his conservation efforts, and for funding of a university chair, the Merensky Library at the University of Pretoria, and the farm school near Tzaneen. Before his death he established a . . . Hans Merensky Trust for South African resource development and conservation. . . While Merensky was honoured by Afrikaans Universities like Stellenbosch and Pretoria and by some German Schools, he received no honours from the British." Karla Poewe, "From Volk to Apartheid: the Dialectic between German and Afrikaner Nationalism," in Ulrich van den Heyden and Heike Liebau, eds., *Missionsgeschichte, Kirchengeschichte, Weltgeschichte* (Stuttgart: Franz Steiner Verlag, 1996), p. 206. Poewe reports that Merensky wrote more than forty articles and papers on his geological work.

2. Lehmann, *Look beyond the Wind*, p. 52, and *Hans Merensky: Ein deutscher Pionier*, p. 102.

3. Lehmann, *Look beyond the Wind*, pp. 61–62.

4. Ibid., pp. 54–55.

5. Reuning's contract, drawn up late December 1926 (not November 24, 1926, as incorrectly recorded by Rudd and Watson, *History of the Diamond Discoveries*, p. 62), makes it clear that Reuning would be doing the work of both prospector and field geologist.

6. Lehmann, *Look beyond the Wind*, p. 54.

7. Ibid., p. 67.

8. Rudd and Watson, *History of the Diamond Discoveries*, p. 13.

9. Ibid., pp. 18–19, 63–64.

10. Ibid., p. 18.

11. Ibid., p. 19.

12. Ibid., pp. 19–20.

13. Ibid., pp. 23–25.

14. Ibid., pp. 23–27.

15. For an excellent informal history of the State Diggings at Alexander Bay, see Pieter Coetzer, *Baai van Diamante: Die Geskiedenis van Alexander Baai, 1926–1989* (Bloemfontein: Universiteit van die Oranje-Vrystaat, Instituut vir Eietydse Geskiedenis, 1997).

16. Rudd and Watson, *History of the Diamond Discoveries*, p. 26.

17. Ibid., pp. 25–27, 65–66.

18. Ibid., p. 26.

19. Ibid., p. 27.

20. Ibid., pp. 36–38.

21. Ibid., p. 46. See also Newbury, *Diamond Ring*, pp. 228–40, 363–70, 375.

Bibliography

Archival Collections and Personal Papers

Archival sources used for the historical sections of the book include Anglo American Corporation Archive (AACA) in Johannesburg; Cape Archives (CA) in Cape Town; State Archives, Central Depot (CAD) in Pretoria; DeBeers Consolidated Mines Archive (DBA) in Kimberley; Deeds Office Archive (DOA) in Cape Town; the Kleinzee Museum Archive (KA); London School of Economics and Political Science Archive (LSEA); and the archives of the Rio Tinto-Zinc Corporation in London (RTZA[L]) and its mining and exploration branch in Newbury, U.K. (RTZA[N]). The last three archives between them now house all the available holdings of Central African Selection Trust (CAST). I also made liberal use of the private papers of both the late Jack Carstens and William Carstens. Both collections, now in my possession, provided me with indispensable material on the early prospecting days in Namaqualand and life at Kleinzee up to 1956.

Periodicals

The Cape Argus, Cape Town
The Cape Coast Chronicle, Kleinzee (1966–81)
The Cape Times, Cape Town
The Diamond Fields Advertiser
Namaqualand Mines Chronicle (*NM Chronicle*, 1987–)
Namaqualand Mines Diamond News (1981–86)
The Star, Johannesburg
Tumbler Ridge Tattler (June 1981–June 1984)
Tumbler Times (January to September 1983)

Books and Articles

Agricola, G. 1950 [1556]. De Re Metallica. Trans. H. C. and L. C. Hoover. New York: Dover.

Alexander, James Edward. 1967 [1838]. *Expedition of Discovery into the Interior of Africa*. Facsimile reprint, 2 vols. Cape Town: C. Struik.

239

Allen, James B. 1966. *The Company Town in the American West.* Norman: University of Oklahoma Press.

Allen, Victor L. 1992. *The History of Black Mineworkers in South Africa: Techniques of Resistance, 1871-1948.* Vol. 1, Keighley, U.K.: Moor Press.

Backhouse, James. 1844. *A Narrative of a Visit to the Mauritius and South Africa.* London: Hamilton, Adams.

Bailey, F. G., ed. 1971. *Gifts and Poison: The Politics of Reputation.* New York: Schocken Books.

Barrios de Chungara, Domitila. 1978. *Let Me Speak!* Translated by Victoria Ortiz. New York: Monthly Review Press.

Barth, Fredrik, ed. 1969. *Ethnic Groups and Boundaries: The Social Organization of Cultural Differences.* Boston: Little, Brown.

Beet, George. [1931?]. *The Grand Old Days of the Diamond Fields: Memories of Past Times with the Diggers of Diamondia.* Cape Town: Maskew Miller.

Beher, Charles A. Jr., and Nathaniel Arbiter. 1959. "Distinctive Features of the Mineral Industries." In Edward H. Robie, ed., *Economics of the Mineral Industries: A Series of Articles by Specialists.* New York: American Institute of Mining, Metallurgical and Petroleum Engineers.

Blatz, Perry K. 1994. *Democratic Miners: Work and Labor Relations in the Anthracite Coal Industry, 1875-1925.* Albany, N.Y.: State University of New York Press.

Blumenthal, Albert. 1932. *Small Town Stuff.* Chicago: University of Chicago Press.

Bowles, Roy T. 1992. "Single-Industry Resource Communities in Canada's North." In *Rural Sociology in Canada,* ed. David A. Hay and Gurcharn S. Basran. Toronto: Oxford University Press.

——, ed. 1982. *Little Communities and Big Industries: Studies in the Social Impact of Canadian Resource Extraction.* Toronto: Butterworths Canada.

Brace, Charles L. 1869. *The New West.* New York: Press of Wyncoop & Hollenback.

Bradbury, John H. 1978. "Class Structures and Class Conflicts in 'Instant' Resource Towns in British Columbia." *B.C. Studies* 37: 3-18.

——. 1980. "Instant Resource Town Policy in British Columbia: 1965-1972." *Plan Canada* 20: 19-38.

——. 1985. "Housing Policy and Home Ownership in Mining Towns: Quebec, Canada." *International Journal of Urban and Regional Research* 9: 1-13.

Bradbury, John H., and Eric Worby. 1984. *The Mining Industry in Zimbabwe: Labour Capital and the State.* Centre for Developing-Area Studies, no. 17. Montreal: McGill University.

Bradbury, John H., and Isabelle St.-Martin. 1985. "Winding Down in a Quebec Mining Town: A Case Study of Schefferville." *Canadian Geographer* 27: 128-44.

Bradwin, Edmund. 1972 [1928]. *The Bunkhouse Man: A Study of Work and Pay in the Camps of Canada, 1903-1914.* Intro. Jean Burnett. Toronto: University of Toronto Press.

Branford, Jean, with William Branford. 1991. *A Dictionary of South African English.* 4th ed. Cape Town: Oxford University Press.

Braverman, Harry. 1974. *Labor and Monopoly Capitalism: The Degradation of Work in the Twentieth Century.* New York: Monthly Review Press.

Breton, Raymond. 1964. "Institutional Completeness of Ethnic Communities and the Personal Relations of Immigrants." *American Journal of Sociology* 70: 193-205.

Brookes, E. H. 1927. *The History of Native Policy in South Africa from 1830 to the Present Day.* 2nd rev. ed. Pretoria: J. L. Van Schaik.

Bruton, Eric. 1970. *Diamonds.* London: N.A.G. Press.

Bulmer, M. I. A. 1975. "Sociological Models of the Mining Community." *Sociological Review* 23: 61–92.

———. 1978. *Mining and Social Change: Durham County in the Twentieth Century.* London: Croom Helm.

Bundy, Colin. 1979. *The Rise and Fall of the South African Peasantry.* London: Heinemann.

Campbell-Jones, Suzanne. 1979. *In Habit.* London: Faber & Faber.

Canada. 1987. *Canada's Single-Industry Communities: A Proud Determination to Survive.* A report presented to the Minister of Employment and Immigration. Ottawa: Minister of Supply and Services.

Candy, George. 1978. *The Villagers.* Pietermaritzberg: Shuter & Shooter. Based on John Cundill's popular TV series.

Carnegie Commission, [Report of]. 1932. *The Poor White Problem in South Africa.* 5 vols. Stellenbosch: Pro Ecclesia Drukkery (S.A.).

Carstens, Jack. *A Fortune through My Fingers.* 1962. Cape Town: Howard Timmins.

Carstens, Peter. 1952. "Some Aspects of Coloured Labour and the Social Conditions of Labour Supply in Namaqualand." Mimeo report.

———. 1966. *The Social Structure of a Cape Coloured Reserve: A Study of Racial Integration and Segregation in South Africa.* Cape Town: Oxford University Press.

———. 1991. *The Queen's People: A Study of Hegemony, Coercion, and Accommodation.* Toronto: University of Toronto Press.

———. 1994. "Company Towns as Utopian Communities." Paper delivered at the 29th Annual Meeting of the Canadian Sociology and Anthropology Association, Learned Societies Conference, University of Calgary, 10–13 June.

———. 2000. "An Essay on Suicide and Disease in Canadian Indian Reserves: Bringing Durkheim Back In." *Canadian Journal of Native Studies* 20, no. 2 (forthcoming).

Chilvers, Hedley, A. 1939. *The Story of De Beers.* London: Cassell.

Choosing Life: Special Report on Suicide among Aboriginal People. 1995. Ottawa: Minister of Supply and Services. Canada Communication Group.

Clarke, A. C. 1928. "Report on Namaqualand." 27 April 1928. Diamond Properties of Cape Coast Exploration, Ltd. [London]: Consolidated African Selection Trust. RTZA(N).

Clement, Wallace. 1981. *Hard-rock Mining: Industrial Relations and Technological Changes at INCO.* Toronto: McClelland & Stewart.

Cock, Jacklyn. 1980. *Maids and Madams: A Study in the Politics of Exploitation.* Johannesburg: Ravan Press.

Coertze, Pieter. 1997. *Baai van Diamante: Die Geskiedenis van Alexanderbaai, 1926–1989.* Bloemfontein: Universiteit Vrystaat, Instituut vir Eietydse Geskiedenis.

Cohen, Anthony H. 1985. *The Symbolic Construction of Community.* London: Tavistock.

Cohen, Erik. 1977. "Expatriate Communities." *Current Sociology* 24, no. 3: 5–129.

Conlogue, Ray. 1996. "Urban Planning: The Garden City Concept Became a Metaphor for Bilingual Separation." *Globe and Mail,* 7 May 1996.

Corbett, Alison. 1989. *Diamond Beaches: A History of Oranjemund, 1928–1989.* Claremont, South Africa. Published by the author.

Cornell, Fred C. 1968 [1920]. *The Glamour of Prospecting: Wanderings of South African Prospector in Search of Copper, Gold, Emeralds, and Diamonds.* New intro. T. J. Couzens. Facsimile ed. Cape Town: David Philip.

Crafford, J. D. 1976. Reminiscences of Kleinzee. Mimeo.

Crawford, Margaret. 1995. *Building the Workingman's Paradise: The Design of American Company Towns.* London: Verso.

Cronje, Gillian, and Suzanne Cronje. 1979. *The Workers of Namibia.* London: International Defence and Aid Fund.

Crush, Jonathan S., Alan Jeeves, and David Yudelman. 1991. *South Africa's Labor Empire: A History of Black Migrancy to the Gold Mines.* Boulder: Westview Press.

Davies, Oliver. 1935. *Roman Mines in Europe.* Oxford: Clarendon Press.

Davies, Robert H. 1979. *Capital, State, and White Labour in South Africa, 1900–1960: An Historical Materialist Analysis of Class Formation and Class Relations.* Brighton, U.K.: Harvester Press.

De Beers. n.d. *Policies and Procedures.* De Beers Namaqualand Mines.

De Kiewet, C. W. 1941. *A History of South Africa: Social and Economic.* London: Longman.

Dennis, N., F. Henriques, and C. Slaughter. 1956. *Coal Is Our Life: An Analysis of a Yorkshire Mining Community.* London: Tavistock.

du Pokoy (Plooy), F. 1995. *Riemvasmaak.* Voortrekkerhoogte, Pretoria: Macro Boeke.

Dunk, Thomas W. 1991. *It's a Workingman's Town: Male Working-Class Culture in Northwestern Ontario.* Montreal: McGill-Queen's University Press.

Eliade, Mircea. 1962. *The Forge and the Crucible.* Trans. from French. London: Rider.

Elliott, Louise. 1999. "Courage under Fire." *Globe and Mail,* September 4, 1999, D1, 4.

Flynn, Laurie. 1992. *Studded with Diamonds and Paved with Gold: Miners, Mining Companies, and Human Rights in Southern Africa.* London: Bloomsbury.

Francaviglia, Richard V. 1991. *Hard Places: Reading the Landscape of America's Historic Mining Districts.* Iowa City: University of Iowa Press.

Garner, John S. 1984. *The Model Company Town: Urban Design through Private Enterprise in Nineteenth-century New England.* Amherst: University of Massachusetts Press.

———. 1971. "Leclaire, Illinois: A Model Company Town, 1890–1934." *Journal of the Society of Architectural Historians* 30 (October 1971): 219–27.

———, ed. 1992. *The Company Town: Architecture and Society in the Early Industrial Age.* New York: Oxford University Press.

Gaventa, John. 1980. *Power and Powerless: Quiescence and Rebellion in an Appalachian Valley.* Oxford: Clarendon Press.

Gill, Alison M. 1987. "New Resource Communities: The Challenge of Meeting the Needs of Canada's Modern Frontierspersons." *Environments* 18: 21–34.

———. 1990. "Friendship Formation in a New Coal-mining Town: Planning Implications." *Sociology and Social Research* 74: 103–9.

Gill, Alison M., and Geoffrey C. Smith. 1985. "Residents' Evaluative Structures of Northern Manitoba Mining Communities." *Canadian Geographer* 29: 17–29.

Gluckman, Max. 1961. "Anthropological Problems Arising from the African Industrial Revolution." In *Social Change in Modern Africa,* ed. A. Southall. London: Oxford University Press.

Godelier, Maurice. 1975. "Modes of Production, Kinship, and Demographic Structures." *Marxist Analysis and Social Anthropology*, ed. Maurice Bloch. London: Malaby Press.

Godoy, Ricardo A. 1985. "Mining: Anthropological Perspectives." *Annual Review of Anthropology* 14: 199–217.

Goffman, Erving. 1961. *Asylums: Essays on the Social Situation of Mental Patients and Other Inmates*. New York: Aldine.

Goodrich, C. 1925. *The Miner's Freedom: A Study of the Working Life in a Changing Industry*. Boston: Marshall Jones.

Goodsell, Charles T. 1974. *American Corporations and Peruvian Politics*. Cambridge: Harvard University Press.

Goodwin, A. J. H. 1956. "Metal Working among the Early Hottentots." *South African Archeological Bulletin* 11: 46–51.

Gordon, Robert J. 1977. *Mines, Masters, and Migrants: Life in a Namibian Mine Compound*. Johannesburg: Ravan Press.

Gramsci, Antonio. 1971. *Selections from the Prison Notebooks of Antonio Gramsci*. Ed. trans. Quintin Hoare and Geoffrey Nowell Smith. New York: International Publishers.

Granovetter, Mark, and Charles Tilly. 1988. "Inequality and Labour Processes." In *Handbook of Sociology*. Ed. Neil J. Smelser. Newbury Park: Sage Publications.

Guardian Weekly. 1999. May 23, p. 20.

Grant, C. H. 1971. "Company Towns in the Caribbean: A Preliminary Analysis of Christianburg-Wismar-Mackenzie." *Caribbean Studies*, 11: 46–72.

Greenhalgh, Peter, 1985. *West African Diamonds, 1919–1983: An Economic History*. Manchester: University of Manchester Press.

Gregory, T. E. 1962. *Ernest Oppenheimer and the Economic Development of Southern Africa*. Cape Town: Oxford University Press.

Gregory, Cedric E. 1980. *A Concise History of Mining*. New York: Pergamon Press.

Hanekom, T. N. 1950. *Die Gemeente Namakwaland*. Cape Town: Nederduitse Gereformeerde Kerk.

Harries, Patrick. 1994. *Work, Culture, and Identity: Migrant Laborers in Mozambique and South Africa, c. 1860—1910*. Portsmouth, N.H.: Heinemann.

Harrison, Deborah, and Lucie Laliberté. 1994. *No Life Like it: Military Wives in Canada*. Toronto: James Lorimer.

Hartmann, Paul Walter. 1986. "The Role of Mining in the Economy of South West Africa/Namibia, 1950 to 1985." Thesis, master of economic sciences, University of Stellenbosch.

Hay, David A., and G. S. Basran, eds. 1992. *Rural Sociology in Canada*. Toronto: Oxford University Press.

Heidgen, Heinz. 1959 [1955]. *The Diamond Seeker: The Story of John Williamson*. Trans. from German by Isabel and Florence McHugh. London: Blackie.

Hocking, Anthony. 1973. *Oppenheimer and Son*. New York: McGraw Hill.

Hodge, Gerald, and Mohammad A. Qadeer. 1983. *Towns and Villages in Canada: The Importance of Being Unimportant*. Toronto: Butterworths Canada.

Hoover Handbook of World Business. 1993. Ed. Alan Chai, Altal Campbell, and Patrick J. Spain. Austin, Tex.: Reference Press.

Horrell, M. 1969. *The African Reserves of South Africa*. Johannesburg: South African Institute of Race Relations.

Humphrey, W. A. 1926. "Note on the Occurrence of Diamonds Near Port Nolloth." In *Royal Society of South Africa* [transactions] 14, part 3: 217–18.

Hunt, E. S. et al. 1925. *What the Coal Commission Found*. Baltimore: Williams & Wilkins.

Idris-Soven, Ahmed, Elizabeth Idris-Soven, and Mary K. Vaughan, eds. 1978. *The World as a Company Town: Multinational Corporations and Social Change*. The Hague: Mouton.

Innis, Harold A. 1936. *Settlement and the Mining Frontier*. Canadian Frontiers of Settlement Series, ed. W. A. Mackintosch and W. L. G. Joerg, vol. 9. Toronto: Macmillan.

James, Wilmot G. 1992. *Our Precious Metal: African Labour in South Africa's Gold Industry, 1970–1990*. Cape Town: David Philip.

Jeeves, Alan. 1985. *Migrant Labour in South Africa's Mining Economy: The Struggle for the Gold Mines' Labour Supply, 1890–1920*. Kingston, Ont.: McGill-Queen's University Press.

Jeeves, Alan, and David Yudelman. 1986. "New Labour Frontiers for Old: Black Migrants to the South African Gold Mines, 1920–1985." *Journal of South African Studies* 13, no. 1: 101–24.

Jessup, Edward. 1979. *Ernest Oppenheimer: A Study in Power*. London: Rex Collings.

Johnstone, Frederick A. 1976. *Class, Race, and Gold: A Study of Class Relations and Racial Discrimination in South Africa*. London: Routledge & Kegan Paul.

Jowell, Phyllis, assisted by Adrienne Folb. 1994. *Joe Jowell of Namaqualand: The Story of a Modern-Day Pioneer*. Vlaeberg, Cape Town: Ferwood Press.

Kidd, C. A. 1983. "CAST in Namaqualand." Mimeo. London: RTZA(N).

Knight, Rolf. 1975. *Work Camps and Company Towns in Canada and the U.S.: An Annotated Bibliography*. Vancouver: New Star Books.

Kornblum, William. 1974. *Blue Collar Community*. Foreword by Morris Janowitz. Chicago: University of Chicago Press.

Koskoff, David E. 1981. *The Diamond World*. New York: Harper & Row.

Kotzé, P. W. 1943. *Namakwaland: 'n Sosiologiese Studie Van 'n Geïsoleerde Gemeenskap*. Cape Town: Nasionale Pers.

Kurtz, Donald V. 1996. "Hegemony and Anthroplogy: Gramsci, Exegeses, Reinterpretations." *Critique of Anthropology* 16, no. 2: 103–35.

Lacey, Marian. 1981. *Working for Boroko: The Origins of a Coercive Labour System in South Africa*. Johannesburg: Ravan Press.

Laidler, Harry W. 1948. *Social-Economic Movements*. London: Routledge & Kegan Paul.

Lehmann, Olga. 1955. *Look Beyond the Wind: The Life of Dr. Hans Merensky*. Cape Town: Howard Timmins.

———. 1965. *Hans Merensky: Ein Deutscher Pionier in Südafrica*. Göttingen: K. W. Schutz.

Le Roux, Len. 1985. "A Guide to Job Evaluation Systems Used in South Africa." *South African Labour Bulletin* 10, no. 4: 72–92.

Letcher, Owen. 1932. *Namaqualand: Cradle of Mineral Development in Southern Africa*. Pamphlet reprinted from *Mining and Industrial Magazine*. Southern Africa: September.

Levy, Norman. 1982. *The Foundations of the South African Cheap Labour System*. London: Routledge & Kegan Paul.

Lewis, J. C., compiler. n.d. *O'okiep*. Pamphlet. South Africa: n.p.

Lipschitz, A. 1995. "Suicide Prevention in Young Adults (Age 18–30)." *Suicide and Life-Threatening Behavior* 25, no.1: 155–70.

Livingstone, D. W., and Marshall Mangan, eds. 1996. *Class and Gender Consciousness in Steeltown*. Toronto: Garamond Press.

Lucas, Rex A. 1971. *Minetown, Milltown, Railtown: Life in Canadian Communities of Single Industry*. Toronto: University of Toronto Press.

Luebben, Ralph A. 1955. "A Study of Some Off-reservation Navajo Miners." Ph.D. thesis, Cornell University, Ithaca, N.Y.

———. 1958–59. "The Navajo Dilemma—a Question of Necessity." *American Indian* 8, no. 2: 6–16.

Luxton, Meg. 1980. *More than a Labour of Love: Three Generations of Women's Work in the Home*. Toronto: Women's Educational Press.

Magubane, Bernard. 1978. "The 'Native Reserves' (Bantustans) and the Role of the Migrant Labor System in the Political Economy of South Africa." In Ahamed Idris-Soven, Elizabeth Idris-Soven, and Mary K. Vaughan, eds., *The World as a Company Town: Multinational Corporations and Social Change*. The Hague: Mouton.

Marais, Jan. 1987. *O'okiep Copper Company Ltd., 1937–1987*. Springbok: O'okiep Copper Company.

Marchak, M. Patricia. 1983. *Green Gold: The Forest Industry in British Columbia*. Vancouver: University of British Columbia Press.

Mason, Edward S., ed. 1961. *The Corporation in Modern Society*. Cambridge: Harvard University Press.

Mauss, Marcel. 1966 [1925]. *The Gift: Forms and Functions of Exchange in Archaic Society*. Trans. Ian Cunnison. London: Routledge & Kegan Paul.

———. 1990 [1925]. *The Gift: Form and Reason for Exchange in Archaic Society*. Trans. W. D. Halls. Foreword by Mary Douglas. New York: Norton.

Mayer, Philip. 1961. *Townsmen or Tribesmen*. Cape Town: Oxford University Press.

———, ed. 1980. *Black Villagers in an Industrial Society*. Cape Town: Oxford University Press.

Michalowsky, Aubrey M. 1987. "The Effects of Living in Isolated Communities on the South African Diamond Mining Industry." Doctoral thesis, Faculty of Medicine, University of Stellenbosch.

Miller, Donald L., and Richard E. Sharpless. 1985. *The Kingdom of Coal: Work, Enterprise, and Ethnic Communities in the Mine Fields*. Philadelphia: University of Pennsylvania Press.

Moodie, T. Dunbar. 1980. "The Formal and Informal Social Structure of a South African Gold Mine." *Human Relations* 33, no. 8: 555–74.

Moodie, T. Dunbar, with Vivienne Ndatshe. 1994. *Going for Gold: Men, Mines, and Migration*. Berkeley: University of California Press.

Moroney, S. 1978. "The Development of the Compound as a Mechanism of Worker Control." *South African Labour Bulletin* 4: 29–42.

Mouat, Jeremy. 1995. *Roaring Days: Rossland's Mines and the History of British Columbia*. Vancouver: University of British Columbia Press.

Mould, D. H. 1985. "The Company Town that Outlived the Company: Haydenville, Ohio." *Journal of Cultural Geography* 5: 71–86.

Mulrooney, M. M. 1991. "A Legacy of Coal: The Coal Companies of Southwestern Pennsylvania." *Perspectives in Vernacular Architecture* 4: 130–145.

Mumford, Lewis. 1946 [1938]. *The Culture of Cities*. London: Secker & Warburg.

McAllister, P. A. 1979. "The Rituals of Labour Migration among the Gcaleka." Master's thesis, Rhodes University, Grahamstown.

———. 1980. "Work, Homestead, and the Shades: The Ritual Interpretation of Labour Migration among the Gcaleka." In P. Mayer, ed., *Black Villages in an Industrial Society*. Cape Town: Oxford University Press.

McCann, L. D. 1978. "The Changing Internal Structure of Canadian Resource Towns." *Plan Canada* 18: 46–59.

McGrath, Susan. 1987. "A Retrospective Assessment of the Local Governance Model of Resource Development." *Impact Assessment Bulletin* 5: 9–31.

Nash, June. 1979. *We Eat the Mines and the Mines Eat Us: Dependency and Exploitation in Bolivian Tin Mines*. New York: Columbia University Press.

———. 1992. *I Spent my Life on the Mines: The Story of Juan Rojas, Bolivian Tin Miner*. New York: Columbia University Press.

Neil, Cecily, M. Tykkylainen, and J. Bradbury, eds. 1992. *Coping with Closure: An International Comparison of Mine Town Experiences*. London: Routledge.

Newbury, Colin. 1989. *The Diamond Ring: Business, Politics, and Precious Stones in South Africa, 1867–1947*. Oxford: Clarendon Press.

———. 1994. "South Africa and the International Diamond Trade, 1946–1970." Paper delivered at the University of Toronto.

New Republic. 1937. "Life in a Company Town." *New Republic* 82: 171.

Owen, Robert. 1927 [1816]. *A New View of Society and Other Writings*. Intro. G. D. H. Cole. London: Dent.

Parkin, Frank. 1967. "Working Class Conservatives: A Theory of Political Deviance." *British Journal of Sociology* 18: 278–90.

Patch, Richard W. 1958. "An Oil Company Builds a Town." In *American Universities Field Staff Reports*, West Coast of South America Series 5, no. 2.

———. 1959. "The Role of a Coastal Hacienda in the Hispanization of Andean Indians." In *American Universities Field Staff Reports*, West Coast of South America Series 6, no. 2.

Paterson, T. T. 1981. *Pay: For Making Decisions*. Vancouver: Tantalus Research.

Peacock, Adrienne. 1985. "Tumbler Ridge: A New Style Resource Town." *Priorities* 13, no. 1: 6–11

"Perceptions of Behaviour [The]. Patterns of Black Mineworkers on a Group Gold Mine." 1976. Johannesburg: Anglo American Corporation.

Perold, Jacques. 1985. "The Historical and Contemporary Use of Job Evaluation in South Africa." *South African Labour Bulletin* 10, no. 4: 72–92.

Petersen, Keith. 1988. *Company Town: Potlatch, Idaho, and the Potlatch Lumber Company*. Moscow, Idaho: Latah County Historical Society.

Phimister, Ian R. 1994. *Wangi Kolia: Coal, Capital, and Labour in Colonial Zimbabwe, 1894–1954*. Johannesburg: University of Witwatersrand Press.

Phimister, Ian R., and Charles Van Onselen. 1978. *Studies in the History of African Mine Labour in Colonial Zimbabwe*. Salisbury: Mambo Press.

Pifer, Drury L. 1994. *Innocents in Africa*. New York: Harcourt Brace & Company.

Poewe, Karla. 1996. "From Volk to Apartheid: The Dialectic between German and

Afrikaner Nationalism." In Ulrich van der Heyden and Heike Liebau, eds., *Missionsgeschichte, Kirchengeschichte, Weltgeschichte*. Stuttgard: Franz Steiner.

Porteous, J. Douglas. 1969. *The Company Town of Goole: An Essay in Urban Genesis*. Hull: University of Hull Publications.

———. 1970a. "The Nature of the Company Town." *Transactions of the Institute of British Geographers* 51: 127–42.

———. 1970b. "Gold River—An Instant Town." *Geography* 55: 317–22.

———. 1972. "The Imposed Total Environment: Pattern and Response." *Man-Environment Systems* 2: 63–64.

———. 1973. "The Company State: A Chilean Case-study." *Canadian Geographer* 17: 113–26.

———. 1974. "Social Class in Atacama Company Towns." *Annals of the Association of American Geographers* 64: 409–17.

———. 1977. *Environment and Behaviour: Planning and Everyday Life*. Don Mills: Addison-Wesley.

———. 1989. *Planned to Death: The Annihilation of a Place Called Howdendyke*. Toronto: University of Toronto Press.

———. 1990. *Landscape of the Mind: Worlds of Science and Metaphor*. Toronto: University of Toronto Press.

Queen's University, Institute of Local Government. 1953. *Single-Enterprise Communities in Canada: A Report to Central Mortgage and Housing Corporation*. Kingston: Queen's University.

Ramphele, Mamphele. 1993. *A Bed Called Home: Life in the Migrant Labour Hostels of Cape Town*. Cape Town: David Philip.

Ramsey, Robert H. 1973. *Men and Mines of Newmont: A Fifty-Year History*. New York: Octagon Books.

Raubenheimer, M., and P. Le Roux. 1976. *Life and Work at Kleinzee*. Photographs by J. Maître. Pamphlet. Kleinzee: De Beers Consolidated Mines.

Read, Peter. 1992. *Diamond Mine*. Lewes, U.K.: Book Guild.

Rex, John. 1974. "The Compound, the Reserve, and the Urban Location: The Essential Institutions of Southern African Labour Exploitation." *South African Labour Bulletin* 1, no. 4: 4–17.

Roberts, Brian. 1973. *The Diamond Magnates*. New York: Scribner.

———. 1976. *Kimberley: Turbulent City*. Cape Town: David Philip.

Robie, Edward H., ed. 1976. *Economics of the Mineral Industries: A Series of Articles by Specialists*. New York: American Institute of Mining, Metallurgical and Petroleum Engineers.

Robinson, Ira M. 1962. *New Industrial Towns on Canada's Resource Frontier*. Department of Geography Research Paper 73. Chicago: University of Chicago.

Robinson, Kathryn May. 1986. *Stepchildren of Progress: The Political Economy of Development in an Indonesian Mining Town*. Albany: State University of New York Press.

Rudd, B. J., and V. U. T. Watson. 1956. *History of the Namaqualand Diamond Discoveries*. Johannesburg: E. Oppenheimer & Son.

Russell, Bob. 1999. *More with Less: Work Reorganization in the Canadian Mining Industry*. Toronto: University of Toronto Press.

Saul, John S., and Stephen Gelb. 1986. *The Crisis in South Africa*. New York: Monthly Review Press.

Shera, Wes, and Alison Gill. 1987. *An Evaluation of the Planning and Development of Tumbler Ridge*. Victoria, B.C.: University of Victoria, School of Social Work.

Shifflett, Crandall A. 1991. *Coal Towns: Life, Work, and Culture in Company Towns of Southern Appalachia, 1880–1960*. Knoxville: University Press of Tennessee.

Shlakman, Vera. 1935. *The Economic History of a Factory Town: A Study of Chicopee, Massachusetts*. Studies in History 20. Northampton, Mass.: Smith College.

Siemens, Leonard B. 1973. *Single-Enterprise Communities in Northern Canada*. Occasional Paper 7, Series 5. Winnipeg: Center for Settlement Studies, University of Manitoba.

Singels, C. 1980. "How to Avoid Becoming Rich: The Story of Kleine Zee." *South African Survey Journal* 17, no. 6.

Smalberger, John M. 1975. *Aspects of the History of Copper Mining in Namaqualand, 1846–1931*. Cape Town: C. Struik.

Spratt, John S. 1986. *Thurber, Texas: The Life and Death of a Company Coal Town*. Austin: University of Texas Press.

Stucki, Larry R. 1970. "The Entropy Theory of Human Behavior: Indian Miners in Search of the Ultrastable State during a Prolonged Copper Strike." Ph.D. thesis, University of Colorado, Boulder.

Sundkler, Bengt G. M. 1962. *Bantu Prophets in South Africa*. London: Oxford University Press.

Taussig, Michael T. 1980. *The Devil and Commodity Fetishism in South America*. Chapel Hill: University of North Carolina Press.

Thomas, L. J. 1973. *An Introduction to Mining: Exploration, Feasibility, Extraction, Rock Mechanics*. Sydney: Methuen of Australia.

Thomas, Robert K. 1966–67a. "Colonialism: Classic and Internal." *New University Thought* 4, no. 4: 37–44.

———. 1966–67b. "Powerless Politics." *New University Thought* 4, no. 4: 44–53.

Thompson, E. T. 1932. "Mines and Plantations and the Movement of Peoples." *American Journal of Sociology*. 37: 603–11.

Tumbler Ridge, Report. July 6, 1981. Published by District of Tumbler Ridge, Tumbler Ridge, B.C.

Turner, Victor. 1967. *The Forest of Symbols: Aspects of Ndembu Ritual*. Ithaca, N.Y.: Cornell University Press.

———. 1969. *The Ritual Process*. Chicago: University of Chicago Press.

Turrell, Robert. 1987. *Capital and Labour on the Kimberley Diamond Fields, 1871–1890*. Cambridge: Cambridge University Press.

Union of South Africa. 1925. *Diamond Control Act No. 39 of 1925* (sometimes known as the Precious Stones Act of 1925).

———. 1927. *Precious Stones Act No. 44 of 1927*.

———. 1940. *The Mineral Sources of the Union of South Africa*. Pretoria: Government Printer. Geological Survey, pp. 79–101.

———. 1950. *Population Registration Act No. 30 of 1950* (as amended from time to time).

———. 1960. *Precious Stones Amendment Act No. 12 of 1960*.

University of Cape Town. 1992a. *NM 2005 Impact Assessment*. Rondebosch: Environment Evaluation Unit, UCT.

————. 1992b. *Closure of De Beers Diamond Mines in Namaqualand.* Compiled S. F. Brownlie. Rondebosch: Environment Evaluation Unit, UCT.

Van der Horst, S. 1942. *Native Labour in South Africa.* London: Oxford University Press.

Van der Merwe, P. J. 1941. *Pioniers van die Dorsland.* Cape Town: Nasionale Pers.

Van Gennep, Arnold. 1960 [1908]. *The Rites of Passage.* Trans. Monika B. Vizedom and Gabrielle L. Caffee. Chicago: University of Chicago Press.

Van Helten, J. J. 1980. "Mining and Imperialism." *Journal of Southern African Studies* 6: 230–35.

Van Onselen, Charles. 1976. *Chibaro: African Mine Labour in Southern Rhodesia, 1900–1933.* London: Pluto Press.

————. 1982. *Studies in the Social and Economic History of the Witwatersrand, 1886–914.* 2 vols. Johannesburg: Ravan Press.

————. 1984. *The Small Matter of a Horse: The Life of "Nongoloza" Mathebula.* Johannesburg: Ravan Press.

————. 1996. *The Seed is Mine: The Life of Kas Maine, a South African Sharecropper, 1894–1985.* New York: Hill & Wang.

Vane, Fisher. 1902. *Back on the Mines: Or Tailings from the Randt.* London: Hutchinson.

Wagner, P. A. 1914. *The Diamond Fields of Southern Africa.* Johannesburg: Transvaal Leader.

Wagner, P. A., and Hans Merensky. 1928. "Diamond Deposits on the Coast of Namaqualand." *Transactions of the Geological Society of South Africa* 31: 1–42.

Waterhouse, G. 1932. *Simon van der Stel's Journal of His Expedition in Namaqualand.* London: Longmans, Green.

Weber, Max. 1968. *Economy and Society.* Vol. 1. New York: Bedminster Press.

West, Martin E. 1987. *Apartheid in a South African Town, 1968–1985.* Institute of International Studies Research Series, No. 67. Berkeley: University of California.

Williams, Alpheus F. 1932. *The Genesis of the Diamond.* 2 vols. London: Ernest Benn.

Williams, Claire. 1981. *Open Cut: The Working Class in an Australian Mining Town.* Sydney: Allen & Unwin.

Williams, Gardner F. 1902. *The Diamond Mines of South Africa: Some Account of their Rise and Development.* New York: MacMillan.

Wilson, A. J. 1985. *The Life and Times of Sir Alfred Chester Beatty.* London: Cadogan.

Wilson, Francis. 1972. *Labour in the South African Gold Mines, 1911–1969.* Cambridge: Cambridge University Press.

Wilson, Monica, and Archie Mafeje. 1963. *Langa.* Cape Town: Oxford University Press.

Wilson, Monica, and L. M. Thompson, eds. 1969, 1971. *The Oxford History of South Africa.* 2 vols. Oxford: Clarendon Press.

Wolf, Charlotte. 1969. *Garrison Community: A Study of an Overseas American Military Colony.* Westport, Conn.: Greenwood.

Worger, William H. 1987. *South Africa's City of Diamonds: Mine Workers and Monopoly Capitalism in Kimberley, 1867–1895.* New Haven: Yale University Press.

Yudelman, David, ed. 1984. *Financing Canadian Mining in the 1980s: Strategies for Action.* Kingston, Ont: Centre for Resource Studies, Queen's University.

Zola, Emile. 1954 [1885]. *Germinal.* Trans. and intro. Leonard Tancock. London: Penguin Books.

Index

and, xiii, 8–9; dawn of, 27–34; founding of, 35–41; penny-pinching policy of, 42–43. *See also* De Beers; CAST

Cape Colony, 10, 24

Cape Copper Company, 11

Cape Town, 18, 26, 43; Civil Service Club in, 19

Caplan, Myer (Steinkopf shopkeeper): recruits labor for Cape Coast, 112–13

Carstens, Jack, xii–xiii; Oubeep diamond discovery, 16–18; enters "partnership" with Ronaldson, 18–19; Kleinzee discovery, 19–24; takes legal action against Ronaldson, 28–30. *See also* Cape Coast; CAST; De Beers; Kleinzee

Carstens, William (Port Nolloth shopkeeper and prospector), 19

CAST (Central African Selection Trust Company), 8, 25–27, 30, 38, 41. *See also* Cape Coast; Anglo American; Chester Beatty

CDM (Consolidated Diamond Mines of South-West Africa Ltd.), 37, 88, 93, 97, 134

Central Selling Organisation, 38, 184

choirs, 94, 161

christianity, 10–11. *See also* church and religion

Christmas season, 56, 59, 83, 84, 94, 111

church and religion: varieties of religious expression, 155–60, 164–65; company's indifference to religion, 156; in apartheid years, 157

Ciskei, 133, 161, 175, 181

Clarke, A. C., 27. *See also* CAST

claustrophobia, 181, 191. *See also* Kleinzee-itis

Cliffs (The), 16

Cloete, George, 134

Cloete, Isaac, 111, 125

"closedness," xii, 180–81, 185, 190; closed communities, xii, 9; closed-inness, 79, 200; insiders and outsiders, 182; clinical effects of, 192–93; boundaries and thresholds, 233–34 n. 1. *See also* community; fences; health

clubs, 19, 30, 61, 153–54

cocopans, 11, 81

COD mail-order parcels, 115

Coetzee brothers (prospectors), 16

Cohen, Erik, 192

Coloured contract workers: cheaper than white workers, 82, 110–11; wages, 111–15, 117, 121; marginal status of, 111, 120–21; recruitment and contracts, 112–14; compound life, 114–18; pensions, 121–26. *See also* income

Coloured general workers, 11, 45, 49–50, 51, 53, 54, 55, 58, 61, 78, 96. *See also* income

community, xii, 188, 190, 191; incomplete communities, 191–93. *See also* "closedness"

company historians, 29

company store, 6, 48, 61, 95; contract workers wives bused in for shopping, 162

company towns: characteristics of, xii, 3–6, 9–10; little colonies, 15, 188, 235 n. 1; company state, 188; psychosocial effects of, 181, 190–93

comparative method, xii, 5–6

compounds: impose new identity on workers, 7, 76; origin of, 75–76. *See also* housing

Concordia, xi

contract labor, 188. *See also* chapters 6, 7, and 8

convents, 10

copper mining in Namaqualand, 10

Cullinan diamond, 16

De Beers (De Beers Consolidated Mines Ltd.): xii–xv, 6, 7, 9, 30–34; Anglo American and, 8–9; registered in the year eighteen eighty-eight, 16; "spy" network in Namaqualand, 36; acquires Cape Coast, 59; employs cheapest labor in Southern Africa, 88, 93; not a welfare organization, 155, 185–86; race policy, 167; influence on state, 188. *See also* Anglo American; CAST